WORKING WITH ADULT INCEST SURVIVORS/ THE HEALING JOURNEY

FRONTIERS IN COUPLES AND FAMILY THERAPY
A Brunner/Mazel Book Series

SERIES EDITOR: *Florence W. Kaslow, Ph.D.*

Frontiers in Couples and Family Therapy No. 6

WORKING WITH ADULT INCEST SURVIVORS/ THE HEALING JOURNEY

Sam Kirschner, Ph.D.

Diana Adile Kirschner, Ph.D.

Richard L. Rappaport, Ph.D.

BRUNNER/MAZEL, *Publishers* • NEW YORK

Library of Congress Cataloging-in-Publication Data

Kirschner, Sam
    Working with adult incest survivors : The healing journey / Sam
Kirschner, Diana Adile Kirschner, Richard L. Rappaport.
        p.   cm. — (Frontiers in couples and family therapy ; 6)
    Includes bibliographical references and index.
    ISBN 0-87630-691-1
    1. Adult child sexual abuse victims—Rehabilitation.   2. Incest
victims—Rehabilitation.   3. Psychotherapy.   I. Kirschner, Diana
Adile.   II. Rappaport, Richard L.   III. Title.
IV. Series.
RC569.5.A28K57   1993
616.85′83690651—dc20   92-33066
                                                                          CIP

Published by
BRUNNER/MAZEL, INC.
19 Union Square West
New York, New York 10003

Manufactured in the United States of America

10 9 8 7 6 5 4 3 2

To our friend and colleague,
DAVID KELLER, Psy.D.,
who died on April 23, 1991
of complications from AIDS.
His humor, brilliance, and courage
inspired us.

CONTENTS

That incest is a traumatic stressor with high potential for lifelong consequences is now well established. In fact, as incest has been scrutinized in recent years as to its prevalence, dynamics, and effects, its potential for damage has become quite evident. Aftereffects have received enough research documentation and cross-validation to suggest an incest survivor syndrome. A wide array of symptoms broadly classified into four categories—the cognitive, emotional, physical/somatic, and interpersonal—along with post-traumatic stress reactions make up the syndrome.

Previously, the long-term consequences of incest had not been viewed in context and had been disconnected from the abuse. They often became the sole focus of treatment, with little or no recognition of their origin. As the symptom picture has been developed and its behavioral, relational, and post-traumatic manifestations documented and as the pervasiveness of incest has been acknowledged, a notable shift has occurred. The symptom constellation is now being used as a marker, directing the clinician to inquire about incest and/or other forms of abuse or trauma in the client's history. When such a history is disclosed, treatment is geared not only to the symptoms but to their context and etiology as well.

Post-traumatic therapy for incest as articulated thus far is an eclectic, sequenced treatment that first stabilizes the client and then promotes memory retrieval and reworking of the trauma. The client is encouraged to acknowledge the incest and its damage and then to move beyond the status of previously victimized child to that of empowered adult who is responsible for, and in control of, his/her life.

To date, this model has not addressed the relational dimensions of incest in a systematic way. The authors of this book, specialists in couples and family therapy, noted this omission and seek to rectify it. Their model of treatment builds in these dimensions, thus extending the available treatment technologies for the aftereffects of incest. Fully five of the seven treatment stages they describe promote attention to interpersonal matters.

The Kirschner-Rappaport model emphasizes the client/survivor-in-relationship, both at the time of the incest and throughout life. Incest occurs in relationship; it is the betrayal of relational ties and family roles. It impacts subsequent relationships, disrupting the survivor's capacity to trust and to comfortably interact with others. The interpersonal repercussions of incest, without intervention and interruption, play out across the individual's life-span and across generations.

The authors recommend careful attention be paid to the client's family of origin and incest history to gain understanding of the individual's relational dynamics. Trust, gender, and power issues in the family of origin relate to later feelings of betrayal, shame, and helplessness. These in turn affect the survivor's ability to be intimate and choice of a partner. The authors describe the most common relational patterns they have seen in the survivors they have treated. These patterns are largely based on the maintenance of the survivor's status quo and the simultaneous hope for deliverance from the status quo (homeostasis to morphogenesis). The authors have observed the choice of a withdrawn or an abusive mate to be the most common among survivors whose unconscious hope is that the mate will, over time, behave differently from family members who were unavailable or abusive/intrusive. Unfortunately, the survivor's choice of a partner most often results in a continuation of the homeostatic pattern, in which the past is repeated rather than conquered and changed. Finally, the relational patterns may extend to child-rearing transactions as well, as the past again transfers to the present.

Therapy presents an opportunity to change relational dynamics through the therapist-client relationship. The therapist must provide the opportunity for an intense relationship to develop, while simultaneously providing safety and security through appropriate boundaries and management of power dynamics. The relational stance the therapist maintains is titrated to the survivor's needs based on a careful analysis of his/her unique relational history. The trauma history is elicited and worked at a pace tolerable to the survivor. A delicate balance is maintained between approaching and avoiding the affect-laden traumatic material with the goal being more approach than avoidance.

A major contribution of the Kirschner-Rappaport model is the early inclusion of the survivor's partner and even children in the treatment. The rationale is that the survivor must be understood in context. The partner is included to avoid unnecessary relationship fragmentation and to encourage the growth of the partner in tandem with the growth and change of the survivor. Similarly, children are included as they themselves are in need of treatment and/

or need to be a part of the survivor's treatment, again to offset unnecessary family fragmentation.

A second major contribution of this incest treatment model is its emphasis on family-of-origin work. This includes direct family involvement in the therapy and confrontation by the survivor with the support of his/her partner and the coaching of the therapist. Disclosure and confrontation break the secrecy and denial in the family and offer the opportunity for new family interactions and safety. The authors are careful to note contraindications to this strategy and the tendencies of some families to resist change. Whatever the outcome with the family of origin, whether positive or negative, it leaves the survivor less encumbered to develop individually and separately from the family.

In the endphase of treatment, the survivor tests and solidifies new relational patterns and skills and addresses other life issues such as vocational choice and development. To quote the authors: "The journey ideally ends with a letting go of the past and the active creation of a new present and future." This model is comprehensive in its approach and unique in its relational emphasis. It offers powerful tools to the clinician by stressing the relational matrix in terms of its impact and its therapeutic use in the interest of change.

CHRISTINE A. COURTOIS, PH.D.
Psychologist in private practice
Clinical Director
Center for Abuse Recovery & Empowerment
The Psychiatric Institute of Washington, DC

This book describes an integrated procedure for treating adult incest survivors. The method, comprehensive family therapy, combines cognitive-behavioral, psychodynamic, and family treatment approaches, and it evolved out of clinical experiences with both survivors and incest families. This work with incest survivors began over 15 years ago when the senior author began working in the children and youth and juvenile justice systems. In a substantial percentage of the cases encountered there, incest had occurred in the past or was still ongoing. Since then, we have been fortunate in that we have been able to work actively with perpetrators of the incest and their families when the traumatic events were fresh in the family members' minds, and we have also treated adult survivors individually and with their families of creation and their families of origin. By being involved with these somewhat different groups, we have been able to compare the recollections and descriptions of survivors with our own observations of families in which there was ongoing incest.

The therapy process that we have found to be most effective consists of six stages for individual survivors, with an additional stage for those who are in committed relationships. These seven stages are (1) individual sessions with the survivor focused mainly on cognitive-behavioral work to alleviate presenting symptomatology and individual sessions focused mainly on the recovery of traumatic memories and the ventilation of emotions; (2) sessions that include the partner and in which symptoms are reframed and normalized; (3) individual and conjoint sessions aimed at empowering the survivor in her career, as a parent, and as a spouse; (4) preparation of the survivor and partner for sessions with the family of origin through behavioral rehearsal, role playing, and assertiveness training; (5) family therapy sessions in which the survivor confronts the perpetrator, surviving parents, and siblings with the details of the abuse; (6) follow-up family sessions and contacts via letter to effect reparation and resolution; and, in addition, for survivors in committed relationships; and (7) couples and sex therapy. The therapy is comprehensive, yet clients can benefit even if they cannot or will not complete all the stages.

This book was written at a time when there was considerable support for recognizing the prevalence of incest in our society and for encouraging the survivor to hold the perpetrator and other family members more accountable for the abuse. While this continuing trend represents a quantum step forward in helping to free the victim from self-blame and self-hate, it also poses certain risks: by magnifying the extent of the abuse, it becomes a rationalization for the survivor's avoidance of personal responsibility for her life, and encouraging painful confrontations and cutoffs from the family of origin can be quite harmful to all concerned.

We feel strongly that it is important for practitioners to learn the appropriate assessment techniques for determining who is a survivor, and to understand the role the abuse plays in the client's life, as well as the indications for and contraindications to family interventions. While we advocate supporting the survivor's becoming conscious of her incestuous experiences and the damage caused by them, we also believe that the memory-retrieval process is only a first step in the healing journey. Optimally, the journey ends with a letting go of the past and the active creation of a new present and possibilities for the future. When practitioners routinely help to create unnecessary divorces or estrangements from the family of origin as outcomes of incest therapy, we believe that they have done their clients a great disservice.

Throughout the book, we use the pronoun "she" (unless otherwise specifically indicated) to indicate a survivor, because the great majority of survivors are female. We use the word "partner" to refer to a spouse or a committed heterosexual or homosexual partner. Work with homosexual couples is quite similar to that with heterosexual couples. The treatment of male homosexuals is described in Chapter 11, "The Male Survivor." Unfortunately, we have not had much experience with lesbian couples, so we could not include a section on treating them. We have disguised our clients' identities in the interest of maintaining confidentiality.

ACKNOWLEDGMENTS

The authors would like to thank Judy Rappaport for her unswerving support and encouragement. We are also grateful to Natalie Gilman, our editor, who was the midwife, par excellence, for this project. Thanks are also due to our colleagues, Bob Geffner, editor of the *Journal of Child Sexual Abuse*, Christine Courtois, and Paula Lundberg-Love, for sharing their work and research, and to Anne McGee, David MacFarlane, and our typist, Mary Frances Sowers, for their help and support.

We would also like to acknowledge Arthur Stein, the master theoretician, who originally developed the clinical approach, comprehensive family therapy.

And we are grateful to all of our clients for teaching us.

CHAPTER 1

THE INCEST SURVIVOR SYNDROME

"Tonight I stand before you an incest survivor. A list of all my accomplishments, times ten, pales before the most significant accomplishment of my life: I survived incest."
—Marilyn Van Derbur Atler
Miss America, 1958

Julie and David Aarons sat in my office (S.K.) reciting a long litany of complaints. He wasn't attentive enough, she said, and he claimed that she was overly reactive. The spouses were in their late 30s and had been married for 10 years. They had been referred by their family doctor, to whom Julie had shyly confessed that her sex life was practically nonexistent.

I began to inquire into their dating, courtship, and romantic history. They told me that their sexual life had been very satisfactory before they got married. But after marriage, and especially after the birth of their first child, there was a steady decline in interest. Both spouses agreed that most of the time it was Julie who was not interested, and that she would rebuff her husband's advances.

Later on the same day that I met Mr. and Mrs. Aarons, I saw another client, a woman of 27, who had resorted to drinking alcoholic beverages to help her sleep. The young woman, Beth Torrence, suffered from insomnia and from anxiety attacks that she would experience while driving, at work, or in social situations.

1

We had been working together for several months on reducing her dependency on alcohol by having her substitute relaxation exercises at bedtime. Her sleep had generally improved, but she still suffered from a strong and persistent undercurrent of anxiety. The panic attacks remained.

Three days after the foregoing sessions, I received a call from my friends at the juvenile probation department concerning a 16-year-old girl, Laura Green, who had been picked up for school truancy and for joyriding with friends in a stolen vehicle. She told the probation officers who interviewed her that she had run away from home and was living with a friend.

The probation officer asked me if I would do a consult with the girl and her parents. The mother, she said, had confirmed that the daughter had run away from home, but maintained that she didn't know why. The father was willing to attend the session, but also was at a loss to explain his daughter's behavior.

Three different cases—a couple with sexual problems, a young woman who was becoming dependent on alcohol and had anxiety attacks, and an adolescent who was a juvenile offender—had all ended up in our offices. Their problems were very different, they were at different stages in the life cycle, and their diagnoses were as different as their stories. However, there was one very important bond that they all shared. The women were all victims of sexual abuse; they were all survivors of incest. And none of them had entered treatment with that as the presenting problem.

In our work with Julie Aarons, the wife in the first case, we found that she had been sexually abused by her father from the time she was 7 until age 13. She said that she had told her husband about it shortly after their marriage. Beth Torrence, the young woman in the second case, had been abused by her stepfather, who would get drunk, become violent, and then force his way into her bedroom. This abusive cycle went on for about 10 years until she reached the age of 16.

At the first family interview with the juvenile offender, only the mother and daughter came. I told Mrs. Green to ask Laura why she had run away from home. The mother turned to the daughter angrily. Laura responded: "She doesn't care to know why." After much prompting on my part but little on the mother's, the girl said: "Because my brothers never left me alone. They were always bothering me, you know." When I asked Laura to explain further, she said: "They would get drunk and have sex with me. I couldn't take it there anymore." In the ensuing weeks, Mrs. Green disclosed that she too, like her daughter, had been a victim of incest.

All clinicians confront the marital, individual, or family problems associated with incest whether they are in private practice or in other clinical settings. Findings from a host of research and clinical studies are presented here that indicate that adult survivors of incest suffer from devastating personal and interpersonal difficulties. The presenting problems that often bring survivors into treatment can be divided into four categories, as described later. These areas of dysfunction and the interactive effects form what we call the incest survivor syndrome—a diagnosis that should suggest the codiagnosis of post-traumatic stress disorder.

The past decade has seen a growing awareness of the prevalence and consequences of childhood sexual abuse. Societal recognition of the severity of the problem has taken place in an atmosphere of open and frank discussions of sexual attitudes, behaviors, and experiences. In this climate, there have been increasing reports of childhood sexual experiences and incest in the general population.

A number of first-person accounts have chronicled the experiences of incest victims. These books, written primarily by women, contain narratives about their incest memories, the aftereffects of the trauma, and their difficulties in recovery. Among the more moving publications are Brady's (1979) autobiography of father–daughter incest, Bass and Thornton's (1983) edited stories of female survivors, Evert's (1987) struggles to recover from mother–daughter incest, and Bass and Davis' (1988) guide for female survivors, which also contains numerous first-person reports of incest. Some of these accounts have even found their way into popular magazines, including a former Miss America's discussion of her incest trauma in *People* magazine.

As more women have come forward with their detailed descriptions of being molested, a small but growing number of male victims have also published such accounts. Lew (1988) has edited the narratives of some of his male patients who are incest survivors, while Grubman-Black (1990) has presented both his own case and those of other male victims.

In the past decade, the subject of incest and its aftereffects has become further publicized as a central theme in various novels and movies. Authors like Maya Angelou (1980), herself an incest survivor, and Michelle Morris (1982) have written powerful and moving fictional accounts of women who have been abused. Movies like Barbra Streisand's *Nuts* have broken the taboo in Hollywood against dealing with incest and its consequences.

Coincident with the appearance of these autobiographical and fictionalized accounts has been the emergence of epidemiological research on the incidence of incest. According to Russell's (1986) landmark study, a substantial number of the women in the population, as high as one in five, has had an incestuous experience at some point in childhood. Most of these victims were sexually abused before the age of 14. Other studies, most notably one by Porter (1986), have claimed that one boy out of six will have been sexually victimized by the age of 16, although the incidence of incest has not been established. Russell (1986) has also observed that the majority of perpetrators are male for both male and female victims.

Because incest occurs during childhood, the victim is especially vulnerable to being traumatized for life. An increasing number of investigators have concluded that the victim's later maturation and development will be adversely affected. Browne and Finkelhor (1986) have reported that about 40% of all survivors end up requiring psychotherapy in adulthood.

There is also an emerging awareness among clinicians in both inpatient and outpatient settings that a substantial portion of their caseloads represent incest survivors. Studies of outpatients have found that from 25% to 44% of all outpatients are survivors (Briere, 1984; Rosenfeld, 1979; Westermeyer, 1978). Carmen, Rieker, and Mills (1984) reported that 43% of the adult inpatients in their sample were victims of childhood physical and/or sexual abuse. Similar results were obtained by Emslie and Rosenfeld (1983) in their study of hospitalized children and adolescents. They found that 37.5% of all non-schizophrenic girls and around 8% of the boys had been incestuously victimized.

As more information has appeared about the prevalence and probable consequences of incest, various theoreticians have called into question some of the sacred cows in psychology. Most notable among these widely held beliefs are Freud's oedipal and seduction theories, in which he claimed that his patients' reports of being sexually abused were merely fantasies arising out of their libidinal drives. In the wake of myriad reports on the reality of incest, these theories have been attacked by both feminist writers (Rush, 1980) and psychoanalysts (Masson, 1984; Miller, 1984). Indeed, Miller's (1981, 1983, 1984, 1990) comprehensive writings on the reality and devastating consequences of child physical and sexual abuse have become best-sellers among the general public and required reading for therapists.

In light of these developments, researchers, clinicians, and theoreticians are studying the relationship between the trauma of incest and the later development of psychopathology. As Miller (1990) points out, it was Freud who first made the connection, about 100 years ago, between adult hysteria and childhood incest, but it was also Freud who turned away from his own discoveries. We are apparently returning to the fertile field of inquiry abandoned by Freud in 1897.

THE INCEST SURVIVOR SYNDROME

While the specific relationship between early traumas and the later development of psychopathology in survivors is still under investigation (Rieker & Carmen, 1986), it has become increasingly clear to clinicians that a host of symptoms are generally related to the complex of experiences surrounding the incest. We need, therefore, to understand better the special needs of this population. In particular, clinicians require a more comprehensive picture of what symptoms their patients bring into treatment and how these presenting problems are related to the incest. Only then can we begin to formulate successful treatment plans. The symptoms include low self-esteem, anxiety disorders and chronic depression, eating disorders, drug and alcohol abuse, sexual dysfunction, and abusive marital or incestuous family relations.

We have tried to classify the most common problems presented by survivors into four areas: cognitive, emotional, physical/somatic, and interpersonal. While other classifications are possible, we have attempted to simplify the task by presenting those issues that most often motivate incest victims to seek psychotherapy. Since most survivors do not describe childhood incest as their reason for seeking treatment, clinicians must be aware of the possibility of incest if their clients present with problems in several of these categories.

But while survivors do not have to present with serious psychopathology in all four areas, they often will fall on a continuum of moderate to high dysfunction in all categories. This nexus of problems from the four areas and their interaction effects form the incest survivor syndrome.

COGNITIVE PROBLEMS

"I'm dirty . . . bad . . . damaged."

"Just a piece of shit—that's me."

"I'm useless, trash. . . good for nothing."
—Incest survivors

The most pervasive difficulties with which survivors struggle are issues in self-esteem and self-concept. Poor self-esteem and chronically negative self-references are commonly reported. Survivors also believe that they are inherently bad because there is something fundamentally wrong with them. In two separate studies, Herman (1981) and Lundberg-Love (1990) reported that nearly 100% of their female survivors felt stigmatized, damaged, or irreparably branded.

Survivors also share a predominant belief that they are unlovable. Whether this faulty belief stems from feelings of guilt or of self-blame over the incest is unclear. Nevertheless, as a group, survivors, despite evidence to the contrary from spouses, lovers, children, and therapists, continue to persist in their belief that they are unlovable and bad.

Survivors may also suffer learning difficulties and have poor attention spans. These disabilities often begin in childhood or early adolescence when the abuse is taking place. As adults, the cognitive problems may manifest as gaps in memories, childhood amnesia, thought disorders, or enduring concentration and learning difficulties.

Several studies have documented the clinical observation that most survivors suffer from some degree of dissociative disorder. Browne and Finklehor's (1986) excellent review of the literature concluded that dissociation is a long-term consequence of incest. Briere (1984) reported that 41% of his sample experienced dissociation, 33% derealization, and 21% out-of-body experiences. Lundberg-Love, Crawford, and Geffner's (1987) study of survivors found that 61% of their sample exhibited dissociative symptoms.

For example, in the second case described earlier, Beth Torrence reported an elaborate series of out-of-body experiences and dreamlike states that took place at night when she was alone. Although she was a brilliant woman, she found that she couldn't concentrate sufficiently to do well at school. In addition, Beth had virtually no memories of her early adolescence, although she repeatedly described herself as being "a bad seed."

Another manifestation of the dissociative disorder is a form of psychological splitting. The survivor develops two distinct aspects of self-representation, a "good me" and a "bad me." In certain cases, the "good me" will overcompensate for the shameful existence of the "bad me" through overachievement or perfectionism. In its extreme form, the splitting process may result in multiple personality disorder, that is, the birth of a number of distinct personalities of various ages and different genders. A recent study by Putnam (1989) found that about 85% of patients with the diagnosis of multiple personality disorder had a history of sexual abuse.

EMOTIONAL PROBLEMS

"I'm terrified of the dark."

"I want to die. Nothing has any meaning for me."

"I heard somebody breaking into the house. I started hyperventilating."
                              —Incest survivors

Survivors often come to therapy with symptoms of anxiety and depression. Anxiety disorders such as agoraphobia are common among these patients. Chronic depressive reactions may occur in adolescence and persist well into adulthood. In our view, these are long-term posttraumatic reactions to the incest.

Let us look at some common anxiety or fear reactions. Nightmares, night terrors, insomnia, and fears of sleeping alone are typical symptoms. Nightmares and night terrors are usually recurrent in nature, with basic themes of being chased, hunted, captured, or suffocated. Survivors who are also parents may be afraid to be alone at night, as well as manifest anxious vigilance when the children are sleeping.

Some survivors present with fears of losing their loved ones, especially their partners or spouses. Profound separation anxieties or abandonment terrors are expressed by some patients as early as in the first
few sessions. Others will report that they are afraid of being killed or
annihilated, even in situations in which there is no imminent danger.
These fears are often expressed as having arisen in night terrors or
nightmares. Clients who are torn between fears of abandonment and
of annihilation will often present as lethargic, depressed, and almost
paralyzed.

According to a study by Briere and Runtz (1986), survivors are
much more likely than controls to consider or attempt suicide. They
are also much more prone to self-mutilating behaviors using cigarettes
or razor blades. These activities reflect the underlying depression
and the lack of a desire to live that are characteristic of this population.
Several studies with college-age women have confirmed higher rates
of depression among both clinical and nonclinical samples (Sedney &
Brooks, 1984; Lundberg-Love et al., 1987).

Some survivors present with deadened affect and a quality of numbness. They can report unspeakable horrors they have undergone
without betraying any emotion. These clients have adhered to the
family rule, "Don't talk, don't trust, don't feel" (Black, 1981).

Still another category of emotional reaction to incest is a persistent
and pervasive feeling of shame. Survivors will often report feelings
of wanting to hide from the world or that they do not deserve to
live. Other survivors suffer from chronic guilt over almost anything—
especially enjoyment. Their children's successes, spending money,
or pleasure in eating are sources of or triggers to experiences of guilt.
These feelings come out early in treatment and are not repressed or
even suppressed as they are with many other types of clients. In
Chapter 4, we explore how the issues of shame and guilt originate in
the family of origin and how they are inextricably part of both the
psyche of the client and the family-of-origin system.

Survivors often display what Seligman (1975) has called "learned
helplessness." In the face of chronic abuse and denigration, the
victims come to experience themselves as impotent and helpless.
They have learned not to assert their desires or will or to express their
feelings or beliefs. The apparent passivity and high degree of apathy
that these clients display are similar in some ways to the passivity and
apathy witnessed in concentration camp survivors.

For example, in the Aarons case described earlier, the couple would fight repeatedly. During those quarrels, Mr. Aarons would drink and become extremely abusive verbally. He would break things his wife loved—a favorite picture, a vase—as he derided her for "not being a woman." Mrs. Aarons would simply weep helplessly in response. She reported a great deal of shame and depression about her problems, and often fantasized about committing suicide.

PHYSICAL/SOMATIC PROBLEMS

"I have colitis."

"It's these terrible tension headaches that drive me crazy."

"I have chronic yeast infections and terrible PMS."

"I binge eat."

—Incest survivors

Survivors also complain of many physical disorders, such as gastrointestinal problems, chronic tension, migraines, insomnia, chronic itching or pain in the vaginal area, and nausea. But unlike some writers who see these as psychosomatic complaints or conversion symptoms (e.g., Courtois, 1988), we prefer to view the disorders as physical reactions to extreme stress, in the same way that we view ulcers.

Abused children face overwhelming fear and stress daily. Since they are unable to flee the situation and are captives of their families, their bodies produce tremendous amounts of adrenaline and norepinephrine. No wonder that they later suffer from chronic gastrointestinal and other stress-related disorders.

Lundberg-Love, Crawford, and Geffner, in their 1987 study of female survivors, found a high incidence of somatic complaints. About 50% of their sample reported gastrointestinal problems, pains, and headaches, while 53% were found to have eating disorders. Sedney and Brooks' (1984) college sample reported chronic tension (41%), insomnia (51%), and anxiety and nervousness (59%). The latter study's findings are extremely interesting for two reasons. The sample was a nonclinical population, which makes the results even more powerful. In addition, the findings suggest that the post-traumatic effects of incest are already in place by late adolescence and young adulthood.

Many female survivors report chronic discomfort, pain, and infection in their vaginal or rectal areas. These complaints, coupled with their ongoing feelings of shame, make it extremely difficult for them to undergo routine gynecological exams. Many of our clients are automatically referred to female gynecologists because they had refused to be examined by a man and then, through inertia, had not gone to see anyone for years. One client would faint each time she was examined and would awaken only after the exam was complete.

Another common complaint is chronic nausea, often experienced in anticipation of or during sex. This condition is especially prevalent when the survivor has a history of incest that included oral sex. Because of the extreme nausea, both males and females will often find it impossible to enjoy either giving or receiving oral sex. We view the nausea as a learned response to the incest. Indeed, like the symptom of helplessness, survivors learn certain kinds of responses at the time of the abuse that were adaptive to the intolerable situation. Over time, these responses take on a life of their own even though they may no longer be appropriate.

Two other types of serious physical problems that will often bring survivors into treatment are eating disorders and drug or alcohol abuse. One recent study has shown that a very high percentage of anorexics and bulimics are survivors of childhood sexual abuse. The study by Lundberg-Love and colleagues, mentioned earlier, found that 53% of their sample suffered from eating disorders.

The survivors in the three cases described in this chapter all suffered from somatic complaints. In addition to her problems with alcohol, Beth Torrence was bulimic. Julie Aarons reported vaginal discomfort and nausea in connection with sexual intercourse. And both Laura Green and her mother suffered severe migraine headaches.

Substance Abuse and Adult Children of Alcoholics

Because many survivors are adult children of alcoholics (ACOAs), they share with that population the additional issues of shame and guilt over being products of highly dysfunctional families. While it is not within our scope here to review the ACOA literature, many of the cases we present show the treatment of survivors who are also ACOAs. These survivors come to treatment with all the baggage of shame-bound families. We would agree with Fossum and Mason (1986), who hypothesized that the compulsive disorders related to eating and drug or alcohol abuse (so prevalent among survivors) can be viewed in part as defenses against their shame.

Many clinicians, including Courtois (1988), have confirmed our clinical experience that incest often occurs in the context of an alcoholic family. As children of alcoholics, survivors are at great risk of becoming chemically dependent themselves. Indeed, recent studies have confirmed our clinical findings that as many as four out of 10 survivors are abusing or have abused drugs and alcohol. Lundberg-Love and co-workers (1987) found that 42% of their sample were substance abusers who tended to abuse more than one type of substance. Similarly, Briere (1984) found that 27% of his female survivors had a history of alcoholism and 21% had a history of drug abuse, as compared with 11% and 2% of nonsurvivors respectively. Herman's (1981) study of incest victims indicated that 35% abused drugs and alcohol.

We have also seen that survivors present with spouses who are drug and/or alcohol abusers. In these cases, the survivor may not be an abuser herself, but functions as a codependent partner. In many instances, the entire pattern of the overfunctioning woman and the alcoholic man who abuses the daughter may be repeated. We have seen a substantial minority of family cases (see Chapter 3 for a presentation of the data) in which the intergenerational transmission of alcoholism, codependency, and sexual abuse has occurred.

INTERPERSONAL PROBLEMS

"I've never had a relationship that lasted more than three months."

"I worry about the children all the time."

"I've been attacked four times and raped twice."

"I have no desire for sex."

          —Incest survivors

Survivors often come to therapy with interpersonal issues as their primary concern. Difficulties in committing to or maintaining satisfying intimate relationships, parenting problems, revictimization, and a host of sexual issues are at the top of the list. Numerous studies have shown that female survivors, in comparison with controls, are severely conflict-laden, experience rage and ongoing hostility toward both of their parents, and hold all women in contempt. Courtois' (1979) data indicated that 79% of her female sample had moderate to severe problems relating to men. Against this backdrop, it is understandable that a substantial number of these women are unable to commit to an intimate relationship. Three studies have corroborated that female survivors are less likely to marry than are nonsurvivors (Meiselman, 1978; Courtois, 1979; Russell, 1986). The data in these studies ranged from a high of 40% to a low of 30% of the women never having been married.

The most pervasive problems faced by survivors in relationships are around issues of intimacy. According to Lundberg-Love, Crawford, and Geffner (1987), 89% reported an inability to trust people, while 86% had difficulties in dealing with close relationships. In Meiselman's (1978) study comparing female survivors with a group of controls, 64% of survivors reported conflict and fear with spouses and lovers as compared with 40% of the controls. Because of their lack of trust and the accompanying feelings of fear and anger, survivors have severe difficulties in allowing significant others, especially partners or spouses, to nurture or give to them. They will either rigidly maintain the caretaking role in the relationship or distance themselves. Often, they will complain, especially in couples work, that their partner does not attend to them, but when the therapist intervenes to rectify the situation, the survivor tends not to cooperate. The survivor's inability to be in the cared-for role stems from both a fear of being dependent and the terror of being hurt again.

Another factor that contributes to the dynamics of rigid roles in the couple is the survivor's basic belief that she is unlovable and not worthy of caretaking. While that belief system persists, transactional work with the couple will not be successful. Later chapters in the book detail typical couples' issues and the individual and marital techniques we use for their successful resolution.

Survivors who are able to get married and have children often experience severe anxieties in relation to the children. They will play out their fears of being abused by being hypervigilant concerning their children's safety, for example, in going to or returning home from school, expressing fears about strangers hurting them, and also worrying about their safety when the children go to sleep. Survivors often become highly anxious about their spouses' or partners' becoming perpetrators, either because they have chosen a potential or actual perpetrator (which is unlikely, according to most studies, e.g., Kaufman & Zigler, 1987) or because they have generalized their fears to include all men.

Some survivors present with children in treatment who have been either physically or sexually abused. These children are often referred by the school because of truancy or serious acting out in class or by the police. For example, in the third case described earlier, Laura's mother, Mrs. Green, had been sexually abused by her alcoholic father and had subsequently married an alcoholic who covertly organized his sons to abuse his daughter. She had been extremely codependent with her alcoholic husband and endlessly catered to all his needs at the expense of her and her daughter's needs. The situation had become so intolerable that Laura had begun acting out at home and at school.

Another serious consequence of incest is sexual revictimization. The study by Lundberg-Love and colleagues (1987) found that 50% of their sample had been sexually revictimized. Other studies have also concluded that survivors are at serious risk of being raped or victimized in nonconsenting sexual experiences. For example, in Russell's (1986) study, 68% of the survivors had been victims of either rape or attempted rape. Revictimization will often bring survivors into treatment as they seek to understand why they are always being hurt.

In the past decade, a number of clinically based studies have corroborated what clinicians have seen in their consulting rooms: the devastating effects of incest on later adult sexual functioning (Meiselman, 1978; Herman, 1981; Briere, 1984; Lundberg-Love, 1990). In these studies, as many as 87% of the women studied reported sexual problems. Studies using nonclinical samples have also shown that survivors as young as college age score significantly lower on a measure of sexual self-esteem than do controls (Finkelhor, 1979). And Courtois (1979) showed that up to 80% of nonpatient survivors reported sexual difficulties.

We have found it useful, following Sprei and Courtois (1988), to classify six types of sexual dysfunction that are often described as reasons for entering either individual or couples therapy. These are desire disorders, arousal disorders, orgasmic disorders, coital pain, frequency and satisfaction difficulties, and qualifying information (Schorer, Friedman, Weiler, Heiman, & LoPiccolo, 1980).

Desire disorders fall into two categories: low sexual desire and an aversion to or disgust with sex. In the Lundberg-Love et al. (1987) study, 67% of female survivors experienced an aversion to sex. Briere (1984) reported that 42% of his sample had low sexual desire. These studies suggest that incest victims have been negatively conditioned to sexual activity. As with other learned responses, these behaviors can be difficult to extinguish if they are not understood in the context of the incest. Maltz and Holman (1987) have observed that since the sexual abuse probably constituted the child's first experience with sex, negative conditioning in survivors is very strong. Chapters 7 and 10 present a variety of individual and couples techniques for helping survivors and their partners overcome long-standing sexual difficulties.

Arousal disorders are common in both male and female survivors. In men, victims have problems with impotence or with maintaining erections during either foreplay, oral sex, or intercourse. These difficulties are seen among both homosexuals and heterosexuals. The sexual preference of the client does not appear to lessen the traumatic consequences of the incest where sexual arousal is the issue.

In female survivors, arousal problems manifest themselves as difficulties with lubrication or as no lubrication at all. If intercourse is then attempted, pain is sure to follow. Many couples (or individuals) who present in sex therapy with this problem are unaware of the symptom's connection with an incest history. Other women may suffer from a lack of sensation or a numbness in the vaginal area that precludes the possibility of arousal. In the Lundberg-Love et al. (1987) sample, 36% reported problems in becoming sexually aroused.

Orgasmic disorders are also common to both male and female survivors. Problems with retarded ejaculation or a total inability to achieve orgasm occur frequently among men. Among gay men, these difficulties may be explained as the result of not "being around the right kind of lover" or other, similar reasons. In Chapter 11, we discuss typical issues facing both heterosexual and homosexual male survivors and the similarities and differences in treating them.

In women, survivors may be able to achieve orgasm only through solitary masturbation. We have found that even manual stimulation by a spouse will often fail to bring the woman to orgasm. In many women, solitary masturbation may be experienced as the only safe way to enjoy sexual activity (Courtois, 1988).

Survivors are often referred by their physicians or gynecologists because of severe coital pain, vaginismus, or dyspareunia. Vaginismus results from involuntary muscle spasms during intercourse. Dyspareunia, defined as pain experienced during intercourse, comes from the Greek word for "unhappily mated as bedfellows." These symptoms can prevent the couple from having sex even though the survivor may want very much to do so.

The study by Lundberg-Love and co-workers (1987) found that 56% of their sample reported unsatisfactory sexual relationships. But as Courtois (1988) has noted, many widely divergent patterns exist in terms of both frequency and satisfaction. In our experience, a substantial percentage of both male and female survivors engage in sexual promiscuity or acting out at some point in their lives. In the Lundberg-Love et al. sample, 58% of the women had engaged in this behavior. Other studies have reported significantly lower figures, but the period of observation involved was considerably shorter than the period of more than two years covered by the Lundberg-Love, Crawford, and Geffner study. In our experience, survivors will often oscillate between abstinence and promiscuity, depending on such life-cycle variables as the length of the relationship, the ages of any children, the "empty nest" syndrome, and the survivor's age. Lundberg-Love (1990) has also observed that survivors may exhibit low sexual drive at one stage of the life cycle, whereas at other stages, they may report more heightened activity. For example, in the Aarons case, Julie Aarons, who had almost no sexual desire for her husband, had gone through a period of promiscuity during her adolescence—a period in which she had had sex with over a dozen boys.

Qualifying information is what Courtois (1988) refers to in describing other variables that affect sexual functioning. These include flashbacks, memories, and other intrusions that are triggered by sex. Dissociation and derealization also can occur during sex. These states are adaptive in the sense that the survivor is at least able to be physically present, but unfortunately they may preclude any sexual enjoyment. Other qualifying information we have found to be important is evidence of physical damage suffered by the victim during the incest. In Chapter 3, we present a transcript in which a survivor discusses how a violent incestuous episode left her with permanent physical and psychological scars.

POST-TRAUMATIC STRESS DISORDER AND INCEST

The concept of the incest survivor syndrome has been developed as a useful guide to clinicians who work with victims of incest. In our experience, survivors who come for treatment suffer dysfunction in every major aspect of their lives. Even those patients who, for example, have successful careers are apt to be unable to enjoy that success and to live in fear of abandonment or annihilation. Such survivors, in particular, will often ask how it is possible that events that occurred so many years earlier could so profoundly influence them today.

How, then, can we understand the onset and intractability of the syndrome and its apparent relationship to the incest trauma? As discussed earlier, survivors have been subjected to conditions of extreme stress. As children, they grew up in families in which they could not exert control over either their parents' behavior, especially that of the perpetrator, or their own boundaries and space. They generally lived in fear and over time developed a condition that we would describe as similar to Seligman's (1975) portrayal of "learned helplessness." Indeed, the Seligman experiments shed light on the stressful conditions under which abused children live and their subsequent reactions to those stressors. In Chapter 4 we describe those experiments and show how victims of abuse become powerless individuals.

Because the incest experience is stressful for most children and they have great difficulty escaping from it, it is quite understandable how survivors develop lasting reactions to being molested by family members. Children's coping mechanisms are ill equipped to deal with a trauma that is outside the range of their expectations of normal family relations. In that sense, incest is a traumatic event as defined by the revised third edition of the *Diagnostic and Statistical Manual of Mental Disorders* (DSM-III-R) (American Psychiatric Association, 1987) in that it is a distressing experience that would upset almost anyone and occurs outside the range of usual human experience.

Furthermore, survivors' reactions to the trauma also meet the criteria set forth in DSM-III-R for post-traumatic stress disorder (PTSD). As we detailed earlier, research has shown that survivors suffer from flashbacks and recollections of the trauma, and also may evidence numbing of affect, feelings of isolation or detachment, dissociative disorders or psychogenic amnesia, hypervigilance, difficulties in falling asleep, and symptoms of anxiety and depression. All of these symptoms are part of the criteria for PTSD in DSM-III-R. In sum then, there can be little doubt that the extremely stressful situations surrounding the incest (including the familial control, denial, and enforced silence) create intolerable psychological conditions for the victim. Over time, these conditions give rise to the reactions that typify the incest survivor syndrome.

We concur with Briere (1984) who has called for a diagnosis of postsexual abuse syndrome. Courtois (1988) also has argued convincingly that PTSD should be used as the principal Axis I diagnosis or as a secondary diagnosis to survivors' other symptoms. The reader is referred to Courtois' excellent review of the current literature on PTSD and the incest trauma.

Along with Courtois, Briere, and others, we believe that the evidence is compelling to consider the PTSD diagnosis in addition to the diagnosis for one or more of the client's other symptoms. It is time for practitioners to have in mind a dual diagnosis when treating clients who are incest survivors and who present with a varied symptomatology. Keeping a dual diagnosis in mind will remind both the clinician and the client (or client family) that the presenting difficulties are responses to and legacies of an intolerable situation. As we discuss throughout this book, normalizing the client's symptoms and depathologizing the survivor are integral parts of a successful treatment plan. The dual-diagnosis view, then, helps to facilitate the normalizing process for all treatment participants, including the therapist.

SUMMARY

Survivors often present in therapy with a variety of cognitive, emotional, physical, and interpersonal difficulties. These problems and their interaction effects form the incest survivor syndrome. Because incest has powerful consequences for the victim, a diagnosis of posttraumatic stress disorder needs to be given in addition to the diagnosis of the presenting complaint. A dual diagnosis will assist the clinician, the patient, and the patient's family in normalizing the presenting problems and in depathologizing the survivor.

CHAPTER 2

DETERMINING WHO IS A SURVIVOR

*"Something strange happened last week while my husband was
trying to arouse me sexually. I remembered someone very rough
lying on top of me, I could almost smell his breath. I was very
frightened and started to cry."*

—A married survivor

Unless we are well known in our communities as experts on survivors
of childhood and adolescent sexual abuse, clients generally do not
come to us with incest as the presenting problem. They come to
therapists with vague anxieties, depressions of unknown origin,
substance-abuse problems, career difficulties, problems with hard-to-
handle children, and complaints about relationships. Since this is the
case, the therapist must leave open the possibility that any of his or
her clients may have been sexually abused and have suppressed the
memories.

The fact that a significant piece of historical information is unavailable to the client and the therapist is, of course, troublesome. Even
worse than this ambiguity, however, are the relational implications;
that is, the therapy commences with a secret or an unconscious lie.
Since the childhood experience of the incest survivor is shrouded in
unspoken, carefully guarded secrets and unconscious "knowing," the
therapy can become a repetition of all that was pathological in the
family of origin. Indeed, the therapist may sense that the client

was abused but for either strategic or countertransferential reasons remains silent. The client knows, but cannot remember or speak. If the spouse is involved in treatment, he may also collude to maintain the secret by withholding information or anecdotes about the survivor's family or about her childhood experiences.

The impact of these secrets is felt most in the initial bonding phases of the treatment. If the therapeutic relationship is constructed on a falsehood or secret, the therapy becomes a place that is too similar to the original family experience. Clients will then recreate and replay their dysfunctional patterns of maintaining secrets with the therapist that will affect the entire treatment process. They will unconsciously expect the therapy to be yet another place where the truth cannot be told and certain subjects are taboo. Under these circumstances, survivors will tend to conceal other important historical and contemporary information, as well as to hide facets of their innermost thoughts and feelings. Therefore, the longer the truth remains unspoken, the more compromised the therapy becomes.

The incest truth must be revealed for more than just the opportunity of working through that particular trauma. A profound cognitive and interpersonal restructuring takes place when clients no longer need to build their self-image or intimate relationships around the protection of others. By revealing secrets, survivors can begin to discover their own needs, wants, beliefs, and goals. In short, they can begin the journey to redefining and transforming their identities as distinct from the people they were in their families of origin.

INDICATORS OF ABUSE

Since most survivors do not enter treatment with the incest as the presenting complaint, clinicians are often perplexed as to how to recognize a victim of childhood sexual abuse. Lundberg-Love, et al (1992) have shown that incest survivors score significantly higher than controls on six of 10 clinical scales of the Minnesota Multiphasic Personality Inventory (MMPI). Survivors reported more somatization, alienation, impulsivity, social introversion, depression, anxiety, and ruminations. Intake procedures that include administering MMPIs and examining the profile patterns may assist the clinician in recognizing a survivor.

Other authors, such as Courtois (1988), have developed intake interviews in which the patient is routinely asked about childhood sexual experiences in the context of taking a family history. The nonchalance of the clinician in eliciting traumatic material can go a long way toward giving the client permission to discuss the incest. Once the incest has been disclosed, the therapist may choose to use a structured questionnaire, such as the excellent one developed by Courtois (1988), to get at more of the details.

Structured questionnaires that ask about current and past sexual experiences can also uncover an incest history. These instruments are especially appropriate for those individuals or couples who present with sexual difficulties. For example, the Purdue Sex History Form (Trepper & Barrett, 1989) not only asks patients about their sexual likes and dislikes, but also if they were physically or sexually abused as children.

We have also found it useful to evaluate all new patients on the presence and degree of dysfunction in the four key areas described in Chapter 1. Survivors, unlike most other clients, will typically report, in the first few sessions, that they suffer from moderate to severe problems in their cognitive, emotional, somatic, and interpersonal functioning. The survivor's profile, then, can be seen in the presence of dysfunction in all four areas and in their interactions.

On the other hand, the absence of pathology in any of these categories may indicate that the client is not a survivor or that the abuse was minimal. Keeping in mind this and the other indicators described in this chapter can help therapists discriminate clients along a continuum of abuse severity and abuse-related disorders. Simply put, the more severe the symptomatology, the more likely it is that the abuse was ongoing and brutal.

Predictors of Abuse

Gerald Ellenson (1985, 1986) has described a number of other factors that may be predictive of childhood sexual abuse. These include:

1. Recurring nightmares with at least one of the following:
    a. Catastrophes that endanger the client or family members.
    b. Children being harmed or killed.

    c. Client or family members being chased by attackers.

    d. Scenes of death or violence.

2. Certain types of obsessions, which include impulses to harm one's child or a sudden feeling that one's child is in danger or is being harmed.

3. Recurring dissociation that involves sudden sensations that the client's child is an unrelated stranger or a sense that the client's past was actually the past of a total stranger.

4. Persistent phobias regarding being alone or in a physically compromised situation.

5. Recurring illusions of an evil/malevolent entity in the home or in the body.

6. Recurring auditory hallucinations of:

    a. Hearing a child or person crying or calling.

    b. Hearing an intruder or booming, frightening sounds.

7. Recurring visual hallucinations of:

    a. The movement of objects or figures in the corner of the eyes.

    b. Shadows/shadowy figures seen in the home.

    c. The appearance of a dark silhouetted figure when in bed at night.

8. Recurring tactile hallucinations involving physical sensations that range from a light touch to being physically pushed or thrown down.

Ellenson (1985) also found that any combination of seven symptoms or more is predictive, while any combination of five symptoms, including at least one perceptual disturbance, or the presence of two perceptual disturbances is highly predictive of incest. The clinician who uses a combination of the methods presented here will be able to determine the presence or absence of incest with a high degree of probability. But the reader is cautioned that timing is everything in the treatment of survivors. Be certain that the client is ready to discuss the trauma before bringing up the material.

IN-THERAPY CLUES

There are other indicators that can point to a history of abuse. These are in-therapy clues to which the therapist must attend. They include dissociative behavior in the session, amnesia or forgetfulness about the contents of the last session, an inability to maintain object constancy with the therapist, the wearing of extra clothing or covering up, or overflirtatiousness.

Here-and-Now Indicators

Survivors often have difficulty staying in the here and now during sessions. Frequently, they will forget what they were saying, seem to drift out the window, will "tune out" the conversation, or will change topics in midsentence. One client would trail off in the middle of her sentences, especially when she was talking about her adolescence. When the therapist gently asked her to complete her thought, she responded: "There's no point in talking about it. What's done is done." In subsequent sessions, the therapist learned that the woman's mother had remarried when the client was 12 years old. Within a year, her stepfather had begun to molest her. The incest had continued throughout the client's teenage years.

Recurrent Amnesia

Another sign of an abuse history is recurrent amnesia about the contents of the previous session. We will often give our clients specific homework assignments between sessions and we carefully observe their reactions to the tasks. When clients "forget" after having agreed to carry out the task, and do so several times, they may be doing something other than "resisting" in the usual way.

In one case, a single parent had agreed that she would sit with her 10-year-old son and help him with his math homework, since he was doing poorly. For three weeks in a row, the client completely forgot to do so. The therapist learned that the woman had excelled in mathematics, and had even taught the subject in high school. He began to suspect that the client was experiencing anxiety when she thought about sitting close to her son. He asked her to imagine sitting next to her boy and doing math. The client began to cry softly, and between her muffled sobs said, "I won't do that to him." Over the next few months, the woman told of how her father had helped her with schoolwork, and then afterward had made her touch his genitals.

The homework assignment had restimulated the memory, and in order to cope, the client had forgotten the task assignment and all the relevant material from the session.

Another variation on the theme of amnesia is the client's inability to internalize the clinician or maintain object constancy. Many clinicians, as a process goal in treatment, ask their clients, either directly or indirectly, to "take" the therapist with them in between sessions. This intervention fosters the internalization of the therapist and strengthens the therapeutic alliance. Some clients, however, are unable to "carry" the therapist beyond the office door. They do not think about the therapist at all in between sessions or about what was discussed in the latest session. In a longer-term type of therapy, this can be considered unusual client behavior.

One male survivor, who suffered from acute anxiety on the job, repeatedly forgot the therapist's name and missed the exit off the highway that led to the office for a period of four months. He would start each session by telling her that he had a lot to discuss, and then would routinely sit in silence. The therapist suggested that he keep a diary so that he could write down his thoughts and feelings during the week. The client responded that he never thought of the therapist, and that if he did, he quickly put her out of his mind. Over a year went by before the client remembered that his father had forced him to have sex with him.

Dress

Some clients will protect themselves by leaving their coats on even if the office is too warm, or by coming to sessions wearing layer upon layer of clothing. If the therapist has a couch with pillows, some clients will create a barricade of pillows around themselves or sink into the couch in the position of children playing peek-a-boo. Some survivors, if given a choice, will sit as far away as possible from the therapist.

At the other end of the continuum are clients who dress in an extremely provocative manner and who begin to flirt with the clinician almost immediately. One client, who came to sessions dressed in a miniskirt, would slouch in her chair and point her legs in the direction of the therapist. The clinician decided to tell her that this behavior was making him uncomfortable. The woman replied that she was surprised to hear that since, in her experience, most men enjoyed looking at her. The therapist asked her when she had first realized that a man had been looking at her and desiring her. With very little hesitation, she said that her brother, who was 10 years older than she was, had told her how beautiful she was when she was 8 years old. Over the next five years, he had molested her in every conceivable way. When she turned 13, she ran away from home and began sleeping with older men who allowed her to stay with them for short periods.

CLUES IN HISTORY TAKING

Careful history taking may also reveal clues about sexual abuse. For example, the client may discuss a woman-friend's sexual escapades or a quasi-sexual relationship with her brother. These anecdotes may be trial balloons to test the clinician's reaction. Or the client may tell a horrible story of child sexual abuse in the middle of a totally unrelated discussion. Out-of-context or tangential references to incest are often signals that clients are sending to alert us to the presence of abuse.

Sexual Promiscuity

We have found that a history of sexual promiscuity, running away from home, or juvenile delinquency is frequently associated with incest. Sexual relationships with older boys or men, especially in adolescence (as in the case of the overly flirtatious client mentioned above), are also a possible sign. One female survivor, who had been arrested for shoplifting as a teenager, had been in court-ordered counseling and never told her counselor that she was being molested at home. She told the therapist that she was initially relieved when she was arrested because she was sure they would send her to jail.

Other clients may tell you that they were promiscuous or stayed out all night "right under their parents' noses." One woman told of how her father waited up for her one night and surprised her when she had sneaked back into the house. She said that her father had "thrown a fit," but then never mentioned the incident again. The survivor had taken his silence to mean that she was allowed to stay out. Moreover, the client also began to realize that if she did stay out, she could avoid having sex with her father. During the course of treatment, the client came to realize, as well, that by not disciplining her, the client's father had tacitly given her permission to end their relationship.

A number of clinicians have also noted that many survivors oscillate between sexual promiscuity and lack of desire over the life cycle. These bipolar behaviors may reflect an underlying bipolarity in affect. Lees (1981), and more recently Lundberg-Love (1990), observed bipolar patterns of affect, cognition, and behavior in some of their female survivors. Patients who present with these patterns may well be survivors. Because of these findings, we have begun to pay closer attention in our history taking to the presence of vacillations between extremes throughout the patient's life.

Overly Sexualized Play

Some survivors, even early in treatment, will reveal that they had been sexually involved with a younger sibling or neighbor. They will discuss how guilty they have felt about their taking advantage of someone younger. Therapists will, at times, attempt to reduce these guilt feelings without adequate exploration of the client's family life. We have found all too frequently that overly sexualized play in a client's background is often a symptom of a dysfunctional family in which incest may have occurred. In our experience, these survivors will more readily reveal that they have molested someone else than that they themselves have been abused.

UNRAVELING THE SECRET

Good clinical judgment dictates that we develop hypotheses about our clients based on data accumulated from a variety of sources. Among such sources are psychological testing; the presence of anxiety disorders along with cognitive, physical, and interpersonal/sexual problems; in-therapy behaviors of patients, including amnesia and flirtatiousness; and peculiarities in patients' histories, including extremes in sexual behavior and running away from home.

Another good source of information is the client's spouse or partner.

Whenever possible, we include partners in the treatment of survivors. Later chapters discuss the rationale and treatment strategies for including partners throughout the treatment. Partners will, if asked, be more likely than the client to disclose an incest history because they usually do not feel particularly loyal to their in-laws. In one instance, a woman who found it difficult to achieve orgasm brought her spouse at the therapist's request. In the first couple session, the husband revealed that his wife had recurrent nightmares in which she was being chased by a dark male figure. The therapist asked both spouses if they knew who the man was. When the wife said no, the spouse chimed in: "Of course you do, honey, it's your father." That remark began the telling of the trauma.

Once the therapist has determined that the clues and signs point toward a history of incest, he or she can slowly initiate some discussion around the issue. Conversations may range from vague nonspecific references to something frightening having occurred in childhood that would account for some of the symptoms to overt and specific questions about parent–child interactions. What we seek to avoid, however, is therapeutic silence or, at the other extreme, the inappropriate and ill-timed remark, "You must be an incest survivor."

The Zeitgeist

In the current zeitgeist of greater openness about incest, we are becoming more aware of therapists who precipitously make interpretations about an incest history. It is crucial to the formation of a successful alliance that the clinician serve as a midwife in the process of disclosure, and not as a battering ram. The survivor must take the lead in the process. Uncovering the incest trauma then becomes an important matter of time and timing. If the trauma is never revealed, the client will terminate treatment without having had an opportunity to work through the abuse and to grow. If the trauma is revealed too quickly, the client will become frightened and either terminate therapy prematurely or suppress the trauma further.

In one case, the survivor was only willing in a vague way to acknowledge that she had been molested. Any attempts on the clinician's part to deal with the topic were immediately sidestepped by the client. This particular dance continued for four months until the client was ready to deal with the issue. She came in one day and announced that since Thanksgiving was approaching, she needed to decide whether to attend dinner at her parents' house. Only then did she begin to tell the story of how her stepfather had abused her.

Once the client has spoken about the incest, the therapist can proceed on much surer footing. The therapist can, for example, determine which methods for memory retrieval will be useful in the particular case. Chapter 7 details the various methods we employ. The essential message we convey to our clients is: "The truth can, will, and must come to the surface and we will both show courage in facing it. And, in this way, healing will take place."

A Cautionary Note

Another danger of the current public disclosures by survivors is an overzealousness on the part of clients and clinicians in defining incest. A small percentage of patients have a tendency to overdramatize or histrionically inflate certain interactions with family members that they characterize as incestuous. Other clients (thankfully, a very small minority) exhibit serious sociopathic tendencies. These patients will unabashedly lie about their family histories in general and about their being abused in particular. Therapists need to recognize that some clients revel in being in the victim role, while others pretend to be victims when they are really exploitative sociopaths.

An example of an overdramatizing client was one woman who claimed that she had been "severely sexually abused" by her brother. In the course of taking a detailed history, the client revealed how her brother would make obscene gestures at her by "giving her the finger" or by telling her, "Go fuck yourself." The therapist asked the woman if the brother had disrobed in front of her, forced his way into her bedroom, or made any sexual advances. She replied, "No." Her answers to these and other detailed questions indicated that while her brother had demeaned her verbally and nonverbally, he had not sexually abused her.

Misrepresentations and false accusations not only are destructive to clients' family members, but also serve to cast doubt on the severity of real survivors' traumatic experiences. Because many therapists, including ourselves, ask clients to confront their family members about incest, it is important that we are as clear as possible about what actually occurred in the family of origin. This caution prevents us from incorrectly unleashing powerful interactional forces that could prove destructive to the survivor, her family of creation, and her family of origin. In the following section, we provide several definitions of what constitutes an incest experience. These definitions are to be used in conjunction with the signs and indicators detailed in this chapter.

WHAT IS INCEST?

As we all know, parenting includes caretaking activities that involve contact with a child's breasts, genitals, and anus. Very few of us would construe the normal daily cleaning and bathing of younger children as a manifestation of abuse. Indeed, parents who do not ensure that their children are clean are typically seen as inadequate or neglectful guardians. Clearly then, normal parenting mandates some contact with a child's private parts.

What, then, constitutes abuse? As many writers, including Glueck (1965) and Rosenfeld (1977), have observed, there is a continuum of parent–child activities of which only some can be considered abusive. For example, in Rosenfeld's schema, the hygienic caretaking described above is considered to be in the midrange or normal part of the continuum, along with hugging and showing affection to the child. Child neglect and total lack of parental affection and attention are at one end of the continuum. At the other extreme are sexual abuse, rape, and other acts of sexual exploitation.

We agree with most clinicians who use the criterion of informed consent as the basis for deciding whether an act is to be considered abusive. In our view, since most children are in a less powerful position than their parents, other adult family members, and older siblings, and are often dependent on them, sexual demands that are put on the children can readily be seen as exploiting the relationship. Any sexual act whose aim is to gratify the adult and which exploits the child's naiveté or lack of power is seen as abusive. Such activities as the adult's exposing himself to the child or disrobing the child for voyeuristic pleasure would fit the definitions of abuse proposed by Benward and Densen-Gerber (1975), Sgroi, Blick, and Porter (1982), and Steele (1986).

Courtois (1988) has elaborated on and extended the definition of incest to stress its similarity to rape.

> Incest is a form of rape—rape within the family, with additional potential for damage to the victim due to the relationship between perpetrator and victim. The relationship increases rather than decreases the traumatic impact of the abuse. The dynamics of incest distinguish it from rape perpetrated by a stranger, the most pertinent having to do with the adult's access to the child by virtue of kinship ties and authority, the secrecy, the betrayal of trust, the child's powerlessness, and the repeated and developmentally inappropriate nature of the violations. Further support for conceptualizing incest as a form of rape comes from the reactions suffered by victims. They can best be described as compounded and intensified rape trauma reactions with some differences due to the special dynamics of incest. (p. 16)

Neither this definition nor the ones mentioned above reflect the current legal standards for what constitutes incest. While incest is forbidden throughout the United States, various states use different definitions for abuse. In general, though, sexual contact, which is usually defined as sexual intercourse, between blood relatives or between other kin such as members of a stepfamily is considered incestuous. Incest, then, legally entails parents, stepparents, siblings, and in-laws.

Some well-respected researchers in the field have taken issue with both the breadth of the proposed definitions and the overly politicized (i.e., male-bashing) nature of the discussions surrounding incest. For example, both Finkelhor (1978) and Rosenfeld (1979) have criticized the incest-as-rape hypothesis as being incorrect factually, since most abuse takes place over a longer time, usually with consent, and rarely or only occasionally involves force or violence.

Yet, despite these apparent differences, we have found that from the patients' point of view, and from their reactions to the trauma, they perceive and experience themselves as having been violated and dirtied as if they had been raped by strangers. As we discussed in Chapter 1, this particular cognitive and emotional reaction has been found in almost all survivors studied.

We have, therefore, found it more useful clinically to use the definition for incest that utilizes the three principles of informed consent, exploitation of the child's naiveté or lack of power, and the sexual gratification of the older person. There are two reasons for this: we seek not to minimize the patient's experience of the trauma, and we seek to prevent the patient's spouse, the perpetrator, and other family members, and sometimes the patient herself, from minimizing the traumatic psychological consequences of the incest. The usefulness of not minimizing the abuse will become clearer as we describe the dynamics of the survivor's family of origin. In the next chapter, we examine the different types of incest and the specific family and individual dynamics associated with each.

SUMMARY

Several important methods have been developed to determine which clients are incest survivors. These include the presence and severity of problems in all four areas of cognitive, emotional, physical, and interpersonal functioning. Other signs can be gleaned from screening questionnaires and paper-and-pencil measures, patient behaviors in therapy, patterns in the patient's history, and information gained from the spouse. In our experience, the more indicators that point to an incest profile, the more confident we are of making the diagnosis. We use a fairly broad definition for what constitutes incest in order to avoid minimizing the trauma with either the patient or her family.

CHAPTER 3

THE SURVIVOR'S FAMILY OF ORIGIN

Family therapists first began to deal with incestuous families in the late 1960s and to observe their structures and interactional styles. In this chapter, we present a brief historical overview of theoretical work on incest families, data on the prevalence and type of incest, studies of perpetrators and their families of origin, and studies of families in which incest takes place. In the process of presenting these data, our own clinical observations, and those of other experienced clinicians, we hope to dispel some myths about the dynamics of perpetrators, their spouses, their victims, and the structures and processes of incestuous families. As each type of incest occurs under somewhat unique circumstances, a discussion of similarities and differences among them is of interest, as well.

This chapter also presents the most commonly occurring types of incestuous relationships with females. (Chapter 11 details the most frequently reported types of abuse with males.) Knowing the key systemic and individual dynamics that characteristically operate in each relationship, as described here, can be enormously helpful to the practitioner. Developing hypotheses, understanding the survivor's marital and parenting issues, formulating treatment plans, and making interpretations and interventions all will be accomplished more readily when the clinician has a deeper appreciation of the survivor's family of origin and the type of incest she has suffered. It is in the context of these family and individual dynamics that the personalities of survivors are formed.

FATHER–DAUGHTER INCEST

One of the most common types of incest, and certainly the most intensely studied to date, is that between fathers and daughters. In her landmark study, Russell (1986) found that about 5% of all girls are sexually abused by their fathers. In describing the families in which father–daughter incest took place, the early family therapists (e.g., Machotka, Pittman, and Flomenhaft, 1967) pointed out that incest had to be considered a "family affair." By this reframing, they hoped to blame no one person and, at the same time, to spread the blame around among other family members, especially the mother. Furthermore, they wanted to create a reality in which all members were also victims, not just the abused child.

In their writings, these pioneers drew a picture of an incest family in which, more often than not, mothers were either physically or psychologically absent. They were emotionally distant from their spouses and their daughters. In the context of this arrangement, men turned to their daughters for comfort, and even sex. The girls could not report these events to their mothers because they were estranged from them.

The distant-mother hypothesis led to other corollaries. One of the most important assumptions that many therapists made was that the mothers really knew what was going on. Clinicians believed that even when the mothers denied knowing about the incest, at some preconscious or unconscious level of awareness, they really "did know." In some instances, the mothers themselves had been victimized as children and had repressed the trauma. Their denial, then, represented not only the family's suppression of truth, but also their own.

An unfortunate consequence of this viewpoint was that some clinicians began to blame women for their husbands', brothers', or sons' behaviors. As Leupnitz (1988) has pointed out, a subtle misogyny is built into any theoretical model that holds the woman responsible for the man's abusive behavior even when it is couched in more neutral language, such as "distant." The mother-blaming interventions only compounded the problems of the victims by further disempowering and denigrating women in families.

Partly as a reaction to this viewpoint, and partly as an outgrowth of the women's movement, some clinicians began to focus more of their attention on either the victim or the perpetrator. Individual therapy to help each of them became a standard prescription. In this model, women were victims of male perpetrators and of a male-dominated culture and, therefore, could not be held responsible.

Our view recognizes the strengths of each position and seeks to avoid their limitations. Father–daughter incest *is* a family affair in that it affects all members and occurs because there have been breakdowns in the structure and process of normal family life. But there are also significant individual dynamics at play in these systems. Only by examining both the family and the individual issues, system, and psyche can we develop a comprehensive model for understanding and treating survivors. Let us then look at some of the key elements that are present in these cases.

In every case that we have ever seen of father–daughter incest, there is a highly dysfunctional marital relationship. The spouses often have few shared interests or friends in common. Courtois (1988) has observed that the spouses may have been incompatible from the outset. The lack of commonality is also mirrored in their emotional distance. The spouses are unable to meet each other's needs for companionship, affection, and nurturance.

The spouses also have very poor communication and conflict-resolution skills. They carry with them long lists of grievances about each other that fester and impede the possibility of intimacy. The spouses will often communicate these grievances to the children or use the children as go-betweens or messengers. This type of triangulation is characteristic of very disturbed marriages and helps to create a foundation for other, more serious problems (Kirschner & Kirschner, 1986).

The inability to communicate directly to each other prevents the partners from functioning as an effective parental team. As a result, consistent discipline, nurturance, and guidance are lacking. Children are often inappropriately put into adult roles. At times, they are asked to be parental caretakers; that is, they are expected to meet their parents' emotional needs while their own needs are ignored. At other times, children are put in the role of parental children; that is, they are expected to take care of their siblings, the household, and themselves because the parents are absent, are intoxicated, or simply have abdicated responsibility.

All three elements—the distance in the marriage, the poor communication skills and destructive triangulation of children, and the divided parental team with children inappropriately cast as parental figures—are features of families with father–daughter incest. Against the backdrop of these elements, the spouses are also unable to share power equally in the family. As a result, one or the other partner becomes the dominant one. In father–daughter incest, we have seen three types of family hierarchies: the father-dominant type, the mother-dominant type, and a third type in which both spouses abdicate authority and put the children in charge. Each of these family types has its own unique features in terms of both individual and systemic dynamics.

The Father-Dominant Family

The first type of family is the one that has received the most scrutiny. This is the father-dominant family. The husbands tend to be more authoritarian and to dominate the family's decision making. These authoritarian perpetrators are the ones who have traditionally been viewed as more emotionally disturbed than most patients, or simply as "evil." Yet, to date, no research study has ever found that abusive fathers are more disturbed than other outpatient men (Meiselman, 1978).

The psychopathology of these men, however, may appear in two areas: alcoholism and sexual dysfunction. There is ample research that shows that possibly up to 50% of all incest fathers can be considered alcoholics (Virkkunen, 1974; Meiselman, 1978). For the dominant male, drinking may trigger episodes in which he both physically abuses his wife and sexually abuses his daughter. In these alcoholic systems, the women serve as codependents and enable the perpetrator through their silence, fear, and distance.

In the male-dominant family, the women are more distant from their spouses primarily because they are devalued in the relationship. In almost all cases we have seen, these women grew up in families in which they and their mothers were denigrated and were not in positions of power. In some instances, these women are reliving their own sexual abuse at the hands of a violent father. The traumatic consequences of having been sexually abused as children and then physically abused as adults become too much to bear. They will become physically ill, severely depressed, or even suicidal. At times, the mothers may leave by escaping to a psychiatric facility where they can be left alone.

Because they themselves either are survivors or have been severely beaten down, mothers in the father-dominant family are unable to guide or serve as effective role models for their daughters. They will often put their daughters in charge of the household and the other siblings, or ask them to be parental caretakers.

It is in the latter role that daughters become victimized by their fathers. Because their mothers lack the power and energy to function appropriately, the daughters are asked to fulfill the fathers' emotional needs. In this way, they function as substitutes for their mothers, as companions at night, and eventually as lovers. While many of these situations do begin simply out of a need for companionship, some perpetrators do not develop a warm or affectionate relationship with their daughters and will simply molest them.

Many therapists believe that the spouses in father-dominant families do not have sex with their husbands and that is why the fathers turn to their daughters. While we have found that where father–daughter incest occurs, there is almost always marital sexual dysfunction (also see Waterman, 1986), the particular sexual problems vary from family to family. There may be disorders of desire, impotence, or premature ejaculation. However, only some of our cases have no sexual activity between the spouses.

Another sexual problem seen in the male-dominant families is sex addiction. These men have sex with their wives frequently, have sex with their daughters, and even conduct affairs with other women. Many of these sex addicts were themselves victims of child sexual abuse. Carnes (1991) has found that 81% of his male sex addicts were sexually abused as children. Of these, 33% of the men had been abused by their fathers or mothers. The pattern of incest leading to sex addiction and to further incest only recently was identified and requires further study.

In sum then, the male-dominant pattern that the pioneering family therapists first described as the prototypical incestuous family does exist, but only as one type of incest system. In these groups, the daughters may act as their fathers' caretakers and/or as substitutes for the mothers. Physical abuse of spouses also is often present, especially when the male is an alcoholic. The sexual life of the couple is dysfunctional, but with differences from marriage to marriage.

The Mother-Dominant Family

The second kind of father–daughter incest family is one in which the mother is dominant. In these families, most financial and child-rearing decisions are made unilaterally by the woman. In many cases, the man will come home on payday and give his wife the entire check. She then will allot him a certain amount of spending money, much as she would with the children's allowance. When we have assessed these families, the hierarchical map shows the wife on top and the husband at the same level as the kids. Often, the incest that then occurs is similar to that between siblings.

The fathers in these families often present in therapy as backward, inadequate men who act like victims themselves. In their histories, we find, almost universally, that they have suffered from physical abuse, abandonment, or sexual abuse. Two different reports have shown that somewhere between 30% and 50% of male offenders were either sexually abused as children or witnessed incest between their fathers and sisters (Pelto, 1981; Kaufman & Zigler, 1987). The sexual victimization of these fathers had apparently predisposed them to view sexual activity between adults and children as "normal."

The traumatic consequences of their own abuse have also left many male survivors with shattered egos and a sense of valuelessness. These men, like the women in the male-dominant families, behave in a childish and passive way.

It has been our experience that some of these perpetrators are also addicted to sex, albeit as voyeurs or pedophiles. Their own victimization has left them basically unable to relate sexually to other adults. They prefer sex with children, compulsive masturbation, or voyeuristic activities at adult bookstores. Often it is when they drink that they become disinhibited and their defenses weaken. At those times, they may turn to their daughters for sexual gratification.

Their wives, on the other hand, despise them for being weak and inept. The women are often encapsulated narcissists who are aware of only their own needs and wants. They are unconcerned about their daughters' needs, except as the daughters exist to serve their mothers. These women have little interest in having sex with their husbands and are only too glad to be rid of them. The victims, in turn, are unable to disclose their pain and betrayal to the mothers because they are not interested. In a very real sense, the fathers and daughters are joined as common refugees from a petty tyrant.

Some survivors from mother-dominant families have reported to us that they voluntarily engaged in sex with their fathers. The survivors, in these cases, also claimed that while they did not initiate such sex, they did enjoy the contact, love, and closeness. However, we doubt whether these survivors, if given other choices, such as a warmer relationship with their mothers, would have willingly continued to have sex with their fathers. Furthermore, retrospective studies of survivors (Russell, 1986; Herman, Russell, & Trocki, 1986) have shown that most adults were not voluntary participants in father–daughter incest. It is clear, however, that under certain circumstances, older daughters may have enjoyed the sexual contact and, in some cases, even looked forward to it. With the latter kind of survivors, the issue of sexual pleasure becomes inextricably woven with the issue of guilt.

In sum then, the mother-dominant family type is characterized by women who are narcissistic and men who are devalued and impotent. The fathers function more or less at the sibling level and seek their sexual gratification there. The daughters cannot communicate their secrets to their mothers because the women are disinterested. The fathers and daughters are bonded as emotionally neglected children.

The Chaotic Family

The third type of family is the more chaotic kind in which the parents have abdicated authority to the children. As Kempe and Kempe (1984) have noted, these families are the ones that often come to the attention of the authorities or child protective service agencies. The children are often found living in squalor, frequently abandoned or neglected, and victims of sexual abuse. They often have sex with each other, and they are also victimized by parents and revictimized by neighbors. In our clinical experiences with families in the children and youth system, these disorganized families often present with parents who are alcohol and/or drug abusers.

The daughters in these families are expected to get the other children fed, dressed, and on their way to school, and then to get themselves off to school as well, while the parents sleep off their hangovers or are simply not there. The daughters' overfunctioning continues after school with preparing and serving dinner and cleaning up. Many times, the girls have to beg neighbors or strangers for money because their parents are at bars or in drunken or drug-induced stupors. At other times, the daughters are expected to find the parents at the bars and take them home. Often, the girl's retrieval of her father from the bar leads to sexual involvement at home.

The three types of family structure have certain common features. While the male-dominant and the female-dominant types may appear more normal or stable than the disorganized families (and in many ways they are), they all share the lack of boundaries, the lack of marital and parental cohesion, the inappropriate triangulation of the daughter, and the expectation that the daughter will be a parental child or parental caretaker.

Because many of the marriages in which incest is found are able to last despite the many problems that arise, some families may alternate between the female-dominant type and a more chaotic one. This is especially true when the women become so exhausted from running the family and holding it together that they abdicate responsibility and become disabled. In the ensuing power vacuum, no one except the incest victim will step forward to replace the mother. The family then becomes a more chaotic type since neither parent seems to want or is able to run the family.

THE CASE OF SUE

Sue, age 27, complained of severe depression that was exacerbated by violent episodes with her lover, who beat her. Sue lived with her two children, had a good job, and was the sole supporter of the family. She was a survivor of an extremely chaotic family history. The excerpted transcript material illustrates some of the typical problems of survivors: depression, low self-esteem, and revictimization. The material is from Sue's initial session with Diana Kirschner.

Sue: I go to the doctor because I'm so upset, I sleep so much, I mean I can go to sleep . . . lay me down, and I sleep all the time. And I'm always tired, and I'm always too thin. I go to the doctor, and as soon as the doctor sees me, he says, you're depressed and you need antidepressants or whatever. I guess they're antidepressants or something, and I say (laughing), "No, you prescribe it to me, I'll throw them out." And it's on my papers that I'm depressed. It's not that I'm depressed, I don't think, but then, yeah, I have a very low esteem of myself. I'm not very good with people, you know, I look at people and I feel all these things for them. I don't understand why people say this about somebody or that, because I'm always looking for the inner part—throughout all my life, I've always looked that there's a good part in somebody. Because I know I have it and nobody's seen that part.

Therapist: You said that no one has seen that good part. What about growing up? Wasn't there someone then?

Sue: Yes. (Crying) But that was where my problems began. I was 6 when I first remembered being hurt. I was sexually abused. My father was about 30, and when he did it to me, he hurt me. And so when I got old enough, when I got the Pap smear, I guess I was about 15, because the court made us go through all these tests to see what we were like. They told me I wouldn't be able to have any kids because I have really scarred tissues or whatever it is in there, but I did! The man that I married was my first boyfriend and I hated men, the sight of them. I mean I still do. They all look like jerks to me unless they talk to me and they're nice or whatever. If they don't say a word, they don't seem like nothing to me. I don't know. Then when I had the kids, you know I had really hard pregnancies and deliveries and everything, but I made it!

Therapist: Where was your mother through all of this?

Sue: My mother was a waitress. She finally left my father because he was beating her too much. Then, she was working all hours to support us, I mean me and my two little brothers. I was around 15 when I remember everything happening. I always had control over my little brothers, my mom wouldn't come home for weeks at a time, and she would always come get us and take us away and put us in homes, and then we'd come back. She never left us any money and I would scrape up and go to the store and try to feed the kids and I wouldn't eat. Well, finally after all these years of all these problems of my mom just splitting—she had men come in and out, and they did whatever they wanted to me. My mom wound up killing herself.

So she died, and then I went to live at my father's. The court ordered us to go stay with him for evaluation for a year. Well, when we got there, the state signed us over to him, plus they took away my little brother too. And then when we were there for about a week, my dad was an alcoholic and he'd beat his wife every weekend or whenever they drank, and they never came home, and then he'd beat us. He'd beat me so bad that it was just too much, and I left and I went into a foster home.

Finally, they committed me into an institution for a while, and then my foster home threw away the papers because they didn't want me back because I had nightmares. I'd see my mom and I'd look exactly like her. And nobody wanted the sight of me, and they took my brother away. And then I stayed in the institution and I got dismissed because they had me on so many medicines like Stelazine, Valium, and other antidepressants, I guess, and plus I was going through all these shocks to try to make me forget my past. I was a zombie, and I couldn't talk. I could think, but I couldn't talk, everything was dead. All I'd do was sit there and hope that someday I would get out. The orderlies knew that I had been abused for so long, you know, sexually, so I had a woman doctor. I guess I had to have my Pap, I guess it was ordered on my chart. So one of the orderlies, or whatever they are, gave it to me, and I was sexually abused again. The hospital arrested the man in my presence, and I was discharged and that was the end of there. So from then on, I've been on my own.

Therapist: Sue, you're doing incredibly well.

Sue: Yeah, I think so. (Crying)

STEPFATHER–DAUGHTER INCEST

The dynamics of incest that occurs in stepfamilies has some similarities to and some differences from the incest that happens in intact families. The commonalities are a distant and dysfunctional marital relationship; poor communication throughout the system, and especially between the parents; and the triangulation of the daughter into inappropriate role functions.

There are, however, several major differences between incest families and incest stepfamilies. It has been our experience that incest

occurs infrequently in stepfamilies in which the mother is the custodial parent and also the dominant parent. The overwhelming majority
of stepfamily incest cases reflect an authoritarian or dominant father
pattern in which the custodial parent, the mother, is devalued.

In these families, the mothers have usually been left economically
disadvantaged after their divorces, and even more important, they
lack interpersonal support. The children have little contact with their
biological fathers and are emotionally starved. Into this family comes
the savior, who appears to rescue the mother and her children. But
often he is only a predator looking for a vulnerable woman with
defenseless children. In our experience, some stepfathers actually
marry into certain families so that they can have access to the female
children.

THE CASE OF ROSA

Rosa was a 35-year-old survivor who was unmarried and lived with
her younger sister, Elena, and Elena's husband. She came into treatment because of chronic headaches, bouts of depression, and a desire
to have her own romantic life. Rosa described how her mother, while
living with the two girls in South America, had met an American
businessman at the bar where she worked. Within one week, the
man had proposed to her and had offered to adopt Elena and Rosa,
who were 8 and 10, respectively, at the time. Rosa's mother told her
that Raymond, the suitor, was willing to move the whole family to
the United States, and that this would be the fulfillment of all her
dreams. Rosa said that within a year of living together, Raymond
began molesting her. At first, he would only kiss and fondle her.
Then he became bolder and insisted on oral sex, and ultimately on
intercourse. The incest continued for three years.

The case was brought to the attention of the children and youth
protective services because Rosa had revealed to a friend that her
stepfather was doing funny things to her. The friend reported the
incident to a guidance counselor, who, in turn, called the authorities.
The mother and stepfather both vociferously denied the charges,
while Rosa maintained her allegations and refused to go home.

Rosa remembered meeting with a family counselor. Within three
sessions, Rosa's mother had confessed that she was afraid that she
would lose her husband and that her family would be forced to leave
the United States. Therefore, she had told her daughter not to tell

anyone about the incest. In this stepfamily, the daughter was given as a sacrificial lamb to the stepfather to ensure his economic support and so that the family would not have to return to South America.

The survivor in this case, Rosa, reported that she was more angry with her mother than with her stepfather, Raymond. Rosa experienced her mother as a pimp who had whored her to the stepfather so that she (the mother) could enjoy the "good life" in America. In her words, "my mother would have been perfectly pleased, if Elena and I would have continued to satisfy Raymond so that *she* could continue to shop in the malls."

Vulnerability to Incest

Survivors have reported to us that certain factors seemed to contribute to their having sex with their stepfathers. One of the most frequently mentioned reasons was the initial warmth and friendliness of the stepfather. These women had little or no contact with their biological fathers and were emotionally starved for male attention. In our view, they were highly vulnerable to their stepfathers' approaches. Following Zubin and Spring's (1977) general vulnerability model, we would say that these girls and their family systems as a whole were extremely vulnerable to a major disorder. In other words, the conditions were ripe for acting out, boundary violations, and, ultimately, for incest.

In the stepfamily case described above, the mother and daughter were vulnerable and the stepfather took full advantage of their relative positions of powerlessness. As Herman (1981) has observed, many mothers are so economically and emotionally dependent on their spouses that even when their daughters disclose the incest, they feel powerless because they fear losing their base of security.

Another factor contributing to the vulnerability of stepfamilies is the relative weakness of the incest taboo. Finkelhor (1979) has hypothesized that the incest taboo is weaker with stepfathers than among biological fathers. This has been borne out in Russell's (1986) findings that stepfathers abuse their daughters at significantly higher rates than do biological fathers.

Our conclusion, then, about stepfamily incest is that, in general, stepfamilies are more prone to incest than intact families because the mothers and children are more vulnerable, the mothers tend to be more dependent and have fewer resources, and the incest taboo is weaker among non-blood relatives.

UNCLE–NIECE INCEST

Kinsey's (Kinsey, Pomeroy, Martin, & Gebhard, 1953) classic study, *Sexual Behavior in the Human Female*, found uncle–niece incest to be the most common form of familial molestation. Russell's (1986) landmark study has essentially replicated this finding. In her sample, Russell also found that the sexual contact tended to be of a less severe nature. Courtois (1988), however, reported that some of her survivors recalled more serious forms of sexual molestation by their uncles.

From our clinical experience, we believe that uncle–niece incest may be so prevalent because it generally involves sexual contact without intercourse. Survivors report fondling and kissing as the most common types of molestation. Because uncles generally do not have frequent access to their nieces, and when they are together may not be left alone for long periods, they are usually not able to have intercourse. Nevertheless, our clients and those of Courtois (1988) and Meiselman (1978) have reported very traumatic aftereffects of uncle–niece incest.

It has been our experience that survivors generally do not tell parents about an uncle's activities. The silence seems to arise out of a combination of the lack of perceived severity of the molestation and the reluctance to tell on the mother's or father's brother. This is the case even in families where the uncle has been known to be inappropriate with his own daughters. For example, mothers will leave their daughters alone with their brothers, even though they know these men to be alcoholic and inappropriate with females. The following case example illustrates some of the family dynamics of uncle–niece incest.

THE CASE OF ELLEN

Ellen was the older of two daughters. Her family and her grandparents lived together in the grandparents' home. Ellen's mother had two brothers who lived nearby. Neither was currently married, although the older one had been married for a brief period. The younger brother, John, was 27 when Ellen was 13.

Ellen remembered that when her parents went out, John would come over, ostensibly to visit his parents. But, he would also help Ellen and her younger sister with their homework. When her younger sister had gone to bed, Ellen would often lie on the couch with her uncle and watch television. It was there that he would fondle and kiss her. Ellen was afraid to say anything to her parents for fear they wouldn't believe her story.

In her therapy, Ellen disclosed that she had also enjoyed the sexual contact with her uncle because she had idolized John and had a crush on him. In time, John began to make advances to Ellen's younger sister as well. Ellen reported that when her sister told her about John's advances, she began to realize that John had used her. Ellen threatened John with exposure if he did not stop. In therapy, she confessed that the secret had been kept for 15 years. Only when problems surfaced in her marriage did Ellen begin to realize how deeply the incest had affected her.

This case shows that age difference is often a precipitating factor in the onset of uncle–niece incest. Relative closeness in age makes younger uncles inherently more attractive to their nieces, and they also may have more in common. Meiselman (1978) has pointed out that in some families, the uncle functions as the only male role model. This gives him more access to the niece, especially if he is living in the same house with her.

MOTHER/STEPMOTHER–DAUGHTER INCEST

Few studies have established the rate of incidence of mother/step-mother–daughter incest. Russell (1986) found that 5% of all sexual abuse of girls and 20% of all abuse of boys involve women. But no data were reported, specifically, for the incidence of mother–child incest.

A recent study by Carnes (1991) of 290 sex addicts illustrates the potential impact of maternal abuse. The findings showed that 15% of the males and 9% of the female addicts were sexually abused by their mothers. Carnes also reported that 11% of the males and 3% of the females were forced to have sex with their mothers. Unfortunately, no data were presented on how many of these sex addicts had themselves become abusers.

SURVIVORS OF MATERNAL INCEST

Survivors of maternal incest have reported that in their families the mother was the dominant figure in the house. With the tacit approval of her husband, the incestuous mother used the child to serve her needs. The child never told the father of the incest and lived in fear of the mother. Often, the mother would use violence to keep the victim in a perpetual state of anxiety. As the daughter became a young adult and left home, there would often be a break in the relationship, usually with the parents rejecting the survivor. This severing of the ties would happen not because the survivor confronted the parents, but because she no longer was of any value to them.

Evert (1987) has written a powerful first-hand account of her years of physical and sexual abuse at the hands of her mother. She focuses primarily on her experiences during therapy, and on the memory-retrieval process, in particular, but she also gives us some rare glimpses into the structure of an intact family in which maternal incest took place. The author describes a scene in which she tried to talk to her father about the possible origin of her mother's depression. According to the story, her father cried and told Evert that all of the mother's problems began when she became pregnant with Evert. He went on to say that the mother refused to speak to him for three months. Later, when Evert was born, the mother refused to name her and thereby acknowledge her birth.

This same father clearly did not stop the mother from physically and sexually abusing his daughter. Furthermore, the author reports in the "Afterword" to her book that when her mother died, the father rejected her completely when he remarried. As is the case with so many survivors, the author had not discussed the abuse with either the father, the perpetrator, or other family members. Yet the father had rejected her anyway.

Evert's family, and others we have seen, seem to maintain their cohesiveness on the basis of selecting a "lamb" for ongoing sacrifice. Unable to resolve their own internal and interpersonal conflicts, the parents tacitly agree that one child will serve as the object of their frustrations. Since in maternal-incest families the mother is usually the dominant parent, she is the one who will select and enact the ongoing ritual sacrifice of the child. The father watches passively and does not interfere.

SIBLING INCEST

Sexual play between siblings is the only type of familial sex that has been acknowledged as a more normal part of a child's psychosexual development. This attitude of normality, especially toward siblings who are close in age, has tended to minimize both the reporting of these experiences and the establishment of some reasonable rate of prevalence in society.

Finkelhor (1979) found that 13% of his sample reported sibling sexual experiences. Of these, 74% were heterosexual and 26% were homosexual experiences. Russell (1986), in her study, found that 72% of the women who were sexually involved with their brothers reported being upset by the experiences. Russell also contended that, in view of her findings, researchers and clinicians should not minimize the impact of sibling incest, especially when it involves an older brother and younger sister.

Our experiences with survivors parallel those of Russell. We have found that two types of sibling incest inevitably leave the survivor with traumatic aftereffects—older brother–younger sister incest and older brother–younger brother incest. In both kinds, the age of the perpetrator, his relative power over the victim, and certain family dynamics tend to play significant roles in the trauma of the molestation. In Chapter 11, we discuss same-sex sibling incest.

Older Brother–Younger Sister Incest

Courtois (1988) has identified three main types of older brother –younger sister incest: when the adolescent male experiments sexually with his sister; when an immature or socially inept brother uses his sister for sex because he is afraid of outside females; and when the brother is violent and essentially rapes his sister.

These three types of incest share a common thread. They can only occur when parental supervision is lax or, at the extreme, totally lacking, as in the chaotic families we have described. In our experience, brother–sister incest will stop when the girl becomes old enough to refuse her brother, usually when she turns 13 or 14.

In some cases, however, it continues. This is typical of the type that involves rape. In these families, the brother's behavior is modeled on the father's behavior. The boy either witnessed or knows of his father's physical or sexual abuse of the sister. He then replicates the father's behavior. This form of abuse continues with the father's tacit approval.

The third type, then, follows the male-dominant pattern in which the women, both mother and daughter(s), are devalued and powerless. In that atmosphere, the older brother can coerce the sister, who is powerless and without protection. We had one case in which two older brothers molested their sister while their father watched.

Russell (1986) has reported that victims of older brother–younger sister incest are less likely to get married as compared with other incest survivors. Courtois (1988) has suggested that sisters, in comparison with daughters, often feel additional guilt or shame over the involvement with their brothers. These women apparently believe that they should have been able to stop their brothers, whereas the daughters tend to believe that they were coerced.

In our experiences, a sister who has been victimized often will repress the incest experiences precisely because she feels that in some way she had "seduced" her brother. One survivor recalled having been told by her parents that she was dressing like a "whore" whenever she went out and like a "tease" when she simply walked around the house. This survivor had developed breasts at the age of 11 and was very conscious of trying to make herself look as inconspicuous as possible. Nevertheless, her family had given tacit permission to the men in the family to view her as a sexual object. Soon thereafter, her 16-year-old brother forced her to have sex with him, claiming that "she wanted it."

The following case study illustrates older brother–younger sister incest. Many of the dynamics of male-dominant families that we have discussed are present in this example. The case study also describes how the adult survivor has created a new family for herself in which she feels "safe" from further exploitation. Chapter 5 details various types of couple relationships that survivors bring into treatment and how they reflect their family-of-origin dynamics.

THE CASE OF ROBERTA

Roberta, age 37, came to therapy with her husband, Bill, age 36, complaining of marital problems. The spouses agreed that Roberta seemed disinterested in sex and had been so for about five years. The couple had one child, Paula, who was 14. Bill said that over the past three years, he could remember only one sexual episode. Roberta agreed with Bill's description and quickly owned it as her problem. In going over their sexual histories, the therapist found that Roberta had been very active sexually during late adolescence and into early adulthood, when she met Bill. In fact, after some quick calculations, the therapist asked the couple if Roberta was pregnant at the time they decided to marry. The answer was that she had been.

Bill said that he was always extremely jealous of Roberta because she was so "loose" sexually. He wanted to marry her, he said, because he believed it would calm her down and then he wouldn't have to worry so much. Much to his surprise, their sexual life began to wane almost immediately, and following Paula's birth never returned to its original ardor.

The therapist questioned Roberta about her family history. He discovered that at about the time she started kindergarten the family had moved to a new neighborhood. Her brothers, who were 4 and 6 years older than Roberta, had no one to play with and would stay home after school. Roberta's father was described as a violent alcoholic who beat his wife and turned on the boys as well. Roberta recalled that her older brother, Jimmy, began beating her one evening after their father had thrown their mother against the refrigerator. When she began to scream for help, her father came upstairs and joined in the beating, telling her that he'd "be damned if she turned out like the old lady." The physical abuse soon spread to Roberta's younger brother, Al. Whenever he got the chance, he would strike out at her and "teach her a lesson."

When Roberta turned 9, the violence evolved into incest. Jimmy, who had turned 15, had become a social recluse. He had no dates and no male buddies. When Jimmy was not working at his parents' store, he would be at home "watching" his brother and sister. Roberta recalled how, one particular day, as she waited for her parents to come home, Jimmy came into her room and pushed her down on the bed. He began to fondle her and to explore her genital area. Jimmy told her that this would be their secret, and that if she let him have fun, he would stop hitting her.

From that day on, Jimmy would force himself on Roberta, eventually having intercourse with her when she was 10. He continued to use violence as a means of coercing her, sometimes in full view of both parents.

When Roberta was 13, her mother was hospitalized for depression. During the hospitalization, Roberta was raped by her younger brother. After the incident, she ran away from home. Only when her father found her did she tell him what Al had done to her. But she never told anyone about her four years of being molested by Jimmy until she was married.

In this case, Roberta's daughter's ninth birthday precipitated a restimulation of the traumatic violence Roberta had experienced as a child. She believed that, in some magical way, if she did not have sex with her husband, she would not have to acknowledge and accept the sexual trauma of the incest.

SUMMARY

Incestuous families are arranged hierarchically in three patterns: male dominant, female dominant, and chaotic. These family types also share in common poor boundaries between subsystems, the lack of marital and parental cohesion, and the expectation that the victim will function as a parental child or as a parental caretaker. Many of the spouses in these families seem to suffer from alcoholism, sex addiction, or sexual dysfunction. Some families, especially single-parent and stepfamilies, seem to be particularly vulnerable to incest.

CHAPTER 4

TRUST, GENDER, POWER, AND THE IDENTITY OF THE SURVIVOR

"I would lie there in bed, pretending to be asleep, hoping he wouldn't come. I would feel that horrifying touch, pulling the blankets down. I felt so ashamed and helpless."
—A 22-year-old female survivor

This chapter serves as a bridge between our studies of incestuous families and those of the survivors' families of creation. In the previous chapter, we described some of the key elements that characterize the structures and processes common to incest families. While hierarchical considerations, such as which parent is dominant, are important to our understanding of incest families, we also recognize that underlying those variables is an emotional underbelly or infrastructure. This infrastructure is composed of basic values and emotional themes common to each family. In particular, three key motifs are transmitted intergenerationally that shape personality and identity. These themes revolve around the issues of trust, gender, and power. This chapter describes how these themes are played out in incest families and how they influence and shape the identity of the survivor.

THE BLUEPRINTS FOR IDENTITY

We all know that families (especially parents) transmit their values and perceptions about living to the children. Important values such as trustworthiness, respect for boundaries, and integrity are conveyed to children through the actions and behaviors of parenting, and modeled for them in the spouses' marital relationship and in the parents' interactions with others.

Parents also convey messages to their children about the meanings of maleness and femaleness, about competition and collaboration, and about power and assertiveness. These messages and values become internalized as blueprints for cognition and interpersonal behavior. In other words, how people think and perceive and how they act on these important themes are greatly influenced by the inner templates derived from their families.

Indeed, personality is formed out of the combination of temperament, other genetic factors, and these blueprints for cognition and behavior. We have found that the most crucial of these templates fall into three categories or themes. And it is the successful resolution of the conflicting issues in the three areas that greatly determines how we view ourselves and how well we can make life work for us.

The three areas involved are trust, gender, and power. Each area contains the potential for conflict and ambivalence. Trust, for example, contains the inherent paradox of trusting ourselves versus trusting others; gender contains the inherent dilemma of maleness versus femaleness; and power contains the basic paradox of competition and self-assertion versus collaboration and cooperation. In each element, we find the seed of its opposite. Because of this, resolving these dilemmas takes a lifetime. The process also requires intimate contact with others. Since the blueprints for these themes are formed in relationships with significant others, so too are they modified or changed in intimate relationships.

For survivors, each of the categories becomes fraught with tension. They are taught to trust family members who have abused them or failed to protect them, but not to trust themselves; they are told not to feel and to be ashamed of their emotions; and they learn that helplessness is what is expected of them. For survivors, then, the blueprints for trust, gender, and power are betrayal, shame, and helplessness. These are the legacies of incestuous families.

THE THEME OF BETRAYAL

From the earliest moments of life, trusting our caretakers becomes of paramount importance to survival. For many clinicians, including Erikson (1950), the foundation for a trusting relationship is based on the mother–child interactions in the first year of life. In their view, all intimate relationships are based on the model that the primary caretaker has provided. It is as if time stood still for the person and subsequent interactions with significant others could only marginally affect the initial primordial blueprint.

Yet, much later in their development, survivors experience interactions that break the trust. To our knowledge, no one has shown that the first two years in the lives of survivors are typically marked by abandonment, neglect, or abuse by their primary caretakers. According to Russell (1986), only 11% of her female sample were abused before the age of 5, whereas 41% reported being abused between ages 10 and 13, and 29% between 14 and 17. The data that show that 70% of survivors are victimized from latency age on correspond to the reports of our clients.

Thus it is as survivors grow up, and especially as they pass through puberty, that they experience betrayal by family members. They learn that the people they had trusted and depended on could violate that trust. This is the betrayal of incest. For most survivors, the betrayal comes as a shock that seriously erodes the trust that they developed in their caretakers in early childhood. When the protector becomes transformed into the perpetrator, the change is traumatic and difficult for the child to grasp. Most victims attempt to explain what has happened as being their fault, and thus is born a lifelong legacy of self-blame and deep shame.

The code of silence typical of incest families also keeps the survivor further away from trusting intimate relationships (Courtois, 1979; Lundberg-Love et al., 1987). The survivor learns that she cannot speak about her deepest thoughts, feelings, and yearnings. Therefore, her thoughts cannot be heard and validated, her feelings cannot flow freely, and her needs go unmet. Over time, this becomes a pattern that she follows: she cannot or will not try to open up and trust anyone completely because everyone has failed her. As a result, survivors will often partner with men who are uncomfortable with expressing feelings or self-disclosure. These partners tend to avoid intimate interactions and corroborate the survivors' expectations that no one is there for them. The combination of choosing nonrelational and even schizoid men and harboring ongoing feelings of mistrust reinforces the legacy of betrayal. These couples' dynamics are detailed in the next chapter.

Another consequence of the denial and betrayal of trust is that it leaves the survivor vulnerable to revictimization by others (Lundberg-Love et al., 1987; Russell, 1986) whose malevolence or exploitative nature is also denied. Because the survivor cannot tell who is and who is not trustworthy, she tends to believe that she has no control over relationships and so she is prone to taking a fatalistic view of life. For example, one client, who had been molested repeatedly over a 10-year period by her minister father, was referred for therapy because she had been raped at college. The young woman reported that this was the second time she had been raped, and that both times the rape had occurred while she was jogging in the park at dusk. The client said, "If it was meant for me to get raped, there is very little I can do about it."

The Betrayal of the Self

Another way in which survivors are betrayed is how family members communicate with them about the abuse. Many incest families use double-binding communications as a way of controlling the victims. For example, when the perpetrator approaches, he may say that the sexual advances are really good for the victim, or that it is her fault for seducing him, or that it is not really sex. The victim, on the other hand, may come to experience abuse as equivalent to attention, affection, and love.

Some perpetrators tell their victims to cooperate, but then, afterwards, call them whores. If the victim tells her mother what happened, the mother may deny it, and yet later refer to the survivor as disgusting and sinful in a way that suggests that the mother knows it's all true. This double-bind communication makes it very difficult for the survivor to trust anyone. What people say, promise, or give to her may turn out to be a trap, an exploitation, or an attack on her. The victim can't really depend on anyone, not even on herself.

While some authors (e.g., Courtois, 1988; Wooley & Vigilanti, 1984) have suggested that double-binding communications are very characteristic of incest families as a whole, our experiences in working with ongoing incest support a somewhat different conclusion. Double binds are used primarily in communicating to the *victim* and less so in communicating to other family members. This is especially true when the perpetrator is the father or mother and the other parent denies or refuses to talk about the abuse. In these situations, the victim is related to very differently than are other family members. In Chapter 9, for example, we include a copy of a letter written by a survivor to members of her family in which she describes the pain of being treated and related to very differently from her three siblings.

In our view, then, double binds are used to control the victim in three ways: to be more receptive to being molested, to not disclose the secret, and to deny to herself that anything is wrong. As Bateson, Jackson, Haley, and Weakland (1956) wrote in their original formulations on the double bind, the outcome for the recipient of these communications is a feeling of being trapped. And we would add that for survivors, having no escape leads to suffering from "learned helplessness."

How does the victim deal with this impossible situation? One way, which has been widely reported by survivors, is to dissociate from the abuse. Lundberg-Love (1990), for example, reported that 61% of her sample exhibited dissociative tendencies. The enduring quality and tenacity of the dissociative symptom speak volumes about the strength of the prohibition against disclosure or the denial mechanisms in the family.

The denial and code of silence that exist in these families also mitigate against trusting oneself. For children to experience their thoughts and feelings as real, they need to be heard and validated by significant others. Survivors have the opposite experience. When they try to speak about the abuse, or about their real needs and feelings, they are not heard. Rather, their beliefs are invalidated. What they are trying to know about is denied by the significant people in their lives.

A survivor may be told, for example, that she is crazy or imagining things. Or she is told that the perpetrator loves her and would never hurt her. As a result, she learns that her perceptions of reality and her reactions to those perceptions are not to be trusted.

This is the second part of the survivor's betrayal—the betrayal of the self, her senses, her body, and her feelings. All of these aspects of the survivor have failed her. They have given her false information about the abuse, because others have told her that it did not really occur. The survivor's senses and feelings are, therefore, not to be trusted.

Without the consensual validation she needs to honor and accept her real feelings, the survivor is forced to choose another route. She betrays her authentic self and becomes false. This choice is born out of a desperate attempt to maintain internal stability in the face of horror. Much like the mother in the movie *Sophie's Choice*, who must choose which of her two children will live and which will die in the concentration camp, the survivor must decide whether to go mad and disintegrate internally or to betray her authenticity.

There is little doubt that this choice contributes not only to survivors' complaints of feeling unreal, but also to their chronic sense of shame. Clients have frequently told us that they are ashamed of how they let themselves down in not admitting to themselves the truth of what happened. They have also reported that they are really not ashamed that they did not confront their parents or the perpetrator, but that their shame revolves around betraying the self.

THE THEME OF SHAME

Erikson (1950) described the second stage of identity development as a struggle between the autonomy of free choice versus shame and doubt. Through this struggle, the young child either will develop a sense of personal wholeness, coherence, and integrity or will emerge with an identity marked by a sense of wanting to hide from the world. Erikson believed that the impulse to hide, coupled with a fear of being exposed, was the key component of the shame dynamic.

Almost all survivors suffer from shame. Rather than being treated as separate, whole people, their boundaries are violated, as the perpetrator intrudes his needs and wants into their lives. Intrusion is often the norm in the survivor's family of origin. Bedroom doors are to be left open or are nonexistent. The survivor may have little privacy while dressing or in the bathroom. She grows up with a sense of no control over what parts of her body will be seen, felt, or used. She grows up with very little sense of personal boundaries. The survivor cannot hide what she feels is bad, dirty, or unlovable. This leaves her in a constant state of shame coupled with the fear of possible humiliation.

Calof (1987) and Fossum and Mason (1986) have hypothesized that shame is transmitted intergenerationally. In incest families, this process takes place through the interaction between projective identification and parental or marital transactions. For example, in father-dominant families, women and girls are experienced as second-class citizens, as objects of ridicule and laughter, or as "things" that can be used as needed for sexual pleasure. As part of a family-wide projective identificatory process, the "bad," shameful, impulse-ridden, or needy aspects of the males are attributed to the survivor and/or her mother. Through the enactment of verbal or physical abuse toward the survivor or her mother, the survivor internalizes the shameful and rejected personality traits as part of her identity. This gives the survivor the sense that she is not like other people—that there is something wrong with her. She grows up feeling that she is a damaged woman. The process seriously undermines her sense of self. Her femininity becomes something to be ashamed of, a badge of inferiority.

As a result of carrying a shamed identity, some survivors choose partners who are verbally or physically abusive to them. They may also couple with men who are abusive to the children. While there are little data to establish a baseline for these patterns, we do know that physical and sexual abuse have been shown to have an intergenerational transmission rate of about 30% (Kaufman & Zigler, 1987). For these survivors, the deep sense of shame is reinforced by their partners' destructive and denigrating behaviors and, when it occurs, by the sexual abuse of their children. These types of relationships are detailed in the next chapter.

Another source of gender-related shame is the moral climate in the home. In the previous section, we mentioned the case of a young woman who had been referred by her college counseling center because she had been raped. In the course of working with the therapist, she disclosed that her father, who was a minister, had molested her from the age of 7 until she left home to go to college. The client, Jane, had been raised in a highly rigid and moralistic environment. Both her mother and father condemned the "loose" social and sexual mores prevalent in their community. Her father would routinely use his pulpit to rail against the "devil's influence in movies and music."

Rock music was forbidden at home, as were dresses or skirts with hemlines above the knee. Jane's younger sister was more defiant of the rules and would often be punished by her father. These punishments included being strapped on her naked backside while Jane was forced to watch.

But Jane was treated very differently from her sister. She remembered how her father would enter her bedroom at night and get in the bed with her. He would tell her that she was the "beautiful devil's child" who had been sent to tempt him—and that he couldn't resist. The minister would force Jane to have oral sex with him, and later, vaginal and anal intercourse. Throughout the 10-year period of the abuse, Jane's father would often come to her and beg her forgiveness for being "weak of the flesh." He would pray that God would be merciful and take him away so that he would "sin no more."

In therapy, Jane disclosed how she had felt exactly like the whores and tramps her father despised. She felt like an evil seductress who was ruining her father. Yet, he had also told her how beautiful and special she was, and Jane experienced that, as well. The paradox of being special and beautiful while being the "devil's child" created a deep wound in Jane's psyche. Whenever Jane would try to manifest some of her talents, her specialness, she would experience her "badness" and her profound shame. She had an enduring sense that she was an inherently evil person.

Calof (1987) has also described how some parents cover the sexual abuse by being overly rigid and moralistic. Like Jane, these victims are told that sexual contact before marriage is evil or that their friends are "bad" for dressing like "tramps," while inside the family they are actually being molested.

Betrayal and Shame

As discussed in the previous section, a survivor usually suffers from two different kinds of betrayal, and with each, she will feel shame. The first is the consequence of being betrayed by someone who was a trusted family member. The survivor blames herself for the change in the perpetrator and feels ashamed that she has somehow polluted those around her. The sense of being "toxic" has profound interpersonal repercussions for some survivors. Many do not want to have children or even to maintain an intimate relationship.

The second way in which shame arises is through the betrayal of the real self. In denying the incest and maintaining family loyalty, the survivor has sold herself out. She knows that she is no longer being authentic—and she cannot run far from that knowledge. Some survivors try to mask or escape the pain they cannot authentically express by abusing drugs or alcohol. In many ways, they are saying, "I have no outlet, no way to lance this raging, infected emotional wound, so I have to cover it over and kill the pain."

The survivor often develops an elaborate false self, designed to gain approval from others and to hide the bad, shameful real self. She may be very responsive to others' needs or requests or demands of her, thankful for any help or attention, overly generous, and eager to curry favor with significant others. But the inauthenticity remains, and, as Kinston (1983) has noted, shame arises out of acts that are carried out to gain parental love or approval but that violate personal integrity.

This inauthenticity also makes it very hard for the survivor to understand her own dreams and visions about a suitable career or profession. It is difficult for her to define her own goals, discover her talents, or choose her true path in the work arena. Because of this, the survivor is likely to suffer from what Kohut (1977) has described as the "nameless shame," a kind of "depression without guilt" that arises in people who are overwhelmed by the belief that their lives have been failures and that nothing can be done about it in the time that remains for them. In Chapter 8, we discuss how to work with survivors on career issues.

In many ways, the plight of the shame-bound survivor reminds us of what Maslow (1971) called the "Jonah complex." In the biblical story, God called upon Jonah to become his prophet. Jonah responded by fleeing and sailing away on a boat, whereupon a storm arose and he ended up in the belly of a whale. There, he reconciled with his destiny and was miraculously saved. He then began his true work. Maslow referred to those who flee from their own potential or from their calling as suffering from the "Jonah complex." The survivor, having learned to mistrust herself, flees and hides from her authentic self in the shame-filled belly of the whale. In this way, she avoids pursuing her true path in life.

Some survivors also suffer from guilt as well as shame. Whereas shame is a sense that one is inherently bad or disgusting, guilt has to do with feeling that one is unworthy because of one's specific actions or behaviors. While most survivors suffer from shame, only those who feel responsible for the incest tend to suffer from guilt about it. In these families, the survivor is told, in one way or another, that she "made" the perpetrator "do it." As a child, she did not understand which of her actions led to the incest's taking place. Thus all actions may be suspect, and she may then generalize the blame to feeling guilty about almost any behavior. The guilt and self-doubt become added roadblocks impeding her path to self-actualization.

THE THEME OF POWERLESSNESS

Survivors suffer from a sense of being powerless in the world. They have difficulty asserting their desires or making demands on others. Generally, they also do not express their beliefs or feelings, except with reluctance. Because survivors often present with a depressive disorder, they may appear apathetic and indifferent. They often feel as though they can do nothing to change their lives or to help themselves.

As a consequence of their perceived powerlessness, survivors often work at jobs that are below their potential. They also tend to avoid careers in which competition, in terms of either educational or other entrance requirements, is mandated. Competition is likely to bring up not only the feelings of impotence, but also the old, unholy triangles of the past, with all the attendant guilt and shame. As a result of these internal prohibitions, it is difficult for many survivors to actualize themselves as competent, successful women. Instead, they suffer from "learned helplessness" (Seligman, 1975). In Chapter 8, we discuss the crucial task of empowering the survivor not only in her family of creation, but also in her career or job.

What are the origins of this condition? In childhood, the survivor's needs for nurturance, guidance, and appropriate limit-setting often were not met. For those who grew up in chaotic families, basic security needs may also have been unfulfilled. Those who grew up in father-dominant families saw their role models, their mothers, behave in passive and victimlike ways, or worse yet, being beaten and abused. And, of course, the survivors were also sexually abused.

Survivors, then, grew up unable to exert control over their parents' behavior, especially that of the perpetrators, or over their own boundaries and space. They generally lived in unpredictable circumstances, not knowing when they would be violated next, or if they or others would be beaten. Calof (1987) has described this unpredictability as reflecting intermittent reinforcement conditions in which the child is loved one day and abused the next, under similar contingencies. The consequence of this systemic context is that many survivors lived in fear and developed the condition of "learned helplessness."

Indeed, the Seligman experiments shed light on the stressful conditions under which abused children live and their subsequent reactions to those stressors. Seligman (1975) created an experimental situation in which dogs were trained to avoid being shocked by learning to jump from one compartment to the next. Then Seligman raised an impenetrable barrier that made it impossible for the dogs to jump and hence to avoid the electric shock. Over time, he observed that the dogs exhibited increased passivity, decreased performance, a tendency to seek isolation, and an apparent loss of motivation. Garber and Seligman (1980) observed that even when the painful shock was absent, neither the passage of time nor reexposure to the same situation seemed to ameliorate the helplessness or the depression.

When we compare Seligman's experimental conditions with those endured by abused children, we can see the similarities: the subjects are trapped, have no control over the situation, and are powerless to stop their oppressors. Seligman's observations of the lab animals' behavior also have several important commonalities with the reports of adult incest survivors: persistent and enduring feelings of intense fear, helplessness, and dysphoria.

Out of this sense of impotence, survivors tend to cling to the only power bases they know: emotional blackmail, sexual blackmail, and besting the parent. Paradoxically, none of these contributes to real power, the real satisfaction of the survivor's needs and wants.

Emotional Blackmail

The only way for some sexually abused children to exert any power or control, or to satisfy the need for some affection or feeling of specialness, is to participate in the incest and maintain the secret. There then exists an implied blackmail—the secret or not-so-secret promise that they won't tell anyone, which leaves them one up on the perpetrator. For some survivors, this power is the only source of feeling any semblance of control in an otherwise chaotic and unpredictable environment. They, therefore, hold on to the secret and the blackmail even after it is no longer necessary to do so. This makes it difficult for them to relate freely and honestly to others or to satisfy the need for full emotional expression.

Sexual Blackmail

Other survivors learn to use a different kind of blackmail, sexual blackmail. They believe that the only way they can have power is through their sexuality. Their bodies become the sources of interpersonal control, especially over men. The promise of sexual gratification and the threat of withholding it become weapons in their arsenals. With these weapons, survivors can feel empowered. However, sexual blackmail interferes with their ability to attend to and satisfy their own real needs for sexual fulfillment.

Besting the Parent

The victim of father–daughter incest becomes the other woman in a very dysfunctional triangle. She has bested Mother in some way by having sex with Father, and yet the victory has devastating consequences. By winning, she has lost any chance of a normal mother–daughter relationship because such a relationship is based in part on maintaining a hierarchy that defines their relative power. By having sex with her father, the boundaries that define her as a child rather than as an adult have been permanently altered so that she can no longer consider herself a child. In some cases, the victim also stops seeing herself as one of the siblings because they are still children and she is not.

Another consequence of besting Mother is that it leaves the victim with no female role model whom she can respect. She typically still feels a secret identification with her mother, who is the inferior one, the one who lost. The loss of the child identity, coupled with the internalization of the inferior and weak parent, leaves the survivor with an emerging sense of herself as an impotent loser.

We consider these three elements as having a paradoxical effect on the survivor's sense of self. This is so because any sense of power derived from emotional or sexual blackmail or from besting the parent serves to undermine the survivor's sense of integrity and remains a festering wound in her psyche. Rather than developing her strengths and personal power based on a win–win model, the survivor learns that power comes at great cost to her and to her loved ones. The victory, then, is truly a Pyrrhic one.

THE WILL TO LIVE

Survivors have a number of inner strengths that come from the will to persevere, in spite of heartbreak, betrayal, or adversity. They have had to learn to parent themselves as best they can, to steady themselves patiently, and to dissociate from traumatic events in order to master them. This is a very useful and adaptive skill in dealing with life's difficulties and disappointments. Survivors can block out the pain of the moment and do whatever needs to be done.

A related strength is self-control. We have seen and heard of survivors who controlled their reactivity and emotionality in order to deal with serious accidents to children or other loved ones. The self-control mechanisms described in Chapter 3 by the survivor Sue helped her to raise her children without assistance under extremely arduous conditions.

Survivors are often quite dedicated to their own healing. Utilizing their own inner parenting process, they will take steps to find constructive ways out of their suffering. At times, this search is motivated by their desire to give their children a better life than they have had. But whatever the motivation, they will tend to persevere with the process if they sense that there is hope for change. We have seen survivors who have been in therapy for 20 years with various practitioners who have overcome their addictions, phobias, or depressive disorders and who are still working on themselves so that they can create a successful intimate relationship. They have an amazing tenaciousness!

A fourth strength that many survivors have is that they can be very good caretakers. If they were parentified while growing up, they can be quite selfless and devoted to their children or partners. Although this trait has obvious downsides, it can also be a considerable asset. If the devotion to others is balanced with self-caretaking and is validated, they can manifest a good deal of creative competence and the self-esteem that goes with it.

A fifth strength that many survivors have is that of compassion. They understand the wounding process that occurs in love relationships, and often show great empathy for the suffering of others. This compassion, coupled with their caretaking ability, often makes them extremely talented healing agents. They can be very creative, empathic health-care professionals and often, when they can find their generative paths, become great therapists, nurses, social workers, child advocates, or certified addictions counselors.

These five strengths are common to many survivors. They serve to counteract and, in some cases, partially to undo the traumatic consequences of the abuse. While it is true that the legacies of betrayal, shame, and powerlessness become woven into the fabric of the survivor's identity, the impact they have on her depends on several factors. As discussed in Chapter 2, we must keep in mind that there is a continuum of abuse severity and abuse-related disorders. In general, then, the greater the native strengths of the survivor and the less severe the abuse, the less damaged the identity of the survivor will be.

On this end of the continuum are survivors whose family members did protect them from the perpetrators or did not prohibit them from speaking out about the abuse. These survivors are able to overcome their sense of betrayal much more readily. Another group of survivors suffer from much less shame. They have been fortunate in finding real acceptance, despite their self-perceived imperfections, by a loving parent, sibling, grandparent, teacher, or mentor to whom they have disclosed the whole story. And there are still others who do not experience themselves as powerless. Their talents and abilities have been promoted and developed by a parent or a member of the extended family, or by a teacher or a mentor, and reinforced through successes.

Yet, for many survivors, the feelings of betrayal, shame, and powerlessness permeate their cognitive functioning, self–other perceptions, and decision making. To help our clients transcend these self-defeating legacies, we have designed specific therapeutic strategies and techniques. The second half of the book, beginning with Chapter 6, describes the treatment process.

SUMMARY

Three important themes are transmitted intergenerationally that shape the survivor's identity. The motifs of betrayal, shame, and powerlessness affect her view of herself as a person, as a woman, as a parent, and as a spouse or partner. The survivor may also have important strengths that help reduce the traumatic aftereffects of the abuse. In the next chapter, we detail how these legacies are enacted in the survivor's family of creation.

CHAPTER 5

FAMILY-OF-CREATION DYNAMICS

"My father abused me, my husband abused me, I feel like a rag, something to be used and thrown away. All I want is someone to love me."

—A 35-year-old incest survivor early in treatment

COUPLE DYNAMICS OF INCEST SURVIVORS

One of the most ignored factors in the treatment of incest survivors is the importance of the couple relationship. The relationship plays a role in maintaining the survivor's symptomatology and blocking the healing of the incest wound. Conversely, a healthy relationship can play a strong part in the promotion of growth and healing, and there are enhanced possibilities for growth when the spouse is included in the treatment. This inclusion of the spouse in treatment, however, is often considered only as an afterthought, particularly when marital difficulties rise to the surface with the peeling away of presenting symptoms.

Some clinicians exclude the spouse entirely because they feel his inclusion might jeopardize their alliance with the survivor. Other therapists may covertly or overtly encourage the survivor to leave the relationship because the spouse is behaving in an emotionally or physically abusive manner. By understanding the kinds of partners survivors choose and typical coupling patterns, as presented in the following, practitioners can coordinate the treatment process so that individual, couple, and parenting subsystems work together, and thus achieve maximum results. Morever, the practitioner also can avoid unnecessary family fragmentations.

CHOICE OF A PARTNER

People who have suffered trauma and abuse as children, particularly through incest, develop a sense of disillusionment, a sense that they are helpless in the face of betrayal, and an ongoing pain—a perception that nothing will ever change. On the other hand, the very act of surviving implies a kind of hopefulness, a feeling that there is a reason to go on, that life can get better. There is an intuitive belief that relationships that have been hurtful in the past can heal. It is this interplay between mistrust/disillusionment and hopefulness that marks the romantic relationships of adult incest survivors.

Survivors are engaged in an ongoing search for completion; that is, to be healed and to grow. In addition to their tendency to repeat old scripts and family programs, as well as to maintain homeostasis, survivors also possess an intrinsic desire to develop the self. This positive movement, or morphogenesis, occurs through therapeutic interactions with others, such as teachers, coaches, counselors, mentors, and ultimately lovers.

These two life forces, homeostasis (to repeat the wounding process) and morphogenesis (to grow through the wounding), collide throughout the life cycle. The oscillation between homeostasis and morphogenesis in normal or healthy individuals is marked by a natural flow— a slow but steady evolution toward mastery of the new experiences with increasing self-esteem and actualization. In contrast, survivors are prone to becoming locked into more homeostatic patterns. Their internal maps, programs, and imprints are marked by negative and conflicted messages, learned and relearned over time. These messages may include: "I've been hurt badly by my father; therefore, all men will hurt me." "I was abandoned by my mother when I needed her most; therefore, all men/women will abandon me." "My father only nurtured me when he wanted sex; therefore, that's what all men want." "My stepfather brutally raped me; therefore, all men will rape me." Survivors mistrust others and anticipate betrayal.

Unfortunately, but not unexpectedly, there are men who, because of their own experiences while growing up, are inclined to behave in ways that are consistent (e.g., abusers or rapists) with the survivor's expectations about lovers and relationships. This unfortunate fact, the survivor's transference to such men, and her tendency to engage in projective identification as a primary defensive mechanism in relationships combine to ceate a recipe for relational homeostatic patterns—that is, patterns in which she repeats and relives her wounding scripts.

But the quest to change and grow through relationships does remain alive to some degree. What survivors are searching for is a desire to be healed and reparented. They seek to have the gaps and deficiencies from the family-of-origin experiences filled in. Therefore, the survivor will choose a partner who will furnish the needed inputs that were missing in the family of origin. For example, if the survivor lacked basic nurturance while growing up, she will unconsciously (or, depending on her level of psychological awareness, consciously) search for a partner who is capable of providing warmth and validation. Perhaps she will find a mate who did receive a good deal of nurturance while he was growing up, but lacked other inputs that the survivor can provide, say, a dose of psychological realness or pain that he might need in order to grow.

In the later stages of treatment, such a trade-off of emotional inputs may be harnessed by the therapist into a strong intramarital coalition (see Chapter 10). However, even though she has chosen nurturance, as the relationship solidifies, the survivor becomes less able to accept it directly. The nurturance is experienced as a foreign input, incongruent with an internal sense of self as a shameful object that says, "I am unworthy of such love." Therefore, the survivor often selects a mate who is capable of being warm and nurturing, and yet typically has helped to create a relationship in which this capacity is not expressed.

Usually, the partner displayed this possibility in the early courting stages of the relationship, and this fostered the energetic infatuation phase of the couple. In fact, what happened during this infatuation phase is a clue to the practitioner as to the needed but missing input from the survivor's family of origin. That initial excitement represents a romantic feeling of healing that plugs into the survivor's hope, "I can be saved; life does not have to be so painful." This represents her longing to be reparented.

THE EMERGENCE OF THE HOMEOSTATIC PATTERN

When the reality phase of the relationship sets in and the partner's own need to be reparented emerges vis-à-vis the survivor, he becomes needier and more childlike rather than parental. He also begins to feel comfortable with having "won her" and his fear of losing her subsides. Beginning to take her for granted, he delivers less. The survivor starts to regress into her hurt-child states as a result of these disappointments. Further bitter hurts and disappointments arise, and once again the survivor feels the pain of being let down and having promises go unfulfilled.

The survivor overtly or covertly communicates these disappointments to her partner, who now feels even more psychologically regressed into his own hurt-child phase when his needs go unfulfilled. He also becomes disappointed and feels emotionally impotent. The new healing input becomes submerged in a sea of resentment. The mate begins to act as if his giving of nurturance to the survivor is unwanted, is unappreciated, or will take something away from him. Thus an acrimonious win-lose mentality develops and supplants the "win-win" attitude characteristic of the infatuation phase.

The survivor has a variety of reactions to and strategies for dealing with such a loss. Survivors who display borderline tendencies may precipitously terminate a relationship when the realization of disappointment strikes and go on to search for other men who will give them the needed input. These survivors may engage in a seemingly endless pattern of addictive-like short-term symbiotic relationships in which there is never a progression or a healthy resolution of the infatuation phase. The same survivor may behave similarly in work situations where supervisors and bosses often become the magical objects of nurturance. The secret fantasy is that such persons will solve all the survivor's problems. The same phenomenon can also occur with friends and, most significantly, with therapists (see Chapter 6).

The reason for this excitation–disappointment or borderline-like pattern of relating is, we believe, that the benevolent input needed for growth cannot be taken wholly, again, because it is foreign to the survivor and incongruent with the enormous self-hate, shame, and recrimination she feels. Thus she unconsciously organizes relationships so that the input is received and lost, is present but unavailable, or is offered conditionally. In this way, the survivor is surrounded by the needed input, but since it is lost or unattainable, there is no threat to the survivor's self-hate—a state that, while problematic in some ways, is comfortable.

The aforementioned example of receiving and then losing the needed nurturant input is based on the overarching themes of the survivor's childhood. Generally, before latency, the survivor had a more normal childhood—a more innocent, golden time that was then obliterated by the incest. This period may have been characterized by improved communication, openness, and reclamations, only to be followed by an often-shocking shift of energy to a new mate, a new child, a new job, or, more pathologically, to the parents' personal problems or their use of drugs or alcohol that leads to traumatic emotional, physical, or sexual abuse.

The second common unhealthy resolution of the infatuation phase is when the survivor, in a posture of learned helplessness, resigns herself to the "reality" that she will never get what she wants in a relationship and proceeds to suppress feelings of deservedness and neediness. This will often result in unhealthy symptomatology, such as alcoholism or workaholism. Or the survivor may overfocus her energies away from the self and onto others, such as children, friends, or co-workers, in the codependent theme, "I'll meet my own needs for nurturance through giving it to others." This strategy, of course, is unsuccessful since people cannot give what they themselves lack. The survivor is likely to have internalized this relational paradigm in a more constrictive family system that suppressed feelings to the extent that one was not encouraged or allowed to acknowledge neediness openly, or in a chaotic family system in which, in order to survive, the survivor had to suppress her needs and become the caretaker.

A third common unhealthy resolution is that in which the survivor receives little nurturance in her love relationship, but through a learned pattern of denial, experiences no discomfort or anxiety about it. The survivor here is satisfied with "crumbs" and has little or no sense of being denied anything. The marriages of such survivors are often presented or described as "happy" or "perfect." In this type of relationship, the key mechanism for dealing with the end of the infatuation phase is denial of the pain of disappointment. In these cases, dysfunction is often manifest in the spouse, who may drink or have affairs. These symptoms are generally kept secret and seemingly are disconnected from any psychic pain. If they rise to the surface in the form of an exposed affair or drinking problem, they are described as separate problems that are not symptomatic of any marital difficulties.

In some extreme cases, there is so much denial that the infatuation phase never takes place. The marriage is more one of convenience than of romantic or sexual love, a fact that is accepted by both parties, sometimes consciously. The marriage is not a source of emotional or psychological energy. In these highly distanced, loveless marriages, there is little or no anxiety, and no urgency to leave the partner or to do anything (such as therapy) to make the marriage better. Such marital dynamics will invariably include illicit coalitions with different, usually opposite-sex, children who fulfill quasi-marital roles for the spouses. Incest occurs in these family systems, and at some point, the family may present with the child as the problem.

A Cautionary Note

Keep in mind that these scenarios or themes are generalizations based on our work with many survivors and their partners. They do not describe a particular case, but rather the general pattern of cases. The implication of this is important.

For example, in the foregoing, we described the type of couple in which the partners collude, through denial and suppression, to maintain the facade of a "happy" relationship. These couples are all too familiar to clinicians. Generally, survivors who participate in this type of relationship come from families that suppress emotions. But not all persons engaged in that marital pattern are incest survivors. Moreover, not all survivors from families who engage in repetitive patterns of suppression and denial have marital relationships such as this. Even the characterization of a family as "denying" or "suppressing" is an overgeneralization, since no family denies everything all the time.

Families are unique; individual response patterns to family dynamics vary along several dimensions, some of which are systemically based (e.g., the specific "script" for each child as it melds with his or her own unique temperament and capabilities) and intrapsychically based (e.g., the unique healing capacities of the individual child as the child interacts with the system). Phenomena such as scapegoating, family coalitions, identified-patient status, intelligence, ability, and permission to look or go outside the family system for stimulation must be included in order to understand any individual case. An exposition of such a formula is beyond the scope of this book. Thus we do not mean to imply that the individual client should be understood simply as a by-product of a dysfunctional system or be stamped with certain characteristics because he or she comes from a particular type of family. What we do mean to say is that such characterizations are useful for making sense of the great mass of clinically generated material.

MARITAL PATTERNS

There are two general types of pathological marital patterns that are established by incest survivors. Both patterns represent strategies by which the survivor attempts to remain in a relationship in reaction to issues around the incest trauma.

The Withdrawn Mate

One such strategy is when the survivor chooses to marry a man who will not challenge her to remember or deal with the trauma because he has become so detached from his own feelings and his own childhood pain. This man might be characterized as withdrawn or nonrelational. He tends to believe that the "past is the past" and that feelings or concerns are best dealt with via a rational, common-sense approach.

More important, there is a lack of active caretaking in relation to the survivor. If the survivor is having a difficulty or a problem, this partner is likely not to notice, and if he does, he will take a passive approach. In other words, the survivor does not experience him as "in there" with her. Of course, she is often conflicted about her partner's involvement. On the one hand, she wants him to be in there, but on the other, she is fearful of the intrusive or abusive implications of such intimacy.

As for the partner, he reports his family life as having been "just fine" or "great." He rarely gets angry, and if he does, he generally denies it. He may appear depressed, but is not inclined to acknowledge being unhappy. Most people would describe him as a "nice guy" or a "good guy." Some therapists might consider him to be "passive-aggressive."

Why does the survivor choose this type of partner? The withdrawn mate becomes a container for all the survivor's positive wishes and hopes for purity: "He is good where I am bad." "He is rational where I am out of control with my feelings." "He is chaste where I am impure." "I am angry, while he is not." "He had a wonderful family life, while I did not."

The unconscious hope is that the spouse will heal her, reparenting her owned "bad" aspects by providing her with his owned "good" aspects. The problem with this is that all of her assumptions about his being "good" are based on projections, namely, her disowned good aspects that she projects onto him. He acts them out for her, in part because she encourages (and needs) him to behave in this way. If he behaves in any other way, she ignores it. Not coincidentally, these are the same projections he assumed in his own family of origin.

The reverse is also true. The survivor becomes the container for all of the spouse's emotionality—"badness" or "craziness." She acts out his denied aspects of self, including his anger at his parents, certain aspects of his sexuality, and his having problems. These represent the sum of his projections. The survivor is inclined also to act in this way because these are the same projections she assumed in her family of origin.

She believes, "I am crazy. When my husband relates to me in this way, this is largely comfortable and acceptable." His unconscious hope is, "I will be healed by my wife, who will show me by example how to get in touch with my feelings, my hurts, my anger, my memories, and my traumas."

Healing cannot take place when there is a denial of such basic aspects of the self. Certain denied aspects of the self can be modified but not transformed. In other words, he might help her become more rational (which is his inclined way of being—he is good at it) and reclaim this disowned part of her self, but only to the extent that it does not threaten his sense of rationality. He is psychically organized by the question: "If my wife is more rational, does that mean I am more emotional?" Typically, he will not risk the horror of exposing the deeper emotional aspects of himself. This system of checks and balances keeps the partners in a largely homeostatic lock.

For transformational change to occur, there has to be space in the marriage for two beings who can be either rational or emotional at any given time, depending on individual need. For this to happen, each spouse must be comfortable with virtually all aspects of the self. Thus the need to project is minimized. This is the state in healthier marriages, where there is a freedom for the self to *be* and a freedom for the spouse to *be*. In other words, if one spouse behaves in a particular manner, that is no reflection on the other spouse. For this situation to take place, there must be a state of psychological whole-ness and separateness, the ability to function as "I" as well as "we."

Many of the marriages or relationships of incest survivors who have not received treatment are marked by two fused part selves, since the very act of surviving without acknowledging or working through the trauma requires suppression, repression, and denial. These mechanisms are the same forces that spur the processes of projection and projective identification. In courtship, a healthier potential part-ner will not remain in a relationship with a survivor because he will experience the survivor as not allowing him to be himself or as not being able to handle his emotional or sexual needs. Also, a survivor will prematurely drop a healthier partner, typically considering such a man "wimpy." The man's emotional neediness, while quite appro-priate, is viewed as "too much."

A survivor who does couple with a more emotional man may go through a process of identification with the aggressor (where the mate takes on the role of the survivor and the survivor becomes the abuser) by being abusive herself. This may be accomplished by the survivor's engaging in sexual affairs. The men with whom she has affairs will usually resemble the abusive father and will be viewed as sexually exciting. The survivor cannot psychologically handle having men who remind her of the "mother" and the "father" in the same person.

With the withdrawn-partner choice, the attempt is to resolve trans-ferential disturbances associated with mother figures. There is an unconscious wish or hope that the mate—as the mother—will come through for the survivor in a way that her real mother never did: "He will see what my mother did not." "He will be active where my mother was passive." "He will set the abuser straight once and for all." The intrapsychic hope is that the survivor will work this through and discover that not all mother figures deny reality and suppress feelings.

The withdrawn mate is outwardly mimicking the mother through the denial of reality, the suppression of feelings, and an unwillingness to challenge his status quo. The key dynamic is the survivor's fear of abandonment, which is constantly played on by the lack of contact by the mate. This may set the stage for the hoped-for healing, where the abandoning mother figure who failed may become actively energized. The longing is to have a fully potentiated "mother" in the form of a healthy mate who manifests directness, openness, and strength. This morphogenic aspect may grow slowly over time as the couple matures, or more quickly with therapeutic intervention.

The Abusive Mate

The survivor's attempt to work through a transference with the father will result in the selection of an abusive mate who outwardly resembles the father. The abusive partner is viewed as exciting, although the excitement is replete with emotional, and sometimes physical, hurt. He can be addicted to sex and want it all the time. He may request or demand that the survivor engage in sexual acts about which she feels conflicted, such as threesomes and sadomasochistic activities. He may have affairs, sometimes flaunting them openly.

It is critical to recognize that, as an example, this hypersexuality is, at the level of object relations, the same as the asexuality of the more withdrawn partner. The survivor cannot work through her conflicted sexual feelings any more or any less with either partner choice. The sex-addicted mate ultimately puts her in a position of her being the more asexual one, although sometimes early in the relationship, she will join in his activities.

The more asexual mate will force the survivor into playing out a more hypersexual role, although sometimes early in the relationship, this partner will have the effect of taming her wildness. In this case, significant others, such as parents or friends, may remark, "Oh, he's good for her, he's really settling her down." When all that is to be gained is attained (modification as opposed to transformation), the survivor will feel too settled down, which will revive her own more hypersexual impulses.

The relationship with the abusive mate seems more passionate, but it is a passion fueled by fears of annihilation and abandonment, the same dual dynamic as in the incest. This is not the passion associated with mature romantic love. This partner is more emotional and often displays dramatic bursts of anger, inflicts physical abuse, or undergoes periods of deep depression. The relational quality of such emotion is abusive; there is no healthy attempt to work through the feelings, but rather the feelings become weapons of blame and recrimination.

This partner is also more active and directive than the withdrawn mate and often tells the survivor what jobs to take, what friends to have, what clothes to wear, and so on. The choice of such a partner sets the stage for the longed-for experience of the father as the benevolent nonsexual nurturer. While the withdrawn mate appears to be indifferent, the abusive mate is hypervigilant. This again mimics the mother–father relational dynamics of the family of origin. The withdrawn mother does not see and the abusive father sees too much.

Again, the morphogenic hope that underlies the choice of the abusive mate is the potential "father as nonsexual nurturer," and the hope in choosing the withdrawn partner is the potential "mother as the benevolent power." In succeeding chapters, we show how the therapist can harness these relational healing elements into a comprehensive treatment plan.

CHANGES IN COUPLE CHOICE

The particular patterns of the choice of a mate vary from survivor to survivor. Some will continually choose the withdrawn mate because the fear of the abusive mate is so great. For some survivors, there is an almost instantaneous negative transference reaction to anyone resembling aspects of the "perpetrator–father." All the hate will have been projected onto the abuser and none onto the silent or distant mother. These survivors will have an extremly difficult time dealing with male employers, co-workers, and friends.

Some survivors will only select abusive men. In these cases, much of the blame has been projected onto the mother. Sometimes, these clients will, later in treatment, actually verbalize this through such statements as, "If the bitch would have had sex with him, he would not have needed to have sex with me." These women often are apologists for the abusive father. They will have few or no female friends, since their annihiltion fantasies and hate are projected onto women.

In other cases, the survivor may switch back and forth between withdrawn and abusive men. In therapy, these women may muse about dilemmas between choosing the "nice guy who does nothing for me sexually" and the abusive "jerk whom I hate but cannot get out of my mind."

A related phenomenon is the postdivorce or postrelationship switch where there is a more conscious decision to do better the next time by picking better. The most common change in choice is to go from the difficult-to-handle abuser to a more withdrawn man, who appears to be more stable and is easier to deal with and control. This union often results in failure as well, since the true problem is not the choice itself, but the dynamics that underlie the choice.

Generally speaking, the healthier the survivor, the more likely it is that she will choose a mate who has characteristics of both the mother and the father. There is less splitting, as well as a concomitant attempt to heal the relationship with both parents. Psychologically, a healthier survivor can switch back and forth between seeing the partner as "mother" and seeing him as "father," depending on the situation. The less role-bound the relationship is, the greater the chance for change becomes.

An important caveat to this discussion is that these partner choices are best thought of along a continuum from less withdrawn to more withdrawn and from less abusive to more abusive. At the less-withdrawn pole are partners who are indeed quite distant emotionally, but when presented with an opportunity to behave differently (e.g., in therapy), respond well and become more open. At the more-withdrawn pole are classically schizoid partners who may require a great deal of individual therapy just to become emotionally available to the survivor. Less abusive partners may behave quite abusively, but are remorseful when confronted. More abusive mates may be psychopathic and likewise require a great deal of individual therapy to accept the fact of their destructiveness. Together with the survivor's growth pattern and willingness to enact empowering maneuvers in the marriage, the point at which the spouse falls along the continuum is a good prognostic indicator of the success and length of treatment.

CHILD-REARING TRANSACTIONS OF SURVIVORS

Some may question why it is necessary to include a discussion of the dynamics of the children of adult survivors of incest. After all, what effect might these dynamics have on the actual treatment of the survivor? First, many adult survivors of incest do not enter therapy with incest as the presenting problem. It is not unusual for them to present initially with the children as "the problem," and with the incest material either not recalled, not emphasized, or not brought to the therapist's attention. When this happens, the therapist needs to be sensitive to the possibility of incest and aware of the specific effects of survivorship on parenting.

Second, children of survivors are often triangulated and projected upon when the incest has not been worked through adequately. The problems of the children may be directly related to the unresolved problems of the survivor or the marriage of the survivor. Third, in the interest of preventing family fragmentation and promoting family integrity and health, we recommend always evaluating parent–child interactions and intervening where necessary into the child-rearing transactions as part of the normal course of therapy with survivors.

There are a host of defensive psychological processes in which survivors may engage with their children. Perhaps the most significant of these, and the most difficult to unravel, is the projective identification process. A common dynamic is where the untreated incest survivor does not acknowledge the part of herself that feels shameful, bad, and responsible for the incest's having taken place. This mother will often subtly or overtly encourage her own daughter to be "bad" or sexually promiscuous. This action can be viewed as an awkward attempt to replay the original trauma by having the daughter act out her "bad" impulses and then be blamed or punished for them. The underlying hope is an impossible desire to change the ending of this repetitive drama in some vague, undefined way. And the survivor herself may do the blaming.

The survivor may give a dual message to the daughter, such as setting a curfew when she goes on dates with boys, but not really enforcing it. Or she may simply not set a curfew at all, saying that she implicitly trusts her daughter. When promiscuous behavior occurs, she may not notice. The survivor mother may also repressively overreact to the daughter's sexuality to the extent that the daughter has little choice but to rebel by being "bad." The therapist must be sensitive to recognizing the dual messages since superficially the parent–child relationship may seem normal.

When the survivor has been in a parentified role as a child, she often resents the normal demands of her children. There may be an implicit message to the children to act as little adults and to suppress emotional neediness. There often are role reversals, with the children being asked to take care of the parents or the household. This pattern often disintegrates in adolescence when the child becomes less interested in pleasing the parent and more responsive to the peer culture. The result may be truancy, other school problems, sociopathy, drug and alcohol abuse, or suicide attempts.

In some cases, survivors present in therapy with problems of repeated sexual abuse of one or more of the children. (See the case of Laura in Chapter 1.) While many therapists believe that victims are likely to grow up and either become abusers themselves or couple with abusers, research studies show otherwise. For example, Kaufman and Zigler (1987), cited in Chapter 3 for their work with perpetrators, found an intergenerational transmission rate of about 30%. This means that while survivors suffer from many problems, over two thirds of them do not have ongoing incest in their families of creation. When incest does recur, these are striking repetitions in which the age of the abused, the relationship of the perpetrator, the reactions to the abuse, and so on correspond to the original abuse.

If there is ongoing sexual abuse in the family, it must be stopped. In undertaking this healing and solving the other problems in the rearing transactions, the survivor will undergo personal growth as she identifies with her children and vicariously experiences being protected and parented properly.

SUMMARY

Incest survivors are on a continual search for psychological completion. Contemporary relationships with spouses or lovers and children represent the major arena for potential growth and repetitious cycles of pathology. Succeeding chapters focus on how our understanding of the incest survivor can be integrated into a comprehensive treatment plan. This approach attempts to address the interpersonal aspect, as well as the other areas delineated in the previous chapters through specific interventions that appreciate the interplay of the past, present, and future.

CHAPTER 6

ROLE OF THE THERAPIST

*"When I first entered therapy, I had no real idea why I was there
or what therapy was about. I didn't know how much I needed
to tell someone about the depth of my pain, the depth of my
suffering, the depth and strength of my anger . . . but he saw this
. . . I know he felt it, too . . . that was the beginning of healing
for me."*

— A 36-year-old survivor early in treatment

CREATING A POSITIVE ALLIANCE

The formation and maintenance of an adequate therapeutic relationship are the keys to a positive outcome in therapy. With incest
survivors, the therapy relationship can be particularly difficult to initiate and maintain, owing in large part to disturbances of basic trust
vis-à-vis authority figures such as expert professionals (i.e., therapists). These clients tend to transfer expectations of being violated
or let down onto the therapist. The intensity of these transference
reactions varies according to the gender and other characteristics of
the therapist. If the therapist is male and the client was molested
by her father, then the therapist may be perceived as a potential
perpetrator of abuse. On the other hand, the female therapist may
be experienced by the survivor in the transferential projection as the
weak, nonprotecting mother.

The therapist cannot avoid this transference quagmire even if he or she tries to step out of the transference and downplays the power differential inherent in the therapeutic relationship by taking a more neutral posture. He or she may be perceived by the client as "mother," and thus as weak, distant, and unavailable. When the therapist attempts to become less distant and to be more powerfully involved with the client (e.g., to offer advice, give directives and homework, or confront), she or he again may be viewed as a potential perpetrator.

To create a positive alliance, the therapist must construct and co-create through the early process of therapy with the client a relational posture that is conducive to growth and, at the same time, will be comfortable enough that the client will remain in treatment. By posture we mean the stance the therapist takes vis-à-vis the client, such as the degree of directiveness, intimacy, advice giving, or self-disclosure. See Rappaport (1991) for a theoretical exposition of therapist relational posture.

The practitioner must be viewed as "different but not too different from" (the new healthy figure) and as "like but not the same as" (the old familiar figure) the client's parents. Other factors, such as the client's age, role in the family of origin, and personality style, will influence how the therapist tailors his or her stance so as to be "more different" or "more like."

The preference is that the therapist provide as much of a new relational experience as possible despite the barriers imposed by negative transference expectations. For example, a male therapist saw a 34-year-old incest survivor who had grown up in a family with a stern nonnurturant mother and a father who used affection as an entrée to having sex. The client, Debbie, would find men who initially were sweet and caring, but when the relationship became fully sexual, would become abusive or abandoning. She also had a very difficult time forming friendships with other women, claiming that they were all "full of shit."

With her male therapist, Debbie was able to accept some nurturance and, in fact, at times seemed to demand "more kindness." But whenever the therapist was more supportive or forgiving, for example, by choosing not to question her about forgetting her check, Debbie typically would withdraw in an aggressive manner by canceling her next appointment at the last minute without a valid excuse. It became obvious that through Debbie's transferential lens she saw the male therapist as using nurturance manipulatively. In time, however, the therapist was able to provide small doses of nurturance until the client was able to experience it as more real; in other words, as congruent with the dynamics of the new relationship. After two years of treatment, Debbie was successfully dating.

With a female therapist, the nurturant input may be viewed as so different from the original maternal relationship that it cannot be trusted. Debbie had previously seen a female therapist whom she described as "sickly sweet." This description of the female therapist may have been a transferential distortion, an accurate reading of an ingenuine therapeutic stance, or both. Suffice it to say that the posture of the therapist must be reflective of authentic feelings and thoughts about that particular client. Ultimately, posture is a synthesis of the formularized understanding identified in this chapter and the real feelings generated via hour-by-hour contact with the client.

It is safe to assume that when Debbie began treatment she took it for granted that the therapist was a typical man out to exploit her. As she slowly began to resolve that negative transference expectation/organization, she began to experience the therapist as being an atypical man. She began voicing such thoughts in a joking manner, "I'll never find a man like you." There were oedipal dynamics present in the case, but what Debbie was saying also related to her unfulfilled longings for mothering and nurturance. A little while later, she cried for the first time in session, relating a scene from a movie in which a mother confronted her upset daughter. When the therapist moved closer and handed her a tissue, she cried harder. At one point, she grew pensive. When the therapist asked her what she was thinking about, she smilingly said, "I guess you're more of a mom than my own mom . . . you're always there . . . you don't criticize me."

TAKING A RELATIONAL HISTORY

In general, with cases of child sexual abuse, the therapist must be cautious with regard to two major transferential factors, namely, power and intimacy. As indicated above, the therapist cannot avoid the dilemma by being less powerful and more distant since she or he will then be in danger of mimicking the weak, nonprotective parent figure. A "hands-off" or "kid-glove" approach is likely to be viewed by the survivor as the therapist's being fearful of his or her own power. The therapist must be perceived as strong and capable of intimate contact without being so overpowering and close that he or she is seen as a potential victimizer tapping into the incest survivor's fears of annihilation.

How does the therapist maintain this precarious balance? The answer to this is that he or she must take a careful history of the key relationships in the family of origin to determine the relational posture that will work best with the particular client. History taking, then, must be woven into the bonding phase of the treatment.

The therapist asks questions regarding the relationships between the client and her mother, the client and her father, and the client and her siblings (particular attention is paid here, of course, if the client was abused by an older sibling). Questions about who was close to whom, who did the disciplining, who was more nurturing, and who was favored, and at what ages, are asked to determine the specific relational dance in which the client engaged with the mother and father. Indirect and triangulated relationships are particularly important since the abused child may have served for the father as a replacement for the mother. The therapist can then learn what attitudes and behaviors the client is most likely to respond to favorably or unfavorably. The clinician can create the specific relational posture for each client based on these data.

All that was experienced in childhood by the client becomes the relational familiar. While much of it may be highly dysfunctional, the client is, to a certain extent, comfortable with and used to being related to in that way, whether by partners or by therapists. Again, not exactly, but similar. The therapist who provides too little of the familiar relational experience will be ignored or disregarded in some manner. A common refrain from clients who were abused while growing up and are in need of appropriate confrontation is that the therapist was "too nice" or was "too easy on me," and "let me get away with too much." Or in other cases, if the therapist's posture is too much like the original parenting experience, the therapist is rejected for being overly abusive "just like my father," another familiar client termination refrain.

Thus the therapist must take the relational history and determine what the client received, both positive and negative, to ascertain what new psychological inputs the client needs in order to grow, such as more nurturance or support or confrontation. The therapist should then provide a mixture of these two inputs, the familiar for bonding and the unknown for healing. The familiar will keep the client connected to the therapist as he or she will be experienced as congruent, that is, understanding of the client's historically rooted internal experience. This bond provides a base upon which to add inputs that are missing and needed.

THERAPEUTIC POSTURE

The therapist must look for verbal and nonverbal cues—such as crying, smiling, excitation, maintenance of eye contact, interest level, and the turning of the body toward or away from the therapist—to determine whether his or her behavior is correct. A correct posture is marked by a mixture of the older familiar and the newer reparative input. Too much of the familiar input will engender a kind of deflated "here we go again" response on the part of the client. An overly reparative posture, on the other hand, will generally produce a wary reaction by the client. The therapist must be attuned to the client's signaling and adjust his or her behavior accordingly.

For example, in a first session with a female survivor, the male therapist attempted to console the client by handing her a tissue as she wept. The client jerked her body ever so slightly, but noticeably, away from the therapist and muttered a "thank you" while she looked away. She then assumed a pained, false smile. The therapist realized that his posture needed to exclude nurturance. This was later confirmed by the client's history, which revealed that her father had died when she was 2 years old and that the only father figure in her life was her mother's lover, who began molesting her when she was 8 years old. The therapist moved into a more distant posture.

With some sexually abused clients, a more powerful intervention such as confrontation should be introduced following or be followed by a discussion; for instance, asking them how they feel about the therapist's intrusiveness or directiveness. If the therapist needs to confront the client, then he or she can do so, but not abusively, thereby avoiding a negative transference reaction based on prior experiences of harsh fathering. Confrontation may be followed by concerned but not overly nurturing responses to avoid a negative transference reaction to "mother." Depending on the nature of the parental relationships, simply asking that kind of question may be perceived as too intrusive in and of itself. Then the therapist must become more reflective and use more of an active listening posture.

In time, the therapist will gather a considerable amount of data about the client. Responses to all aspects of the therapy (including issues regarding fee setting, fee payment, timeliness, and reaction to other clients), no matter how seemingly minor, are essential information. For example, the client's comments regarding the client seen in the previous hour provide a wealth of data regarding issues of competition. The reaction to how and when one ends the session gives a clue to fears regarding abandonment. Using the data available, the therapist creates a relational yet authentic posture tailored for each client.

The therapist's careful respect of boundaries is of critical importance. The reactions elicited by going a few or several minutes over the set time or calling the client at home for whatever reason are critical to note, since boundary violations are the hallmark of clients' relational histories. Again, this does not mean that boundaries are never approached, since survivors need to experience that the therapist is not afraid of them, that is, "I can cross the supposed boundary without taking advantage of them or exploiting them." Indeed, in some cases, great healing can take place if the therapist shows special interest or investment in the client and gives her extra time or a timely phone call. When there are no "strings attached," the client learns slowly to trust that the therapist will not take advantage of her. This process can help significantly in repairing the trust-betrayal dilemma.

Crossing the Boundary

A boundary crossing does not have to be a boundary violation. For example, one of us (R.R.) received a phone call from Sarah, an incest survivor, canceling her upcoming appointment. After determining that her reason for canceling was insufficient, he pressed against her boundary and challenged her as to why she really wanted to cancel the session. Sarah then unleashed a litancy of excuses, culminating in an exasperated, "I just have too much to handle . . . I'm seeing my mom . . . my (boyfriend) . . . I don't need any more demands . . .

besides I'm giving you plenty of notice . . . why can't you just let me skip a week?"

At this point, the therapist was inclined to give in to Sarah's request. Through a process of projective identification and transference, Sarah was organizing the therapist to feel and perhaps behave as if he were the perpetrating father who did not respect her boundaries. The therapist's inclination to concede reflected this organization through his internal dialogue, "Oh, no, I *am* disrespecting her space. I am just like her abusive father." The therapist had to remind himself that he was not behaving abusively, nor was he violating her boundaries through the dialogue. He said, "Wait a minute, we have an agreement about meeting weekly and working together on your difficulties, and challenging your request is not a violation. In fact, it is part and parcel of my investment in you."

Again, it is important to note that in this therapeutic situation, the therapist cannot remain neutral, since the client was looking for "OK" or "not OK" signals from the therapist. Any questioning of Sarah, no matter how neutral sounding, would be perceived by her as challenging and abusive. An immediate "OK" signal might have indicated to Sarah that the therapist was afraid of approaching the boundary she had erected, perhaps as a defense against his unacknowledged aggressive impulses or as an abandonment such as the one experienced with her mother.

Moreover, some may argue that the therapist could have supported, or even applauded, Sarah's request as a sign of increasing assertiveness. This, too, would be a mistake since Sarah was in an overprotective state of self-defense against a perceived attacker whose threat to her was magnified and distorted. If the therapist had supported Sarah's request, he would have unconsciously conveyed to her that he was the threat that she imagined him to be.

Sarah arrived at the session agitated. The therapist remained steadfast in his assertion that there appeared to be no reason to skip the appointment and that it was important for her to be there. He followed with an in-depth exploration of thoughts and feelings about the preceding week's session. Over the course of the session, Sarah revealed that she was feeling overwhelmed by the psychological material being generated and all that it implied. At a key point, the therapist asked Sarah why she had not just admitted this and asked that the session be organized around a less anxiety-provoking topic.

(Note that this request would have been an appropriately assertive response to an accurate reading of reality as the therapist may have unwittingly gone too far with the more anxiety-provoking material.) Sarah responded that she didn't think the therapist "would listen anyway." She then laughed and said, "Don't say anything . . . I know that's ridiculous . . . I guess it's just how I felt."

The therapist and Sarah processed how she could feel more in control of the material being generated and of the pace of the sessions without having to distance herself from the therapist or dissociate from the feelings or memories. The therapist assured her that he would be responsive to her need to slow things down. At this point, Sarah disengaged from her negative transference reaction and validated the therapist's strong stance by saying, "Now don't let me get away with anything. I might say I need a break, but if you think I need to go forward, then push me. That's why I like you, you're not afraid to push me."

Some incest survivors will allow more of a therapeutic bond than others, depending on their particular histories. Other mediating influences play a role. The client may have found a teacher, coach, or friend in childhood with whom she was able to have a close relationship. Survivors raised as scapegoated, rebellious, and oppositional children often initially will adapt to the therapy much more readily than will those raised as compliant, overly dependent children. This is true because the former's frame of reference is, at least at superficial levels, outside the family, with the therapist representing another outsider to whom they may adapt. Of course, in time, often six months to a year into treatment, the therapist becomes the new engulfing insider and someone to distance from or rebel against. These clients will suddenly terminate treatment, often citing the need to go it alone for a while.

Paradoxical and often indirect interventions (e.g., symptom prescription) generally work best in engaging these clients when their counterdependency rears itself in the therapist–client interaction. With one young male survivor, the therapist congratulated the client on terminating his therapy at just the right time since he was on the verge of resolving the deepest issues stunting his personal growth. "This is a great time to leave," said the therapist. "This way, you can still take all your problems with you." The client decided to remain in treatment since the therapist again had moved into an "outsider" position and he was again free of feeling engulfed, a common relational response of the counterdependent client. After approximately two years of treatment and several more paradoxical interventions, the client was able to accept more direct interventions about his tendency to flee the emotionality of intimate relationships.

MAINTAINING THE THERAPEUTIC BOND

A common therapeutic error is to go beyond or underneath the presenting problem too quickly in the haste to address the "real" or larger concerns, such as the recovery and working through of incest memories. We must always remember that clients are coming to us for a specific reason, as well as to satisfy deeper unconscious wishes, including the uncovering of trauma. However, it is through the resolution of their presenting problems that clients may be freed to open the door to look deeper and wider into their lives. The presenting problem has more than symbolic meaning to the client. It represents a habitual response to stress that has also served as a protective bandage covering the deeper wounds.

Still, the seeds for deeper change need to be planted as early as the first session. The therapist is free to make references to unresolved aspects of the client's life, and then to drop them if necessary. The client who comes to us complaining of insomnia, for example, may be told that her difficulties with men are apparent as well. It is important to do this since, at the deepest intrapsychic level, people are in a constant search for completion. The therapist must balance attention to the presenting problem with attention to latent conflicts and difficulties.

Many survivors are inclined to terminate treatment after resolving their presenting concern without addressing the deeper issues that bring up enormous dread and horror. But if the therapist can provide a solid holding environment through this transitional stage of therapy, the client will remain in treatment. The desire to flee treatment arises because the removal of the presenting problem and the protective function it has served is frightening to the client. The opportunities for real intimacy with the therapist arise in the form, "If we don't talk about my depression or anxiety, what will we do?" A host of terrors and fears are revealed, including those surrounding the incest memories. Suppressed material about early traumas may rise to the surface as the appropriate conditions have been set. That is, the presenting difficulty has been removed or diminished and the client remains in a positive alliance with a potential healer who has already planted the seeds of expectations for further growth.

Why Clients Terminate Treatment

If the therapist has not set the stage for the therapy to continue, many survivors terminate treatment abruptly at this point. The most common termination theme is, "Thank you very much. You've helped me so. I'll be sure to call you if I need you." Or the client may, to the chagrin of the therapist, simply vanish. Positive-change reports are followed by a seemingly mysterious series of missed appointments, sudden financial difficulties, or work assignments that rarely had interfered with the sessions previously. In some cases, more disturbed clients may quickly turn from positive to negative transference following some misperception, miscommunication, or minor therapeutic error.

It is essential that the therapist take responsibility for continuation of the treatment at such a point, since it is a prime opportunity to provide a corrective transactional experience. The symbolic reenactment of the hurtful parent–child dynamics has emerged strongly and can be brought to a corrective resolution. The survivor is used to being wronged or mistreated and continues this stance when viewing the therapist as the perpetrator of abuse, or, alternatively, to feeling let down when the therapist is viewed as the protective parent who abandoned the child in a time of need. In the first instance, the therapeutic mistake is generally perceived of as overdirectiveness, confronting, or even bullying on the part of the therapist. Typically, the therapist, sensing that the client is about to flee treatment prematurely, has turned up the heat inappropriately in some way by trying to get the client to address a charged issue so that the client can see that it is not time to terminate.

The client, in reacting to this combination of real therapeutic error and negative transference, will tend to verbalize her upset. The therapist may be accused of being "just like my father," of being too intrusive or overpowering. This is a tremendous opportunity for the therapist skillfully to point out that she or he is not the parent, to apologize for the error if appropriate, and to reengage the client. This is, in fact, a reenactment of exactly the sequence of events that the survivor longed for in childhood. She can now internalize these aspects of the therapist. Moreover, the therapist becomes more of a whole person with various facets that resemble those of the original parent and others that do not.

A more real relationship will begin to develop between the client and therapist as the working through of the transference takes place. The client will often appropriately attach herself to the new, good "parent" figure as she lets go of the negative aspects of her biological parents. The therapist must have worked through his or her own engulfment terrors and intimacy fears so that he or she allows the client to develop a healthy dependency. This is the only way in which the client can have a reparative transactional experience.

Healthy dependency, in our view, is dependency that takes place in the context of a reparative relationship where the intent of the therapist is to have the client grow to the point of individuation; that is, dependency in the service of independent growth. Dependency must always be followed by an explicit or implicit demand for progressive movement. We define progressive movement as the mastery of new behaviors or the conquering of old debilitating fears. With incest survivors, the expectation will be for their courageous willingness to uncover, explore, and work through that trauma. In this sense, movement toward the therapist is followed by a movement that will ultimately allow the client to move away from the therapist. Stein (1980) has called this process of human development progressive abreactive regression (PAR).

In the second instance of threatened termination, where the therapist is perceived as the weak, ineffectual, or abandoning parent, the client may leave treatment prematurely shortly after the presenting problem has been addressed because somehow the therapist has not acted differently enough from that parent figure. This event often is cocreated through a process of projective identification. The client passively signals the therapist to let her down by, for instance, going to several sessions without bringing in material on which to work. The therapist, of course, feels ineffectual during this time, and in anger may pull away from the client emotionally (i.e., through countertransference, often in the form of client blaming, "She doesn't want to change enough"). As the client feels the emotional cutoff, she unconsciously distances further from the therapist. The pattern repeats itself as the distancing of one begets the distancing of the other.

The cycle can only be broken when the therapist deals with his or her countertransference reactions, reengages the client, and recognizes that the client's pulling away is a transference reaction. The survivor can then see it, as well. The therapist as the benevolent authority figure takes primary responsibility for maintaining the alliance when problems arise in the relationship.

The client can then be powerfully reengaged. Generally speaking, offering a client insight into how she enacted this projective identification process may modify or slow down the distancing process, but it is not reparative. The repair occurs when the therapist behaves differently—as a remedial reparental agent—and the client experiences that change fully and emotionally. With many clients, providing insight after the transformative event has taken place is quite helpful to them in understanding themselves better, as well as for application to other situations.

Working Through Negative Transference

If the client does not feel the therapist's strength (without abusiveness), she will reexperience abandonment terror as there is no penetrating good object available in the therapy. Her internal experience will be one of "here we go again." Being let down as the result of such a therapeutic error, in combination with the transferential expectation of being let down, will, in most cases, cause the client to flee treatment.

These clients generally will not talk to the therapist about being let down or how the therapist is "just like my mother." Therapists are usually attuned to the more obvious negative transference reactions where the therapist is perceived of as a perpetrator as a result of overactivity or doing too much. However, doing too little or being underactive may be a more common error with incest survivors; it is just that these clients are less inclined to relate to the experience in the same way that they do when they feel that a boundary has been actively violated. The misdeeds of the silent partner who did not intervene to stop the abuse are more insidious and difficult to pin down. It is more unusual for a client to blame the therapist for not being "in there" enough. Culturally rooted expectations that therapists will be "remote" and "clinical" also subtly encourage the client not to voice her feelings.

Therefore, the therapist should be keen to hear clues to this negative transference reaction. Complaints about the therapist—such as, "You can't be there all the time," "I have to do this myself," "You have your own family, other clients, etc."—can be indicators that the client does not feel connected enough to the therapist, no matter how rationally the client presents such material.

The working through of this transference, however, is just as significant, since the client experiences a great deal of guilt and consternation over her suppressed rage at the nonintervening parent. The rage she feels toward the perpetrator is actually easier to confront, since the harm was caused directly. But this working through is different from the working through of the negative transference reaction to the perpetrating parent. When perceived as a weak, uninvolved, and abandoning parent, the therapist must be willing to take on the responsibility of engendering a firm stance by confronting the client's relational dynamics. This means that the therapist must firmly address out-of-session dynamics such as no-shows and cancellations by calling the client at home if necessary. In-session dynamics, such as disregarding the therapist by not following through on mutually agreed-upon tasks or homework assignments or casually forgetting what issues they have been working on in treatment, must also be confronted in a timely manner.

For example, one of us (R.R.) spent a three-month period in therapy processing a 28-year-old female incest survivor's dating dynamics with men. This included sexual promiscuity, shame, and guilt over premature sexual involvements that the client, Jan, admitted were her only way to "feel connected." Client and therapist made a contract that she would not have sex with a date before discussing it with the therapist. Jan kept to the contract until, at one session, she casually discussed getting drunk at a party and going to bed with a man whose name she "didn't even remember."

The therapist challenged Jan on breaking their contract. Jan responded by saying that the challenge was silly since she hadn't even thought about the contract at that point because it only applied to dates and "this was no date." When the therapist continued to press further, asking how seriously Jan took her treatment, Jan became silent and somewhat dissociative. For several minutes, the therapist continued to ask her what was going on in an increasingly softer, more nurturing manner.

Finally, Jan spoke: "Who cares anyway, nothing ever changes." When the therapist asked her what this meant to her, she talked about having felt hopeless about the contract's working for her, even before the incident. The therapist asked her why she hadn't said anything then. He also pointed out that she had reported feeling better about herself during the time the contract was in place. Jan responded by agreeing that she did, in fact, feel better when she didn't go to bed with a man on the first date. She also said she realized that, as a result, men had treated her better, but that it also scared her. Jan and the therapist then talked of her fears, the primary one being the fear of having to be herself with men, rather than "just playing a role."

The therapist empathized with Jan and her fears, but also said that he was upset with her for not taking the contract seriously and that he expected her to behave differently in the future. Jan asked why he was being so hard on her. The therapist immediately responded, "Because I care about you." Jan began to cry and described how her mother never seemed to notice when she was acting out as an adolescent. In an upbeat tone, the therapist then said, "Well, I'm noticing," and they both laughed. In the last 10 minutes of the session, the therapist offered insight into the dynamics of the drunken one-night stand. He also developed specific strategies for helping her to deal with these situations, such as arranging with a girlfriend ahead of time to go home with her. Jan recontracted with the therapist to help her and approached future sessions with more determination and maturity.

In general, a typical sequence of confrontation unfolds as follows: The therapist confronts actual client behavior, such as forgetting to work on a mutually agreed-upon task. The client will often act as if it isn't important, which is a signal to the therapist to continue to confront. A genuinely remorseful client posture is generally a signal to back off. The therapist confronts the client's cavalier attitude further by pressing the key issue of how seriously the client takes her treatment, the therapist, and, most important, herself. The client at this point may bring up a more real (i.e., emotionally charged) issue, such as, "Who cares anyway, nothing can change." The therapist must first explore these despairing thoughts and feelings. Then he or she must strongly confront the client's hopelessness by offering himself or herself and the treatment as a new opportunity for change. The therapist then asks the client for a recommitment to the treatment at a new level with higher expectations. He or she then may request that the client follow through on the original task with increased fervor, which creates the possibility of positive reinforcement. The client will experience a renewal or regeneration of hope.

If the therapist can deliver on the promise to continue successfully to confront the client's hopelessness, a transformation will take place. The client will, in effect, introject the therapist as the new good parent; that is, as the conscious and strong mother figure who is not afraid to confront reality. The alliance with the therapist also opens the possibility for honest family-of-origin work (see Chapter 9). Through this process, the client will become stronger and more willing to deal with reality.

There are, of course, a small percentage of survivors who will stay with a therapist who does not facilitate change, and thus the aforementioned abandonment-triggered dynamic does not apply in these cases. These are generally clients who grew up in tightly controlled, closed family systems, which they were not allowed to leave, and so they developed a learned helplessness response. The therapist must watch and overtly push for continued growth, since these clients' expectations for growth are miniscule. It is not that they are satisfied clients. Generally, they are dissatisfied with their lives, but have no inclination to voice that dissatisfaction or, for that matter, to expect that anyone, including themselves or another therapist, can do anything for them.

DEALING WITH THE CLIENT'S AVOIDANCE OF INCEST MATERIAL

In the more usual case, though, the client does indeed attempt to flee the treatment. The survivor is trying to avoid the exposure of childhood traumas and deep intrapsychic wounds. Quite often, suppressed incest material is close to the surface. It is critical to note, however, that it is not just the content of the material from which the client is distancing; the client has managed to live with that pain for many years. Rather, it is also the exposure of the events in a relational context; that is, the possibility of introducing new pain to the system that the client is endeavoring to avoid.

The new pain is the process of making it real by talking about it out loud, by naming and exploring it. The closely held myth, which has been reinforced via family invalidation and cultural suppression, is that if we don't talk about it, it didn't happen and it's not real.

If the therapist believes that incest material is present (see Chapter 2), it is critical that he or she strategically move to help the client bring the material to the surface. Although the client's anxiety may become acute at that point, it is generally still manageable. As long as the material remains lodged, the client's anxiety is essentially overwhelming, highly difficult to manage, and impossible to address.

The suppressed incest material will only be released when the client is in touch with childhood memories and childlike parts of the self. Therefore, it is necessary that the therapist continue to maintain a benevolent nurturant–authoritative stance and good-enough object relations with the client, so that the client then feels safe enough to access her child parts. The therapist must engage and reengage consistently and continuously. We must emphasize that therapists too often allow clients to "coast" or to terminate treatment hastily, citing the client's inability or unwillingness to deal with deeper issues. Often the therapist's unwillingness to extend himself or herself is the more problematic variable. It is our belief that practitioners should err on the side of caution by strategically keeping clients related to them and focused on the treatment.

In the context of a caring holding environment, the therapist can manage negative transference reactions that are sure to occur and, in fact, need to occur for deeper healing and transformation to take place. Indeed, this posture is in itself a corrective experience for the client since it displays a strong concerned investment that the client did not experience growing up.

INCLUSION OF THE PARTNER

There is substantial evidence to support the notion that it is beneficial to include the spouse to some degree in the treatment of anxiety and depressive disorders (Barlow, O'Brien, & Last, 1983, 1984; Bland & Hallam, 1981; Coyne, 1987). Given that survivors often suffer from such disorders (e.g., Sedney & Brooks, 1984; Lundberg-Love et al., 1987; Lundberg-Love, 1990), it follows that the inclusion of their spouses in treatment is indicated. Conversely, not including the spouse in the treatment may lead to deterioration of the marriage or the partner relationship, even though there may be temporary improvement in the functioning of the identified patient (Coyne, 1987; Hafner, 1977; Milton & Hafner, 1979).

The client who presents for treatment is embedded in a particular context. For an adult, the key context is the significant love relationship. If the client who presents for treatment is living with someone or is married, inclusion of the partner is necessary. Positive change on the part of the client may lead to unnecessary fragmentation of the marriage if the partner and the relationship do not develop concurrently. Moreover, the spouse is a potential ally for the therapist if he is bonded with adequately.

If the partner is left out of the therapy, the treatment may fail because the spouse may consciously or unconsciously seek to undermine individual gains, since they threaten a change in the relationship. The partner who is not included in the therapy may develop a negative transference reaction to the therapist, who is perceived as a competitor or saboteur. Often the partner is working at cross-purposes to the goals of the treatment. While the therapist may, for example, be encouraging the client to work on retrieving incest memories, the spouse may say something like, "Why bother remembering this stuff? After all, your father is 72, what good will it do now?" Furthermore, the client may unconsciously or consciously encourage competitiveness or use the therapist's statements as weapons in the couple's disagreements.

For all the reasons described above, it is best to include the partners of coupled survivors in treatment. Typically, the therapist bonds with the partner around the presenting issue. He or she starts by asking the partner to serve in a helping or "consultant" role, if complete entrance into therapy is too threatening. In the best of circumstances, the partner is able to acknowledge his own involvement in some of the relationship problems that have been presented.

The therapist should never accept the incest survivor's claim that "he wouldn't want to come here," "he's against therapy," or "he thinks it's my problem and my problem only," without exploration and, in some cases, confrontation. Exploration of the client's own desires to maintain the status quo by not addressing the marriage at all or her secret wish to ultimately leave the couple relationship should take place. The therapist should stress the importance of the partner's involvement and educate the client regarding the possibility of the loss of the partner if one grows and the other does not.

The longer individual treatment takes place in the absence of the partner, the more difficult it will be for the mate to enter into a positive working relationship with the therapist, since the therapist's alliance with the survivor will seem impenetrable. Therefore, the therapist must not wait until the survivor is "ready," but instead secure the survivor's commitment to include the spouse as early as possible. If the survivor cannot or will not bring him in, the therapist must gain permission to enlist the spouse's support directly via telephone contact. Contrary to expectation, calling the spouse directly is generally effective, if the therapist treats the spouse as one whose presence will be helpful and important to the treatment.

To the greatest extent possible, in the mind of the therapist, the spouse of the survivor is considered a "client" with as much reason to be a part of the therapy and as much in need of treatment as the survivor. When the entire family or the marriage is presented for treatment, this can be more overt and is easier to implement in sessions. If the survivor presents herself as the problem, then the partner's full entry into the treatment is a priority goal. If the therapist maintains this systemic view, as well as an intrapsychic view, this goal can be transactionally reached within three months or so. In relatively few cases does the partner of a survivor present for individual treatment.

A critical companion viewpoint is that, despite appearances, neither partner is intrinsically healthier than the other. Each member of the couple is functioning at the same basic level of interpersonal skill and personal selfhood. In other words, the abilities of each member of the couple appropriately to contain his or her own emotionality, to allow the emotionality of the partner, and to read the relational reality of situations are about the same. If one partner's level of personal development were significantly higher than the other, he or she would find the relationship unfulfilling and ultimately would leave it. What may differ is one partner's willingness to grow psychologically.

Interestingly, some clinicians will tend to see the survivor as healthier than her partner. This perception largely depends on which partner manifests the pathology initially. If the symptomatic survivor is engaged in individual treatment and is able to reduce her symptomatology, to become more assertive, and to develop new skills and behaviors, the partner will begin to appear less healthy by comparison. Very often, this is when a referral to couples therapy is made. By that time, however, the partner may be resentful because of the intense relationship he has with the survivor's therapist. He may not trust the referral or there may be conflicts about whom to work with and whether the individual or the couples therapist is the one who is "right" or is "better." By the time the partner agrees to couples work, the survivor may be ambivalent and resentful. The homeostatic forces of the couple will allow for either partner to play the "resistant" role. Many of these cases end in unnecessary and preventable divorces.

The key to prevention is to follow the rule of always including the partner in treatment with the same practitioner, except in the very unusual cases where there may be physical danger to the survivor or the therapist. Engaging the resistant spouse poses challenges for the clinician, but in the long run it is a major predictor of treatment success. In one case, a resistant husband was asked by the therapist to help his wife's therapy along. John was able to supply a wealth of information about the survivor and her family. The survivor, Mary, actually became more comfortable and said she looked forward to couples sessions. John liked the therapist and began to open up to him about many personal issues that were unrelated to Mary.

In other cases, the survivor resists bringing her partner to treatment. In one instance, the survivor, Cindy, had recently married. She refused to involve her husband in treatment for fear that he would not want her when he found out that she was "defective." In a year's time, with trust built and the therapist's remaining steadfast in his refusal to leave the husband out, she complied by bringing James to a session.

Cindy sat through the session in near panic as the therapist attempted to bond with James. After the session, the therapist and Cindy processed how she felt. Cindy reported fearing that the therapist would like James more than he liked her. This perception was a transferential distortion left over from her relationship with her biological father, who had abandoned the family when Cindy was 8 years old to marry his longtime girlfriend. The therapist insisted that he would not do anything consciously that would hurt her and that he wanted to include James in treatment only because he believed it be in Cindy's best interests.

If the therapist had not insisted on including James, Cindy would have been deprived of the opportunity to work through that significant distortion. Simply talking about it, no matter how emotional Cindy became in the process, would have been insufficient. In the couples session, Cindy reexperienced the trauma and a "new ending" emerged. In other words, this time Cindy did not lose her "father." As a result, she was able to trust authority figures more and to allow herself to be in competitive situations that could involve triangulation and the fear of losing approval.

The therapist must search for an effective reparental posture for the partner of the survivor that is also based on his unique relational history. (See previous sections on creating a positive alliance.) Even when the partner is absent from treatment, for whatever reason, the therapist can still send messages home to him based on the partner's relational expectations and needs.

For example, in one case in which the husband initially refused to participate in treatment, the therapist told the survivor that her husband had done "a wonderful job" of protecting her from emotional abuse by her father at a Thanksgiving dinner held at the parents' home. She had reported a particularly unhealthy interaction, after which her husband strongly but sensitively suggested that they leave earlier than planned. The therapist surmised that the spouse was in need of a small dose of nurturance from the therapist as a healing input from a "father" figure.

After the survivor told her husband about the therapist's validation of him, he began to suggest that the survivor "ask (the therapist) what he thinks" about a problem or "talk to (the therapist) about that." Later, at a strategic point, the therapist called the husband to discuss some of his concerns. The husband readily accepted the therapist's invitation to a session and was open to meeting with him regularly.

INCLUSION OF CHILDREN

There are two ways in which the children of the survivor may enter the therapy. The first is the more obvious situation in which the children themselves are part of or are the major reason the survivor seeks treatment. For example, in one case, a single-parent survivor contacted the therapist because her 15-year-old daughter was acting out at school and in the community. In the first session, the mother revealed that she had been molested by her stepfather in her early teens. The first six months of therapy focused primarily on the daughter's maturational difficulties, which were not unrelated to the mother's arrested development as a result of her own traumatized childhood.

In another case where the children were the presenting problem, the mother did not reveal the incest material until one year into family treatment. In both cases, the therapist viewed the presenting problem through the widest lens possible. That is, the problems of the children were seen in the context of the larger family system, which naturally included the parents' current functioning and histories. This more comprehensive approach allowed sufficient room for the disclosure of other relevant material, such as the incest.

The second situation in which it is appropriate for children to enter the treatment is when the adult survivor or the couple is the main focus of the therapy, while at times problems with children are discussed. This may occur quite naturally if an adequate therapeutic alliance has developed. Generally speaking, clients do not feel bound by the original therapeutic contract, which may only include work on certain aspects of the client's life, such as love relationships or the incest itself.

It is best, as discussed previously, if the therapist broadens the contract for treatment as early as possible. In one case, for example, the therapist pointed out in the first session how the survivor's relationships with her children were adversely affected by her reaction to the incest trauma. In general, the better the therapeutic alliance, the more access the therapist is allowed to various aspects of the client's system.

If the alliance is marked by varying degrees of mistrust, the client will offer the therapist less access to problems involving the children. The survivor may never mention issues with the children or may only drop hints of problems. She may, for example, casually mention that her 8-year-old daughter is being held back in school or that her 16-year-old son was arrested for drunk driving over the weekend. When questioned by the therapist, the survivor may indicate that this has nothing to do with her problems or her therapy.

In some cases, the survivor may simply announce that she has sought separate therapy for her child without consulting with the therapist. In these cases, either the therapist has not "spread" the problem sufficiently or the therapeutic alliance is quite fragile, since a strong alliance is marked by a positive transference in which the therapist is viewed as an expert on human relationships. When several therapists are treating various aspects of one problematic system, the potential for splitting, cross-transferences (both negative and positive), and professional rivalry, particularly when the therapists are operating out of different orientations, is enormous. Therefore, it is usually in the best interests of the family that one therapist manage the entire case, even if it is necessary to include other therapists adjunctively at various times.

In most cases, problems with children can be dealt with directly through family therapy sessions. Additionally, in individual and conjoint sessions with the partners, behavioral rehearsal, modeling, and role playing can be used to build parenting skills and to improve the couple's teamwork.

In one case, the survivor began to talk about her 5-year-old daughter's bed-wetting. The therapist suggested that the client and her husband bring Amy to the next session. In discussing the dynamics around bedtime, Amy revealed that she missed having her mother tuck her into bed, which her mother hadn't been doing since she began studying at night to prepare for a state licensure examination. Amy said she told her this several times, but apparently her mother did not listen. Not coincidentally, it was at about the same age (age 5) that the mother had been molested in her bed at night by her older brother. Mom may have been trying to avoid the memories by not putting her daughter to sleep.

The therapist asked the client to tuck Amy in at night. The husband was directed to "check in" and process with his wife each night to see what incest-related feelings were coming up for her. Each week, the therapist tracked the progress and trouble-shot the triadic interaction, such as confronting the husband when he "forgot" to check in or glossed over traumatic material brought up by his wife. In individual sessions with the husband, the therapist taught, rehearsed, and role-played active listening skills. The husband used his new skills at home and his wife began to tuck Amy in. Within a month, the bed-wetting problem had abated.

This example demonstrates how the therapist served as a reparental agent for the husband by directing, confronting, and educating him. The husband, in turn, helped the survivor to nurture their daughter by meeting Amy's needs for nighttime comfort. This kind of chaining effect, from spouses to each other and then to the children, is, we believe, more economical therapeutically than referring the daughter to a child or play therapist and, by the same token, referring the couple to marital therapy. The independent, marital, and rearing transactions of the family are closely interwoven. Therefore, the most powerful therapeutic interventions take these interconnections into account. In any case, it is important to note that because all aspects of family life are interconnected, there will be a chain reaction to any therapeutic intervention, whether intended or not.

SUMMARY

The initial phase of therapy with survivors of incest is marked by the creation of a positive alliance between client and therapist. Invariably, there will be breakdowns in the therapeutic alliance that are due mainly to issues of power, intimacy, trust, and difficulties in interpersonal relating that depend on family-of-origin experiences. If these negative transference reactions are managed appropriately, these same breakdowns also provide the possibility for a corrective transactional experience and significant reduction of the post-traumatic stress reactions of the survivor.

If the survivor's partner is included in the treatment, the therapist can avoid sabotage, prevent unnecessary family fragmentation, and, even more important, fully harness the healing capacities of the couple. With the solid therapeutic bond in place, the partner enlisted for treatment, and the child detriangulated from the survivor or the couple, the survivor is ready to confront the memory-retrieval process as described in Chapter 7.

THE INITIAL PHASE OF THERAPY

"Until I started coming here, I really didn't believe that I was molested by my uncle. He was like a vague shadowy figure lurking in the dark. Now I'm starting to know what happened, and what he did to me."

—A successful lawyer

In the initial phase of treatment, the therapist focuses on symptom relief and the memory-retrieval process with the survivor. If the client is in a committed relationship, the clinician also develops a therapeutic bond with her partner. The format for treatment, then, is individual sessions with the survivor and less frequent meetings with the couple.

This chapter describes the techniques we use for relieving some of the more common anxiety and depressive disorders. It also discusses the therapeutic role, strategies, and techniques needed to facilitate memory retrieval and the role of the partner in the process. The three goals of the memory-retrieval process are the abreaction of anger, terror, sadness, and mourning that are the emotional hallmarks of incest survival; the lifting of the taboos on knowing and speaking about the incest; and the desensitization to trigger stimuli associated with the trauma that bring up unpleasant thoughts and feelings.

SYMPTOM RELIEF

It is important for the therapist to facilitate symptom relief during the beginning phase of treatment. As we noted in the opening chapter, survivors suffer from a host of cognitive and emotional difficulties, and it is typically these symptoms that bring them into therapy. They must be addressed first, because, in many cases, they are so debilitating that clients are unable to function as parents, partners, or workers.

The first step in the symptom-relief process is to normalize clients' symptoms by reframing them as reactions to the incest. The clinician may offer straightforward explanations like, "Being anxious in strange situations or feeling like you're a bad person is totally understandable when you've been abused as a child," or, "Feeling anesthetized during sex is common in incest survivors." The therapist must accept and then help the client to accept the symptoms as "normal" reactions to the abuse.

The clinician can also educate the client about the typical and "normal" kinds of problems that survivors have. These include chronic depression; suicidal thoughts and gestures; eating disorders; somatic disorders, especially in the rectal area or reproductive organs; phobias; low self-esteem or lack of assertiveness; substance abuse; memory difficulties; sexual dysfunction; trust and boundary issues in relationships; and parenting difficulties. In more severe cases, symptoms may include dissociation, multiple personality disorder, self-mutilation, child abuse, or chronic victimization. (See Chapter 1 for a more complete discussion.)

Even the more severe symptoms need to be normalized. For example, in a case of self-mutilation, the therapist might say, "Of course, you cut yourself. Growing up in that family, you never felt like you existed and the attacks were so random and violent. So you learned to cut yourself. It was an attempt to make things right. It makes you feel strong and puts you in control of the pain."

But even though the therapist makes these normalizing interpretations, he or she does not indicate that self-destructive behavior is condoned. In this case, the clinician might go on to say, "But now you don't need to cut yourself. We are working together to help you feel real and in control. I know you really don't want to cut yourself and I don't want you to, either."

Often, referral to an incest survivors' group as an adjunctive treatment is helpful. Hearing about other survivors' similar situations, thoughts, and behaviors tends to free the survivor from the experience of feeling crazy, dirty, alien, or different. There is nothing more normalizing than participating in a group subculture where the "unknowable" is known, the "unspeakable" is spoken, and the "secret craziness" is shared by others. The result is a relaxation of vigilance in regard to memories, thoughts, and feelings—a freeing of the self to express repressed feelings and to speak the truth.

Some survivors have reported that reading others' accounts of being abused has helped to normalize their difficulties. Books such as *The Courage to Heal* (Bass & Davis, 1988) and *Victims No Longer* (Lew, 1988) are educational and have a normalizing effect. Watching movies about incest can be used therapeutically, either as part of a session or as a homework assignment. Some suitable movies in this regard are *Nuts, Sybil,* or *Something About Amelia.* Partners are also encouraged to watch these movies, both for their educative value and to support the client.

As the therapist normalizes the client's symptoms, he or she needs to educate the survivor in regard to the need for the memory-retrieval work. While reframing, desensitization, or other behavioral techniques are useful in alleviating some of the presenting problems, memory retrieval helps the survivor to overcome the trauma and the subsequent denial. In our experience, successful treatment follows a biphasic path: the therapist works progressively to help the client overcome old anxieties and fears while teaching new skills and constructive behaviors and regressively by exploring the incest trauma, recovering memories, and facilitating the ventilation of deeply buried emotions.

COGNITIVE-BEHAVIORAL TECHNIQUES

In the progressive work, cognitive-behavioral treatment is the approach of choice for the various anxieties and phobias that survivors usually exhibit. When a client worries obsessively, we will have her set aside 15 or 20 minutes of daily worry time during which her goal is to become as worried as possible. A variation on this technique is to have the survivor make a tape of upsetting thoughts about awfulized scenarios of the future and replay it daily for 30 to 45 minutes. Both of these techniques require the clinician to check up on the client to creatively modify the assignment and ensure cooperation and follow-through.

For phobias, exposure is the treatment of choice. This starts with imagery practice in which the client imagines a series of scenes that elicit increasing gradations of anxiety and distress. Then she is asked to construct a list, rating each scene on a scale from 1 to 100 in anxiety-provoking intensity. The client is trained in a number of relaxation procedures. As she relaxes, each scene is presented to her in the order of increasing anxiety. When the client can master the imagery with minimal anxiety, we recommend actual exposure to the feared objects and situations as the next step. This allows for habituation of the fear.

For example, in the Beth Torrence case, described briefly in Chapter 1, Beth suffered from anxiety attacks relating to social situations in which she would be speaking to more than two people at a time. She was quite frightened that she would "sound like an idiot" and that no one would like or respect her. This was a serious problem because Beth wanted to enroll in some computer courses to further her career and was afraid to do so for fear she might have to speak in class. The therapist had Beth make a tape on which she described all the interactions she was afraid of having. The tape included scenes in which people would turn and laugh at her, or insist that she was wrong, or tell her that she was stupid and sounded like an idiot. The therapist asked Beth to play and replay the tape for 45 minutes each day, during which time she was to try to become as upset as possible. Beth resisted the idea at first, but the therapist, in a benevolent way, confronted her: "The only way to master fear is to stare it down. Who is going to run your life, you or your fears?" Beth agreed to do the homework assignment. First, she listened to the tape in the office with the therapist. Then she took it home and listened to it for a week. At the next session, Beth reported that the tape hardly upset her at all and that her worrying had diminished.

The therapist then suggested that Beth attend several social functions to which she had been invited. In the past, Beth had avoided these situations because of her phobia. Beth was still frightened, but the therapist taught her some simple deep-breathing techniques to use right before she approached any group at the party. Beth went to the functions and she was able to converse with five different groups of people. She reported that she had initially thought that she was going to "faint," but by the time she got to the fifth group, she felt only moderately uncomfortable.

Beth was also planning to attend a friend's wedding. The therapist rehearsed Beth so that she could speak to several groups of friends and relatives at the wedding, and then give a short toast to the bride and groom. After the wedding, Beth reported that she was so anxious about the toast that speaking to the smaller groups was not anxiety-provoking at all. The therapist encouraged Beth to continue planning and completing similar activities. Over time, Beth lost her anxiety about speaking in front of groups and was able to enroll and participate in the computer courses.

Beth also suffered from insomnia. To help her, the therapist used a hypnotic technique to access some of Beth's most positive memories from childhood. When Beth was a child, she had a favorite teddy bear, given to her by her "good" uncle, which she would hug to comfort herself when she was frightened. As the therapeutic relationship unfolded, the clinician built on this memory of constructive self-soothing. She had Beth relax and remember the scene in which she comforted herself with the bear. While in a very deep state of relaxation, Beth was able to access the scene very fully. The therapist suggested that whenever Beth was having difficulty going to sleep she access this scene using the relaxation procedure. Beth practiced the technique at home for several weeks and her sleeping improved. The therapist then presented her with a teddy bear as a gift to use for self-comforting. The bear represented the therapist and the therapeutic relationship as a transitional object. Beth was delighted and successfully used the relaxation techniques and the bear to help herself sleep.

Many survivors suffer from depression as well as anxiety and insomnia. In treating this symptom, sometimes a short course of an antidepressant medication can be helpful to lift the depression enough so that the survivor can work on her other issues. We have found that some clients cannot escape their malaise even if they have recovered incest memories and overcome many of their other symptoms. For these clients, antidepressants such as Prozac are necessary for treatment to be successful.

Cognitive restructuring is also helpful in treating a depressed survivor. The therapist helps the client uncover some of the "catastrophisizing" thinking patterns (Ellis & Harper, 1975) that are at the root of the depression. The client is then taught how to short-circuit the negative pattern whenever it appears.

Asking the survivor to keep careful track of her thoughts and how they affect her moods is another very helpful technique. She can write down these thoughts and then symbolically throw them away or pair them with the more rational thoughts that she would like to have. For instance, Beth would frequently have the thought, "I am no good. I want to die." She was asked to do a role play, using the empty chair technique, with the two parts of herself, the attacking part and the protective part. The latter self argued that she was a good person, that the incest wasn't her fault, and that she had always been a valiant fighter. The therapist asked Beth to insert these rational thoughts into her mind every time the negative thoughts appeared. The therapist also emphasized these positive qualities during her sessions with Beth, so as to help her internalize them.

We have found that a regular program of aerobic exercise is also an excellent antidote to depression. For those clients who are willing and able to start exercising, it can be extremely effective and helpful. Not only does it tend to lift the depression physiologically, but it also results in gains in self-esteem, self-discipline, and self-confidence. We have seen many clients benefit by taking control of their own bodies, strengthening themselves, and reshaping themselves so that their body images improve. Meditation can also be quite helpful in similar ways. In addition, it tends to reduce anxiety.

Clients who suffer from migraines and other tension headaches or from chronic backaches should be referred for medical assessment and care. If medication does not alleviate the condition, relaxation training and biofeedback can be utilized effectively for certain clients. For many survivors, however, permanent relief does not come until they have recovered traumatic memories and released the repressed emotions.

For drug and alcohol problems, there must be a strong emphasis on stopping the addictive behaviors. Twelve-step programs like those of Alcoholics Anonymous (AA) or Narcotics Anonymous (NA) can be extremely helpful in this regard. In referring a client to such a program, the practitioner must make sure that the client sees the group as complementing the therapy rather than as replacing it. Otherwise, the other aspects of treatment that need to be conducted may be jeopardized.

The progressive work described takes place in both the individual and couples sessions that are conducted during the initial phase of treatment. While working on these activities, fragments of memories may surface. The therapist can then begin the memory-retrieval process in the individual sessions with the survivor.

THE ABREACTIVE PROCESS

The first goal of the retrieval process involves not merely remembering the incestuous events, but also disclosing them and abreacting the emotions associated with those events, no matter how terrifying, repulsive, or depressing they may be. This process is a kind of reliving of the material within the safe haven of the therapist's office. As the events are exposed in this way, the shame connected with them can begin to fade.

The process can be quite difficult, as most incest victims have had to become thoroughly defended in order to survive. Much of the defense revolves around denying what happened in order to preserve the "good parents," as Alice Miller (1990) describes so well. When the survivor was a child, the need for safety and caretaking and the anxiety about not having them led her to construct the image of the "good parents." Parental behaviors that did not fit this mold were attributed to the "bad self" and forgotten. In this way, the child could feel safe. This process also required the repression of the child's rage and murderous feelings at the parents' actions. Thus, as horrifying behaviors are remembered, a host of annihilation terrors emerges. The survivor may be afraid that the parent(s) will die. Because of the mechanism of projection and a fear of loss of control, she may also feel that she herself, or her own children, will die. In addition, the actual memories are often so traumatic that a significant pathological effect results from the process of remembering.

Along with all the horrors that are stirred up during the memory-retrieval process, various symptoms may also surface. The client may become depressed, act out by attacking herself or others in some way, or self-mutilate or become suicidal. Thus the memories must emerge at a pace the client can tolerate. As ego strength and attachment to the therapist grow, more and more material can surface.

All along the way, the therapist must be vigilant to the appearance of severe dissociative states, serious depression, and the tendency to act out destructively. If the client becomes overly reactive, the memory work must be shelved temporarily, and the therapist must supply extra contact via phone or in person. The extra fueling and feeding are part of the corrective reparenting experience that helps to offset the effects of the incest trauma. If the therapist does not provide the additional contact or continues to probe for memories, the acting out or self-destructive behavior can reach a dangerous level.

For example, in one case, as particularly gruesome incest memories began to surface, the client ran out of the office crying, and the therapist was not successful in pursuing her. The therapist did not phone her to calm her or slow down the affect that had been unleashed. Two days later, the client locked herself in a motel room, called the clinician, and threatened suicide. The therapist was able to talk her out of hurting herself and made time for an emergency session. Later that week in supervision, the therapist discovered that the client's memories of being mutilated had aroused his own fears and anxieties and had generated a subtle withdrawal of interest in her as a defense against hearing any more upsetting material.

Countertransference Issues

A prerequisite, then, to being successful with survivors is the therapist's work on his or her own issues in regard to incest, abuse, and the experience of pain. The therapist must be completely open to hearing about the incest traumas in order for them to emerge into the client's consciousness and be shared in the therapy. Otherwise, the therapist will act out in subtle ways, as in the preceding example, or unconsciously cue the client to keep the repression going.

Among the countertransference issues that interfere with treating survivors are the therapist's own experiences with incest or physical abuse that threaten to emerge if the client remembers, the clinician's discomfort with sexual issues, the therapist's fear of his or her own anger and that of the patient, and the need to protect the client from pain and discomfort.

Some therapists have themselves been victims of childhood sexual or physical abuse. When issues and feelings remain unresolved, they will often surface as inappropriate countertransference reactions in the treatment. These responses may include avoiding the topic of abuse when it comes up, becoming overly stimulated by the material in a voyeuristic manner, blaming the patient for not stopping the perpetrator, and expressing rage at the molester or other family members when the client is not ready to do so herself.

In all cases, but especially with survivors, the therapist must communicate a stance of comfortableness about discussing sex. Since these clients often feel that they are "dirty" or "bad," they will quickly sense whether the therapist feels any discomfort or is uneasy about dealing with their sexual history. Survivors will then tend to project their own self-blaming and self-recriminating thoughts onto the therapist and to believe that the clinician sees them as "dirty." In fact, in many cases, the patients may project their negative assignations onto the therapist anyway, regardless of the clinician's attitudes toward sexuality.

Thus no matter what the initial focus of treatment, the therapist must convey and engender a posture of openness about discussing sexual matters frankly. This is accomplished through a timely, yet direct exploration of the client's sexual history, current sexual life, thoughts and feelings about herself as a sexual person, and sexual fantasies. Over the course of therapy, this material will emerge as the bond between client and therapist is strengthened.

Another problematic area for clinicians is the expression of anger and rage. Some therapists become frightened if the client ventilates rage or appears to lose control over her emotions. These clinicians have reported to us that they fear for the client's safety, their office furnishings, and their own safety.

Therapists who are uncomfortable with expressing anger themselves may tend to tone down the patient when she begins to discuss her conflicted feelings about family members. Indeed, it would be far more comfortable for both therapist and patient to discuss matters in a completely rational manner devoid of emotional outbursts. By toning down the patient, the therapist seeks to ensure that not only do family members not become the targets of her anger, but neither does the clinician himself or herself.

Furthermore, in order to maintain family loyalty, it is in our clients' scripting to tell us that their childhoods were "fine" and without serious problems. Thus it is crucial, in the session, to encourage the expression of anger and negativity toward family members in addition to the positive feelings with which clients are more comfortable.

However, if the client senses that the therapist is uncomfortable with expressions of negativity, she not only may stop ventilating, but may also suppress certain memories that trigger the powerful emotions. Examples of therapists' statements that will impede the memory-retrieval process are: "Well, they did the best they could, given their own backgrounds." "Let's not blame them." "Let's move on; this negativity prevents you from forgiving them and yourself." Any of these types of interventions, if done before the client has fully discharged the anger and negativity, will tend to result in a retreat from further exploration.

Therapists, therefore, need to accept the basic belief that love and hate can coexist in a relationship and that the resolution of this ambivalence comes about through experiencing and accepting each fully at separate times and in separate places. Ultimately, acceptance and letting go of the trauma are the natural outgrowths of the appropriate discharge of sadness and anger.

We have seen many therapists who, because of their own countertransference reactions, grow impatient with clients to whom they have given permission to express negativity and to "be themselves." They will signal their clients to change the topic or begin talking about forgiveness prematurely. This type of double-binding communication is all too familiar to survivors. As discussed in Chapter 4, many parents of survivors use double-binding communication as a way of controlling their children. It is tragic when therapists make the same error.

Another common therapeutic error is becoming overly nurturant or protective toward the survivor. Some therapists believe that they have or should have a magic pill to give their patients that will make up for their suffering. These clinicians try to avoid dealing with painful areas of the survivor's life in order to minimize causing the patient to grieve and be upset. *Nothing the therapist does or says can undo the past.* Only by showing courage in the face of unspeakable horrors can the therapist help the patient confront and work through the pain.

Triggering Memories

When there is some question in the therapist's mind regarding the actual history of incest, he or she can review some of the predictive factors discussed in Chapter 2. Often clients either will have no memories or will have memories that they dismiss as not important or meaningful in their lives. These two problems become the first wall of resistance in treatment. When a client has no memories, but just a vague sense of a shameful violation or suspicion regarding incest and a number of the characteristic incest survivor symptoms, the therapist must start with a detailed history and, it is hoped, bring the memories back to consciousness.

The therapist looks for gaps in childhood memories by reviewing the client's history in two- to three-year periods, starting from age 2. Often there are almost no memories from periods when incest actually occurred. The therapist can target these periods for further investigation. A useful exercise involves the investigation of the client's home life during this time. The client can be instructed to draw a picture of the apartment or house, the layout of the rooms, the furniture, and so on. The therapist can then use guided imagery in which the client regresses to the targeted age period and moves around the house, discussing experiences and reactions. The client can then free-associate to various parts of the house or the furniture. An alternative path involves the use of family pictures from the client's childhood. These can be brought into sessions. Critical pictures with possible perpetrators can be used for an in-vivo gestalt role play, where the client is urged to talk freely and say whatever comes to mind, or in role play at the age at which the incest may have occurred.

Some clients will remember certain years from school and completely block out others. In one case, the survivor recalled her first-grade teacher and some of the class activities, but drew a complete blank for second and third grades. The therapist had the client ask her mother to fill in the missing pieces. The client's mother revealed that her brother, the patient's uncle, had moved in with them at about that time. The client then began to remember, first the school, then her bedroom, her dolls, the uncle, and finally the incest.

Often the memories begin to return in fragments and there is only partial recall. Keeping a journal or diary can be helpful in retaining and reconstructing the retrieved memories. The fragments may be very charged and trigger anxiety attacks, or may generate somatic reactions such as nausea or pains in the body. Ellenson's (1985) predictive symptoms, which are described in Chapter 2, can also be viewed as precursors to recall. For example, a client reported that she became anxious and nauseous whenever her current lover approached her from behind. She had a sense of being pushed. After she was encouraged to explore the feeling, she reported vague memories of being held down by someone who was behind her. In working on this fragment, she remembered more and more fragments in which she was being abused by her older brother.

In general, exercises that facilitate the loosening of the breath and the expression of aggression tend to bring up memories. The client can be asked to pound on pillows or foam padding and just breathe through her mouth. Sounds will often emerge with the breathing and pounding. The therapist can then ask the client to exaggerate those sounds or to lie on her back on a foam pad and pound her fists and feet in tantrumlike behavior. Or she can simply be asked to make a fist, gesture with it, and say "No" over and over. When the therapist keeps this going for a while, the client will usually sense that the perpetrator is the one who is really being addressed. At that point, the therapist can have the client describe or role-play the perpetrator. Sometimes the therapist can take on the verbal role of the perpetrator to facilitate the abreaction. Of course, such work should be performed only by therapists who are trained in these psychodramatic techniques and who are well versed regarding the necessary guidelines and safety precautions.

For example, a 34-year-old client showed a number of signs of incest trauma. She had a great fear of intimacy with men, she viewed sex as repugnant and frightening, and she had large gaps in her memory from age 9 through age 16. She initially had entered treatment for depression and a sense of meaninglessness in her life. After about nine months of treatment, the therapist strongly suspected either physical or sexual abuse in the client's childhood and had her draw a picture of her home at age 10. When she came to the hallway on the first floor, she expressed a vague sense of anxiety. She then remembered always being frightened of the basement in that house. The therapist asked her to imagine walking slowly down the steps, and the client reported that she felt suffocated and had pains in her neck. As the sensations intensified, the client reported that she was frightened and wanted to stop. The therapist stopped the process immediately and validated the client for daring to open up.

Over the next two months, the therapist suggested that they try the exercise for a time-limited period. The client finally agreed to a five-session program. The therapist respected this pacing, each time taking the client further and further down into the basement. On the fifth journey, the client started sobbing uncontrollably and remembered being dragged down the steps by her father. Subsequently, she remembered episodes of violent and forceful intercourse with him in the basement.

If the therapist is unable to help the client unearth memories, but has a strong sense that incest actually did occur in the family of origin, he or she should discontinue the memory-retrieval work and continue working on other issues in therapy. However, the therapist should make a statement such as, "Yes, it probably did happen, and at some point you'll get to it," which acknowledges the probable incest and programs the unconscious for future memory retrieval. If the therapist does not make such a statement, he or she runs the risk of retraumatizing the client with a form of denial or "not hearing."

THERAPEUTIC STANCE

The memory-retrieval process revolves around exposure and acceptance: the exposure of the incestuous events and shameful feelings associated with them and the therapist's acceptance of the events and the survivor. The process starts with education and reassurance. The therapist must educate the client about the importance of memory retrieval. He or she must explain that it is not a panacea that will magically cure all the client's life ills, but a process that will help her make sense of her moods and behaviors, a process that *ultimately* will help her to feel better about herself and less constricted in her life. The therapist must also explain that it will get worse before it gets better, and that there is a normal process of healing in which the memories come up at a pace that is tolerable, and along with them will come self-hate, shame, and guilt and depression and rage. As all this is processed, the negative feelings will tend to subside, and, as the client integrates the memories, she will feel more whole, real, and clear about her own dynamics and what she needs from loved ones in order to heal the wounds.

The practitioner must also reassure the client that she can handle the memories. When the incest was particularly bizarre or involved physical or ritual abuse, the client may be afraid that she will go crazy, die, or lose herself in the process. The therapist must explain that he or she will help to slow down the rate of retrieval so that is it not too disturbing. In addition, the therapist must give the client a vote of confidence and solidly focus on the strength of the client's ego in handling the material. This is all important.

As the memories emerge, the therapist must take on the role of a strong and comforting parental figure who is attending to a trauma-tized child. The first job is to find out exactly what happened. The therapist plays the role of a soothing, anchoring presence, a kind of fair witness, who accepts the disclosures. He or she does not touch the client, unless there is a touch that is an agreed-upon physical safety anchor. The clinician is not to be too verbal or intrusive, but only to ask occasional questions about what happened or what is happening as the client relives the experience. These questions are important because the client is up against the taboo of secrecy—the rule of not talking that kept the incest going in the family. It is important that the client report exactly what happened. This exposes the shame to the light of day—the normalizing acceptance of the therapist.

Sometimes the traumatic memories produce somatic symptoms: difficulty in breathing, a feeling of pain in certain parts of the body, or even a sensation of dying. When this happens, the therapist needs to be more active and to reassure the client that the difficulties and pains will pass, that they are just part of the memory-retrieval process, and that it will be okay. Sometimes, soothing repetitive words in a calming voice are helpful: "It's all right. I'm here. It's all right. I'm here." In such instances, an agreed-upon touch on the arm may be needed to keep the client sufficiently anchored in the present to relive the past safely.

After the client has cried and emerges from the incest scenes, the therapist can be more active and comforting. The practitioner needs to prize the client for being brave enough to face the memories. This involves acknowledging the tremendous courage needed to face the specter of horror and of possible abandonment and separation from the "good" parents. The therapist can also begin reprogramming the client regarding her gender identity at this time. "You are not disgusting, dirty, or shameful; you are a brave and beautiful warrior!"

If the client is ready, the practitioner also can express and model rage at the perpetrator. In addition, the therapist can anchor in an image of the good parent by describing how he or she would have reacted if he or she were the other parent. For example, the therapist might say something like, "I'm furious at your father for hurting you like that. You were just an innocent little kid. If I had been your mother, I would have thrown him out of the house until he got himself therapy. I never would have let him touch you again!"

Dealing with Shame and Guilt

Shame is the sense that the survivor's very being is bad or awful and it is experienced by almost all survivors. It dissipates through the process of exposure and acceptance. The Rogerian stance is an ideal mode for this healing. The therapist helps the survivor to expose and discuss the shameful activities and to air her feelings of being soiled, damaged, or rotten. He or she has to know the full extent of the survivor's imperfections and weaknesses and still accept her as okay. It is this acceptance of all of the client's perceived flaws that is crucial to healing her shame.

In the stance of a reflective witness, the therapist restates what was or is. The client might say, "I sucked my father's cock." And the therapist might reply, "Yes, you sucked your father's cock. Uh huh. What else?" Or the survivor might say, "I stink! I'm repulsive." And the therapist will repeat, "You feel like you stink." These responses, which are the opposite of the family's typical mode, are very healing of the shame. The acceptance allows the survivor to reflect on herself and her statements and to evolve beyond the hiding state of pain. Of course, it is critical that the therapist teach the survivor's partner, if she has one, to be seeking, reflecting, and accepting of her disclosures about the incest and her shameful feelings. Otherwise the relationship will work at cross-purposes to the therapy and continue the shame process.

Many survivors also suffer from guilt, or the sense that they have committed sinful or bad acts. The survivor needs to be exonerated from any guilt she feels about the incest. She must come to understand that the guilt for that is owned by the perpetrator. Remorse, confession, reparation, and the seeking of forgiveness constitute the healing process for guilt. The therapist can discuss this process and suggest it for other behaviors that the survivor may feel guilty about, such as not protecting a younger sibling from the perpetrator.

DESENSITIZATION TO TRIGGER STIMULI

Often, as the client works through her incest memories, she will identify other symptoms related to stimuli associated with the incest trauma. A survivor may report, for example, that she is nauseated by the sight of male genitalia, or that she is terrified of basements (where the incest took place), or that she can't stand oral sex (the form the incest took). Once again, progressive work is needed. Such reactions must be treated with educative and desensitization techniques so that they do not constrict the client's life.

The therapist works to normalize clients' thought patterns with regard to stimuli. For instance, the practitioner can have the client who is repulsed by male genitals write down all of her thoughts about them. Usually, a list is generated: "It's too big." "It'll hurt me." "He'll lose control." The therapist can then have the client write down the phrases she would like to associate with male genitals and actively pair them with thoughts and experiences involving various sexual activities. During this process, the therapist can relax the client and educate her about sex so that more positive thoughts can emerge regarding the troublesome stimulus. For example, the therapist might talk about how a more relational and sensitive man will become aroused more through his feelings about his partner and the couple's relationship than through simple lust.

With desensitization techniques, the therapist can use relaxation and imagery training to combat the anxiety (Lazarus, 1976). For instance, one survivor could not stand the idea of a man gazing at her or kissing her with an open mouth. The therapist had her relax and envision a scene that was made just for her, "safe, secure, beautiful, and peaceful," a scene in which she could see all the beauty, hear just the right sounds, a place that felt just right." She had the client practice putting herself in the scene and staying with it. Then she asked the client to write a description of scenes containing the troublesome gazing and kissing behaviors. She had the client remain "in" her good scene as she read the descriptions to her, pausing if there were any negative reactions (as signaled by an upraised finger). In this way, the client learned more positive associations to the two particular stimuli and was later able to date more effectively.

EDUCATION AND INCLUSION OF THE PARTNER

When a client is in a committed relationship, it is of the utmost importance that she be supported in her progressive work and in the memory-retrieval process by her partner. The therapist is with the client for only one or two hours a week, while the lover spends considerably more time with her. Since the partner is a strong transference figure for the client, he is in a strong position to help or hinder her mastery of fearful situations, the memory-retrieval work, and attendance at groups and classes.

In terms of the progressive work, the spouse has to be educated as to the importance of the survivor's attending AA or performing the activities about which she is phobic. He needs to be taught to be as constructively helpful as possible whenever the survivor needs to practice her new behaviors. For example, in one case, a survivor was afraid to travel over bridges. The therapist planned a trip with the couple in which they would cross and recross several bridges. The spouse was to drive the car and coach the survivor in relaxation and deep-breathing techniques. The trip went well and the survivor subsequently learned how to drive a car.

It is critical that the partner be ready for the memory-retrieval process by the time it starts to take place. As the memories surface, the client is apt to react with depressive withdrawal or negativity in the relationship. If the partner is not included, he is likely to sabotage the work—intentionally or unintentionally. He can easily retraumatize the client by attacking her verbally, getting her to repress or forget material, or arguing against the treatment. For example, in one case, the survivor exposed the details of her father's incestuous involvement with her. Unfortunately, her spouse was allied with the father, for whom he worked. When the client began to tell her spouse about the traumatic memories, he became enraged and defended her father. In other cases, the partner may attack the therapist verbally, not cooperate, or try to terminate the therapy by refusing to pay the fees.

All of these undermining behaviors can be minimized or avoided by strategic bonding with the partner and enlistment of his help from the outset of treatment. When the therapist begins the retrieval work, he or she should secure the survivor's permission to educate the partner about the process. Then the clinician should conduct couples sessions in which the incest and the memory-retrieval process are discussed.

In these sessions, the practitioner educates the partner about the nature of the problem and the tremendous consequences the incest experience has created—consequences that affect not only the client's emotional health and happiness, but also her day-to-day relationship with the partner, and the way in which they have been parenting the children. In one case, for example, the therapist described how the survivor's depressive problems and eating disorder had started at age 13, when the father began abusing her. He also pointed out how the survivor froze up at the husband's advances and had never allowed the spouse to put the children to bed at night, all of which had a direct link to her father's nighttime incestuous behavior. Upon hearing how many of his difficulties with his wife were tied to the abuse, the husband was eager to help her and quickly joined the therapeutic team.

The practitioner should also educate the spouse about the importance of the memory-retrieval process and the difficult journey it entails. This includes a description of how symptoms will sometimes flare up and worsen before they get better. The therapist should especially highlight the bravery of the survivor in undertaking the journey and the importance of the partner's support throughout. He or she should close the therapeutic contract with the partner by describing how the couple could grow and become much closer through the shared experience.

Once the partner agrees to help, the therapist needs to contract to teach him the necessary therapeutic skills. These include listening, empathy, and nonjudgmental validation. The spouse must also be taught to take the survivor's "side" and not to defend other members of the family. This particular stance is extremely important because he is the new transference figure for the survivor. He can become the good parent psychologically who identifies with and protects the survivor's innocent inner child. He must honor the telling and repeated retelling of the abusive incidents as part of an important healing process. As he plays out this role, he is actively repairing the old wounds and laying the groundwork for a truly healthy, growth-promoting marriage.

SUMMARY

The initial phase of treatment involves both individual and couple sessions (with partnered survivors) in which both progressive work and regressive work are conducted with the survivor. The progressive work targets symptom relief and the building of new skills and healthier behaviors. The regressive work revolves around memory retrieval. To help free up the survivor, the practitioner must assist in the accessing and processing of the traumatic memories. Ideally, the process should include full exposure through recall and emotional abreaction; acceptance by the therapist of the client's "imperfections"; the normalizing of reactive thoughts, emotions, and behaviors; and desensitization to noxious trigger stimuli.

It is of critical importance that when clients are in committed relationships, the progressive and regressive goals are targeted with the assistance and close alliance of the spouse. In this way, the client can grow and free herself of symptoms; in the process, the couple's teamwork is promoted and family fragmentation avoided.

CHAPTER 8

THE MIDPHASE OF THERAPY

*"The envelope sat for four days untouched, on the cocktail table,
before I could bring myself to touch it, never mind open it. The
long-awaited letter of acceptance—a miracle in my eyes. I remain
determined in this endeavor, despite my fears. I can hardly
believe it."*

—From the diary of an incest survivor in treatment

By the end of the initial phase of treatment, the survivor has recognized the psychological damage done to her by the perpetrator and the nonprotecting members of the family. She has come to realize the consequences and aftereffects of the incest trauma and to shed the veil of shame and feelings of unworthiness. Her presenting symptoms have either abated or drifted to the background. Generalized anxieties and dysphoric moods, framed in the context of the survivor's abusive background, have improved via the use of a variety of cognitive-behavioral techniques.

The midphase of treatment poses both a crisis and a turning point for the survivor and therapist. The survivor has fewer symptoms; she has reclaimed more of her memory and integrated the realization of having been unjustly hurt. She must now take steps away from viewing herself as the traumatized child to seeing herself as a responsible adult. This represents the difficult but necessary movement toward empowerment. The therapist must now assume a more active and directive stance vis-à-vis the survivor in an attempt to address

121

the problems in her relationships with her partner, children, and family of origin. This chapter focuses on therapeutic goals and strategies of the midphase, and, in particular, on overcoming resistance that may arise during this period.

EMPOWERING THE SURVIVOR

The midphase of treatment is the turning point and essentially represents the heart of the treatment process. The horror of the incest and its aftereffects have been described aloud. The taboo of silence has been broken in therapy sessions. However, although these critical gains are necessary, they are not sufficient for energizing the client's movement toward self-fulfillment and actualization. To accomplish these goals, the survivor needs to be empowered.

By the midphase of treatment, the therapist has helped the survivor to move beyond living as a shameful, unknowing, and traumatized adult-child through the progressive and regressive therapeutic techniques described in Chapters 6 and 7. Through the regressive work, the survivor has now returned psychologically to the times of the original abuse. Some survivors will actually report feeling like they're "9 years old again," for instance. The survivor is no longer behaving "as if" she were an okay adult while denying the traumatized child-self. The survivor, therefore, has moved from a position of being a pseudoadult to experiencing her real inner hurt child with all of its emotions and pain. Moreover, that needy and frightened traumatized child has been soothed throughout the memory-retrieval phase via therapeutic support, reassurance, and empathy. While the therapist must maintain the empathic bond, she or he must now add more active, directive, and confrontational techniques to the treatment plan.

The more active therapeutic stance is necessary in helping the victim reclaim the power that was taken away. The therapist must assist the traumatized and arrested inner victim-child to grow up and become stronger. To accomplish this goal, the therapist must act as a mentor or reparental figure. Interventions aimed at empowering the survivor in her personal life and in her career are required to help her move from feeling like a hurt child to feeling and acting like an empowered adult. What differentiates a child from an adult is personal power and independence—the ability to determine one's destiny and the opportunity to be insulated from and less vulnerable to the actions and behaviors of others. As discussed in Chapter 1, quite often the survivor has developed a response of learned helplessness as an aftereffect of the sexual abuse. This response, while once adaptive, inhibits normal progression toward growth.

Empowerment of the survivor occurs in four areas of her life: development of a new marital contract (if the survivor is in a committed relationship); building parenting skills, if appropriate; working on career issues; and confronting the members of her family of origin. These are dealt with simultaneously in the midphase of therapy, although, of course, one area may take precedence at any given time. In addition, change in one area necessarily effects change in another. These growth areas are synergistically interrelated and cannot be conceptualized or approached in only a discrete or linear fashion.

RESISTANCE

Treatment may get bogged down in this phase because of the survivor's resistance to change. A certain comfort may have been achieved after she has braved the incest horror. Fears of annihilation have abated in that the secret was revealed and she did not die. This realization results in transformational change at the foundation level of the ego. The evolutionary drive toward completion conflicts with, and may temporarily lose out to, a homeostatic malaise.

Growing up requires change and struggle, but most of all it involves the possibility of loss. Loss of spouse and of family of origin becomes a real possibility if the survivor moves in the direction of empowerment. Systemic forces are locked against the survivor because the couple's interactional patterns have helped to maintain her powerlessness. Fears of abandonment may arise, along with such questions as: "How do I have a relationship with my family, knowing what I know now?" "How do I deal with my husband, who seems threatened by the changes I've made?" "How do I tell him I'm not happy with our relationship, how I feel about his not really understanding me or our lovemaking?" "What can I possibly do to fix the damage I've done to my children?" "I see now why I've been so afraid to do what I really wanted to do with my life, to be a writer, but how do I switch careers now? It's so hard to start over."

These issues are the natural by-products of the initial growth phase and represent the survivor's desire to begin anew, to start over, to get it right this time. But loss of the old self and the current couple relationship threatens the survivor's sense of security. She is afraid of unbridled movement toward growth. A new kind of disillusionment may then set in. The possibilities are available, but they seem imposing, unnerving, and too difficult to achieve.

COUPLE TRANSACTIONS

An issue that arises in the midphase with coupled survivors is the growing disappointment, disenchantment, or frustration with their current love relationship. The husband she once admired for his quiet strength now appears withdrawn and avoidant. The husband who seemed so outgoing and talkative now appears wooden and false as she gets in touch with her more real self.

These feelings of disenchantment are a natural outgrowth of the initial phase of treatment. They represent a healthy questioning that comes with maturity rather than accepting the pseudomutual life of a false self. Once the incest secret is lifted, all relationships can be examined critically and improved.

If the practitioner was successful in bonding with the spouse or lover in the first phase of treatment, engaging him for couples work is not difficult. If, on the other hand, the therapist is perceived negatively, has not engaged the spouse, or has alienated him or allied with the survivor against him, the chances of helping the couple grow are greatly lessened.

In virtually all of our cases, the spouse has already become a part of the treatment, although typically he has not entered therapy as an individual client with his own set of problems and issues apart from those of the survivor or couple. He may like the therapist personally, appreciate the work he or she is doing with his spouse, and recognize that there are some couple issues that need to be addressed. However, he may be reluctant to request individual therapy sessions and may participate minimally if he is asked to attend. Still, even if the spouse is only somewhat connected to the therapist and the therapy, the chances for the couple's growing together are quite good.

When the survivor begins to bring up her unhappiness or confusion about the relationship, the therapist must help her clarify what is missing or unavailable. When the survivor (or partner) initiates these discussions at the outset of treatment, we discourage too much attention being paid to the couple. But in the midphase, full attention is given to the couple's problems. As a result of the scrutiny, the survivor may experience feelings of anger at the spouse and a desire to leave the relationship. In the face of these emotions, the therapist must insist that the relationship is probably capable of changing and fulfilling many of her needs. The therapist must give the message that in order for change to occur, the survivor must become more open to and demanding of her spouse, and the spouse must also want to change and enter treatment.

This three-pronged intervention inspires hope while reinforcing the integrity of the relationship. Thus the therapist must allow the survivor to express her feelings of growing frustration and anger while, at the same time, she works on the relationship. In addition, the therapist needs to communicate to the survivor that she is going to have to learn to be powerful in an intimate relationship and so it might as well be this one. This will kill her fantasy that a great relationship with a new lover will magically take place. Moreover, acting out in the form of an affair must be strongly discouraged. The therapist may, however, use the survivor's affair fantasies as material for helping her to explore what she really wants in a relationship.

The survivor, therefore, must understand the message from the therapist that she is responsible for getting what she wants out of a relationship. If her spouse appears to be inadequate, emotionally withdrawn, or abusive, she has a responsibility to alter the situation. We do not mean that this should be done in a codependent way, but rather to help the survivor to see herself as powerfully in control of her own destiny. The goal of couples work is that the spouse and the survivor will each take 100% responsibility for enriching the marriage.

The reality of this work virtually always requires that the survivor be the catalyst in creating change within the couple. This is so because she entered treatment first, has been more invested in the treatment, and as a result of partially removing the wall of secrecy and shame, has transformed herself more. The spouse may have been attempting to undermine the survivor's gains since they represent a perceived threat to the relationship and he never bargained for that; that is, he did not seek treatment himself.

As the survivor talks more about her unhappiness in the relationship and the problems are explored, clarified, and understood, she may be reluctant to do anything to change matters. Fears of being let down or abandoned by the partner are very common for survivors and may intensify as the reality of challenging the status quo sets in. Survivors often begin to protect or defend their spouses when the therapeutic conversation focuses on changing the relationship. One survivor talked about "what a good guy (her husband) was, how he tried, but you know, he's kind of limited." The practitioner must challenge such assertions, as well as confront the survivor's feelings of hopelessness about change. The fear that the spouse will abandon her if she talks with him about her unhappiness in the relationship must be heard by the therapist as an understandable reason to be reluctant and scared, but as an inadequate excuse not to proceed.

Direct and frank dialogue with the spouse, of course, is a process and not an all-or-nothing, take-it-or-leave-it proposition, although the survivor may experience it as such. The therapist must encourage the survivor to take incremental steps toward improving the relationship. Smaller and slower steps are suggested for survivors who have more dysfunctional relationships, are more emotionally dependent, or are less frustrated with their partners.

The therapist, however, must encourage some affirmative action on the part of the survivor. Otherwise, the survivor will continue to experience a sense of powerlessness. With a more disengaged partner, the therapist will typically encourage the survivor to talk to the spouse about a particular problem in the relationship. It is best to choose one problem rather than a litany of complaints, in order to reduce the spouse's defensiveness. If the survivor's anger tends to get out of control, the therapist coaches her on using less offensive expressions of anger. Exploration of disaster fantasies, role plays, and behavior rehearsal may also be used in session. The therapist may also offer to be available via telephone following the confrontation or arrange for a brief telephone contact before the encounter to bolster the survivor.

It must be noted that if there is any danger of physical abuse, there is only one way for the survivor to gain empowerment, and that is by leaving the spouse. In these extreme cases, the therapist must assist the survivor in locating a safe and anonymous living situation (such as a local women's shelter).

In virtually all instances, the goal of these techniques is to empower the survivor so that a new marital contract may emerge that is consistent with the survivor's more authentic self. To accomplish this goal, the survivor must challenge the stability of the marriage so that the spouse gets the idea that for the marriage to survive, he will have to adapt, change, and transform himself. When the spouse begins to understand that the relationship is changing, he will, on his own, seek the therapist out for himself. He will request an individual appointment to discuss things or specifically ask the therapist's assistance with a problem of his own. By completing the confrontational task, not only has the survivor upset the systemic balance of the couple, but a desired outcome is that the spouse may recognize his own abusive, controlling, or withdrawn behavior as problematic.

The therapist must be ready to receive the spouse when he approaches with his personal issues. Depending on the spouse's intrapsychic makeup and relational history, the therapist may be very welcoming, very tough, or both. In one case, a survivor was married to an aggressive and often verbally abusive "macho" husband. The survivor made a series of increasingly confrontative and empowering maneuvers, including a generalized refusal to act as if everything were fine between them. She stopped attending joint social functions, preparing meals, and talking to him about his difficulties at work. Her husband, who had said that he would never go to therapy, called the therapist (S.K.), requesting to see him "as soon as possible." He showed up at the session clutching a women's magazine that contained an article on the psychology of abusive men. He was teary throughout the session and talked of his fears of losing his wife if he didn't change. The therapist congratulated him for showing "real courage."

Factors in the Spouse's Transformation

This kind of transformation is not uncommon, and the therapist must be aware of three factors here. First, some practitioners might view the abusive mate's transformation as somewhat false and tend not to believe it. It is important to remember that the empowerment of the survivor triggers the dormant abandonment fears in the spouse.

He can afford to be macho as long as his abandonment fears remain untriggered. When the survivor shakes her partner at his foundation, his latent personality traits will appear suddenly and dramatically. In the case just described, the qualities that emerged were the more feeling and sensitive sides of the abusive man.

Second, as much as the survivor has hoped for such a transformation, she may tend not to believe it either. A change at the spouse's core will provoke a corresponding change at the survivor's core. For example, as the macho spouse claims his desire for intimacy and no longer maintains his distance, the survivor's latent fears of engulfment, which had never appeared previously, may be provoked. She may refer to him as "wimpy" or claim that she "didn't want him to change like that." She may also report to the therapist, "It's too late now. I wanted him to change a long time ago." Obviously, on a systemic level, the homeostatic lock of the couple may stay in place if the therapist is passive. The therapist must be ready to switch "sides" and to confront the survivor about her reversal and resistance, even though she may claim to feel indifferent or cold toward her spouse.

It is important that the therapist understand the concept of projective identifcation during any unbalancing maneuver so that neither spouse is viewed as inherently healthier. Therapeutic "side taking" may become unhealthy triangulation of the therapist. In general, the practitioner switches sides on the basis of which spouse is espousing *and* enacting the healthier viewpoint, where health is defined as the creation of a win–win marital relationship.

Third, the therapist must be ready for further shifts in the personality of the spouse and be prepared to manage them appropriately. In the case of the macho spouse, after about a month, he began to become hostile again because, he claimed, the survivor was "giving nothing back." The therapist challenged him not to be a quitter and not to expect instant results, explaining that his wife must be given time to experience him as different.

Empowering the survivor usually is very effective in getting her partner more invested in the couple's growth, as well as in his own individual work. In some cases, however, the survivor remains resistant to having her spouse become more involved in treatment despite obvious marital problems and perhaps her own complaints. Sometimes, the therapist is unwittingly organized by the survivor (and couple) to serve as a kind of "mate substitute" for the survivor. Under these circumstances, why should the survivor bother to confront her partner when the therapist provides all the active listening, nurturance, and support? Moreover, the therapist, survivor, and spouse may be repeating and reenacting some drama from the family of origin of either the spouse or the survivor, or countertransferentially, the therapist's family of origin. A common reenactment scenario with survivors is to have an incestuous emotional "affair" with the therapist while the spouse plays the role of nonprotecting outsider.

Again, in comprehensive family therapy, we accept as a given that the therapist cannot be neutral and is always triangulated by the client and couple. The only question is how to manage the triangulation appropriately in each case. In general, in the initial phase of therapy, the therapist focuses more on the survivor in order to provide a corrective emotional experience, to infuse hope, and to open the survivor to the possibility of creating healthier relationships in the natural (nontherapy) environment.

With this focus, the therapist must be careful to avoid becoming a component of the homeostatic system who is used by the survivor and couple to avoid growth. A general rule of thumb is that dependency on and triangulation of the therapist are acceptable if the survivor and couple are working hard at challenging themselves as they move toward growth. This represents dependency in the ultimate service of independence, parallel to the dependency that occurs in healthy parent–child relationships. If this is not happening, the therapist should attempt a more demanding stance with the survivor and should ally more with her partner, if possible.

Use of Indirect Interventions

If directive strategies toward empowerment of the survivor are not working, then the therapist may employ indirect strategies designed to raise the counterwill of the client. There are two potent paradoxical interventions that may be helpful here. One is a nurturing paradox of the order of, "That's okay, we'll just have to work on your accepting your husband as he is. So he doesn't really listen to you and doesn't want to help out around the house or with the kids . . . maybe this is as good as we can get." This strategy tends to reverse the survivor's magical thinking that things will just change by themselves, a fantasy that has protected her from facing the reality that her life will not change if she does not take affirmative action. The goal of the intervention is that the survivor will fully experience the idea of a lifetime of unhappiness and lack of fulfillment, which will provide the impetus for action.

It is necessary that the therapist carry the intervention to a believable extreme, giving the survivor an encapsulated portrait of what her life might look like in the absence of change. The foundational terror of engulfment may provide the "juice" for growth. The healthy response is to feel engulfed and then to do something constructive to alter the situation. If the survivor can block the therapist's message (i.e., maintain the magical-growth fantasy), the intervention was made too lightly or was abandoned too quickly by the practitioner. If the survivor becomes overly anxious or depressed, the intervention was too strong and the therapist should immediately abandon the paradox and reaffirm the therapeutic bond. As always, the survivor's relationship with the therapist is paramount. That bond should not be jeopardized by the therapist's inappropriate insistence on a particular time frame for growth.

The second indirect intervention that may be effective in bypassing the survivor's and couple's resistance is a disciplining paradox that is associated with a fear-of-loss strategy. The therapist may accentuate the distance between the partners and talk about the inevitable dissolution of the marriage if change does not occur. This intervention is designed to raise the fear of abandonment in the survivor or couple, which is being denied as the partners, in reality, slowly drift apart. Again, the mates are fending off this foundational fear. They may cognitively note marital problems and emotionally experience the pain and disappointment, but at a foundational level deny the abandonment terror that is present as they disconnect from each other.

The Fear-of-Loss Strategy

When there is continuing abusive or withdrawn behavior by the partner, it may be necessary to implement the fear-of-loss strategy. In this maneuver, the therapist and survivor use the spouse's fear of abandonment to fuel personal and interpersonal growth. Carefully implemented, the strategy can be quite successful in ultimately stopping the abusive behavior. The therapist, in effect, works to reverse the power structure of the relationship by encouraging the survivor to take the upper hand and to discipline the partner's abusiveness or withdrawn behavior through the strategic use of abandonment.

The tactics range from sleeping in another room, refusing sex, or leaving for a night or a weekend, to legally separating for a month to a year, or even filing for a divorce. In each case, the therapist cocreates with the survivor a fear-of-loss strategy based on the couple's history and tolerance for anxiety. Often the survivor can start with a less threatening maneuver based on prior attempts at fear of loss. If this is not effective, she can then escalate to a stronger maneuver.

In general, the behavior should be strong enough to let the partner know that the survivor means business, but not so strong as to destroy all hope for the marriage. The behaviors are designed to empower the survivor so that she uses her anger in a way that frees her from her sense of impotence in the marriage, and to motivate the partner to grow out of his infantile behavior. The fear-of-loss strategy alters the contingencies that have supported the negative behavior since it so aversive and punitive to the abuser. As the homeostasis is upended, real change can occur in the couple.

It is critical to emphasize that the fear-of-loss strategy is based on an innately healthy process that is built into the infrastructure of well-functioning couples. More secure individuals will threaten to leave, and actually do so in the face of ongoing dissatisfaction with their spouses. Indeed, in many cases, the survivor will initiate such a move as a by-product of personal growth that has naturally set the stage for her overcoming her abandonment fears. In all cases, though, the therapist must understand the fear-of-loss dynamic and the effect it may have on the partner.

It is the *absence* or *overuse* of the loss dynamic that is the sign of a dysfunctional couple. Because of an overpowering fear of abandonment and engulfment, some mates behave as unhappy, frustrated, and powerless stuck persons, while members of other couples constantly threaten to abandon each other. The role of the therapist is to assist these couples in including a healthy fear-of-loss component in the marriage, where, ultimately, the maneuver will not be used simply as a tactic, but as a powerful, benevolent tool to assist in the partners' growth.

There are several contraindications to the use of the fear-of-loss strategy. Safety is always the primary consideration. The experience of abandonment can fuel a great deal of anger and acting out. If the survivor's partner is likely to become dangerously violent, no fear-of-loss strategy short of going to a secure shelter is indicated.

In the majority of cases, safety is not an issue. But there are still a number of considerations to take into account in using a fear-of-loss maneuver. First, if an adequate therapeutic bond or a holding environment to help contain the anxiety that is aroused is lacking, the therapist must continue to try to secure a better therapeutic alliance with each spouse. Second, if the partners are constantly threatening to leave each other, loss is generally not a motivating factor. Instead, engulfment is the major dynamic at work and interventions should be organized less around loss and more around slowly increasing intimacy. Third, the survivor must be sufficiently empowered to carry through on her threats of pulling away from the partner. Otherwise, the intervention will fail, with the homeostatic pattern even further locked into place.

Sometimes during a fear-of-loss move, significant others in the survivor's life, such as family members, ministers, or friends who have a direct influence on her, might work to undermine her resolve. The fear of abandonment is primal; thus significant others may unwittingly and inappropriately overidentify with the partner who is being left. Years of the survivor's having been mistreated will be overlooked and a newly found empathy for the partner may emerge. This is especially the case when the partner actively solicits sympathy and advice from the survivor's family and friends. Therefore, the survivor must be well connected to the therapist and be sure of herself in enacting the maneuver so that when this occurs, she can remain steadfast.

A CASE EXAMPLE

The following transcript is from a consultation session with a survivor and her husband, who refused to participate in treatment. The survivor is in the midphase, and as a result of her new assertiveness, made a fear-of-loss move and stopped having sex with her husband. He then agreed to come in for the consult. The consultant, Dr. Diana Kirschner, uses a disciplinary paradox and a therapeutic fear-of-loss strategy throughout the consult (as noted) to gain the husband's cooperation in joining his wife in treatment.

Sophie: The sexual part he wants from me, I have difficulty with, because I feel that it's just something I'm giving to him and not receiving back. I don't feel it's a meeting of minds or souls or whatever you would say. It's just something he comes and takes and that's it.

Morris: If it were something I just come and take, the two months we weren't doing it, I'd have took.

Sophie: And you didn't.

Morris: Right. So you can't say it's something that I'm really forcing on you.

Sophie: That's true.

Morris: I think it happened after New Year's Eve. My New Year's resolution was that I would have sex with her twice a week. It just seems that after I said that, it was the end of it. I don't know.

Here we see Morris' view of Sophie as an object for his sexual pleasure—his New Year's resolution does not take her wishes into account. This represents a repetition from Sophie's family-of-origin experience.

Therapist: Yeah, go on.

Sophie: The feeling is very difficult with my father (the perpetrator) and I feel it's some sort of block. Sometimes I feel like I'm damaged goods for Morris. He doesn't understand what it (the incest) has done to me mentally. It's just right now I'm going through some very difficult times. My sister has no memory of abuse, and is starting to pick up pieces of memory. . . . (In the family) it's supposed to be something you shouldn't talk about, just forget it ever happened and get it over with.

It is essential to recognize that the therapist, as we have discussed previously, cannot be neutral here. She is instantly triangulated. If she does not forcefully take a stand with the couple, she will be playing the role of the "nonprotective mother." The therapist decides to act as the powerful protective mother figure who simultaneously empowers Sophie.

Therapist: Morris, she needs to talk about it.

Morris: I know, well, she did talk to me about it.

Therapist: A lot. Not once. Many, many, many times—crying about it. She has to talk about it a lot.

Morris: Yeah, well I, the part that bothers me, believe me it's nothing like what she's said, like as far as her being used or whatever. That's . . . nothing like that ever came to my mind. She's still my wife. I still love her, I still do whatever I can for her. But going back to what happened to her, OK, I just felt that I should know about it before he (the therapist) did. He stirred up this whirlwind.

Here we see the negative effects of not including the spouse in treatment. He feels left out, competitive, and angry.

Morris: Number two, if it bothered her so much, why didn't she say something in the first 5, 10, 15 years? Number three, it's still on her mind, OK, but her father's in his 70s right now. What good is it gonna do? I mean, she wanted to expose him or say something to him, get it out of her system . . . I mean, the guy's getting old, what's it gonna do? So I feel the best thing to do is to forget about it. There's nothing that you could do that's going to repair the damage. She was brought up and her mother knew about it or whatever. It's not going to help things out.

We see that Morris identifies with Sophie's father and has more empathy for him than for Sophie. This is an obvious and major problem in the marriage.

Therapist: Morris?

Morris: Yes . . .

Therapist: You have to get on her wavelength. Not only do you have to listen, but you have to follow her lead. And let her take the initiative, especially in matters like this.

The therapist attempts to correct Morris' misaligned identification. At the same time, she attempts to unbalance the system so that there is allowance for Sophie to be in charge. Previously, the system functioned only as long as Morris was "in charge."

Morris: Well, what does she want to do?

Therapist: I don't know what she wants to do. Your job is to help her undersand that and then support her in whatever she wants to do.

Morris: What do you want to do?

Sophie: I want you to work with me through it.

Therapist: Tell him exactly what to do.

Sophie: I need him to help me work through it. I do. You see my sister's husb . . . I see my sister's husband being so supporti . . . (sobbing)

Therapist: Yes, and you don't have that.

Morris: Your sister is different from you.

Therapist: (to Morris) Stop!

Morris: That wasn't . . .

Therapist: Morris, you are blowing it with your wife. You are acting in ways such that you will lose your wife. Now. You're doing it now. I've seen many, many couples with this kind of dynamic, and you are in danger. You're in danger of the marriage's breaking up, the way you're conducting yourself.

The therapist is using the fear-of-loss strategy by amplifying the effects of Morris' continuing to ignore the needs of Sophie. At the same time, the therapist is providing a corrective transactional experience for Sophie. By straightening out the perpetrator father/husband, the therapist "protects" Sophie in a way that her mother did not protect her as a child. We will see later how this strengthens Sophie's resolve in correcting Morris herself. Moreoever, the therapist is continuing to unbalance the contemporary system in favor of Sophie's position, which will have the effect of correcting the overt power imbalance in the relationship.

Morris: Well how many years does this process go on? I mean, she was hurt, but is this . . .?

Sophie: I was hurt, Morris, but I could not say a word to anyone for 27 years. I carried it within myself for 27 years. Bob (the therapist) was the first person I had the strength to even tell it to, because I felt that as a professional he could understand it. Because I knew you wouldn't . . .

Morris: I understand it . . .

Sophie: No you don't!!

Therapist: Tell him what he doesn't understand.

Sophie: The emotions are blocking me right now. He doesn't understand the pain, he doesn't understand how I've been robbed by my father. I'm blocked . . .

Therapist: (to Sophie) It's good. You're doing good.

Sophie: Something was taken from me before . . . before I even knew what it was. Sexual experiences that made me . . . it was really painful. And I can't remember what happened with my father, all of it . . . but I need to work through it, and I can't work through it. My sister's six years younger than I am, and she's just beginning to work through it. She still denies my father. But Morris doesn't even understand what it's like for me with my father. What it felt like for me on my wedding day.

Morris: Look, I still love you.

Sophie: (crying) Yeah. I know that. But you don't understand me. My daughter asked me how we ever got married, because we're so different.

Morris: Don't tell me that when we got married . . .

Therapist: Shhh! Morris, you don't talk when you listen. When you listen, you do not talk. Just listen. You're doing a good job of listening. Keep going, Sophie. So she asked you why you got married when you're so different.

Sophie: We weren't that way when we were married. We've grown . . .

Therapist: Apart. So maybe it can't work.

Sophie: Why?

Therapist: You're telling me that you're so different. As you grow and discover who you are, you're telling me that you're so different.

Again the therapist uses the fear-of-loss strategy, this time less directly with Morris and more generally with the couple. She does this because her bond with Morris is tenuous and continued direct pressure on him could result in an angry or withdrawing reaction. Moreover, by "spreading" the fear of loss, the maneuver contains less of a disciplinary component and more of a reality-based "this is just the way it is" tone that may affect Morris differently. This kind of fine-tuning is necessary when using the fear-of-loss strategy as the therapist must carefully read the reactions of the couple and adjust the intervention accordingly.

Sophie: What do you think, Morris? We're talking about whether or not the marriage can work.
Morris: Whether or not what?
Sophie: The marriage can work.
Morris: She loves me, it'll work. I love her, it'll work. I mean . . .
Sophie: Marriage is not a perseverance contest, Morris. It's a giving and a taking.
Morris: And I think I give some. As for the perfect marriage or the best marriage out there, I don't think I ever said ours was the best marriage, but it's a good marriage compared with the other people I've seen.
Sophie: Well, you haven't seen very many marriages, Morris.
Morris: No, but I've seen more divorces come into the office than marriages, well almost, anyway. And I listen to them.
Sophie: Those are the people getting divorced, is that what you're saying?
Therapist: (to Morris) So you don't think that you're in danger here? That this thing is just gonna . . .
Morris: Well, you're telling me that I'm in danger.

Despite the therapist's use of the fear-of-loss strategy, Morris avoids feeling the effect.

Therapist: I just don't feel any meeting. There's no meeting, no coming together place here.
Sophie: I agree with you.

For the first time, Sophie allies with the therapist's point of view that serious consequences could result from Morris' refusal to enter treatment with her.

Morris: So it sounds like I have to change my ways. Is that right?

Correspondingly, for the first time, Morris recognizes his problematic behavior more genuinely.

Therapist: I don't know if that's even possible.

The therapist continues with the fear-of-loss strategy. If she had immediately embraced Morris' statement, Morris almost certainly would have switched back to his original position. In that case, the therapist would be unable to resurrect the fear-of-loss maneuver. Significantly, the therapist waits for more substantiative movement by Morris.

Morris: Why do you say that?

Therapist: You two have completely different styles, completely different world views, completely different visions of what's happening and what you want to happen.

Morris: We had the same at one time.

Therapist: I don't know. It doesn't look good to me. You have things you have to do, which are your identity and your selfhood . . .

Sophie: Part of my identity is being Mrs. Morris Fine.

Morris: Do you like being Mrs. Morris Fine?

Sophie: I said that's part of my identity.

Morris: It doesn't sound like a very happy identity.

Sophie: I was trying to say that my identity is not just being myself. My identity encompasses other people, other things than just myself.

Therapist: Does that mean you want it to work?

Sophie: Yes. But I don't see how.

Therapist: I don't see how.

Sophie: I don't see how.

Morris: If there are disagreements, it doesn't mean that somebody can't agree. When you say you don't see how, I don't understand that. It's just like saying forget everything and that's it. I mean, I'm sure you must see a lot of other people that you say are so far apart, and that we are . . .

Therapist: But usually there is some way they come together. Especially during a consultation with me, and I haven't felt you two come together at all. She has a lot of work to do in resolving this incest thing. She really needs you in on it, but it's difficult for you to understand.

Sophie: Even more than the incest issues. I've accepted the incest,

I've understood what's happened. But I would like an understanding from Morris of the process.

Therapist: Yes! And of your heart and soul. As I said at the beginning,
he needs to really learn how to listen and to be very deeply tuned
in to you, which is extremely difficult for him. He's very busy
defending himself, "But I do love you, I do!"—instead of just
listening and really attending to what's happening inside you.
It's very hard for him. You're obviously committed to therapy
and believe that therapy heals—he's not particularly interested.

Sophie: He thinks it's the worst thing that ever happened to me, that
these therapists put crazy things in my head.

Morris: I never said it was the worst thing that happened to you.

Sophie: But you have. I guess you never said that therapists put crazy
things in my head?

Morris: I never said "crazy things," I said therapists put things in
your head. I didn't necessarily say "crazy things."

Sophie: I disagree.

Therapist: See, here we go again. It's endless.

Sophie: It is.

Therapist: It's endless, it's always in the same direction.

Sophie: I'm incapable of getting my feelings across to him.

Therapist: (to Morris) I mean, you're going to have to be willing to
turn yourself inside out, and really . . .

Morris: I have to change 100%, sounds like it.

Therapist: You have to turn youself inside out and get into Sophie.

Note how the therapist has remained in alignment with Sophie,
who has been disempowered in the marital relationship. Again, this
stance is designed to correct the power imbalance. She is also a strong
role model for Sophie—note Sophie's use of "we" in the next segment.

Sophie: We're not saying change, we're saying grow.

Therapist: I think it's just too hard for you.

Morris: When you say grow, what you really mean is to change.

Sophie: It's keeping pieces that are good, pieces that you have forgotten.

Morris: I always thought I was a good person.

Sophie: I'm not saying that you're not a good person, but you've

turned into a sarcastic, argumentative . . . it's gotten worse.
Sarcasm is a form of anger, but you don't recognize that. I can't
see us retired for life like your parents live, the constant bickering
and arguing.

Morris: They've been married for 58 years.

Sophie: Marriage is not an endurance contest, Morris.

Morris: It's not an endurance contest. You're right. And I don't want
to end up like them. I'm willing to go with you to the therapist.
I guess I should have done it a long time ago.

After this session, Sophie sent the consultant flowers to thank her
for her help. Morris entered treatment with the therapist who had
been seeing Sophie and participated in couples and individual sessions.

A good outcome in the midphase of treatment with regard to couples work takes place when both the survivor and the spouse are
equally invested in the treatment process. When this occurs, the
spouse is able to own his own dysfunction and difficulties. He sup-
ports and fully understands his spouse's need to confront her family
of origin since he is open to the spouse's point of view. If he is not
empathic, he is at least more engaged in the therapy and, therefore,
more open to the therapist's influence. The therapist can then educate
him about the importance of confronting the survivor's family of origin
and what her emotional needs may be throughout that process

CHILD-REARING TRANSACTIONS

With the spouses more firmly committed to themselves, each other,
and the treatment, work on improving the child-rearing transactions
in the family may commence more fully. As discussed in previous
chapters, there may be illicit coalitions, enmeshments, and disen-
gagements in the contemporary family of the survivor. The practitioner must now help the parental team to address and correct this
dysfunctional system. Generally speaking, there is less resistance to
work on the rearing transaction than on other foci of the midphase, if
the spouse is an active participant in the therapy.

If the survivor is a single parent, every attempt is made to include the other parent in the treatment at this point. He is treated as a critical family member. If there is estrangement or a severe conflict with the survivor, the therapist must fully discuss these issues with the survivor and obtain permission to contact the other parent directly. If he is in need of individual therapy, a referral to another practitioner is necessary.

Quite often, survivors are more inclined to give to their children and to "do right" by them than to give to or care for themselves. Survivors often project onto their children positive characteristics that they deny in themselves, such as hope and the ability to change. This is, of course, a problem in that, when the survivor's children see themselves being treated with more care and respect than the survivor accords to herself, feelings of guilt may block positive growth. This speaks to the need for the therapist to be working both intrapsychically and systemically. Then, as the survivor more apropriately parents her children, she, too, gets her own needs met via therapeutic input, which serves to increase self-deservedness and self-esteem.

The therapist may utilize a host of strategic, structural, and communications techniques to restructure and reorganize the family system. Moreover, because the therapist is in a positive reparental posture, role modeling, education, advice, and suggestions are effective in bringing about changes, as long as the therapist considers their intrapsychic and systemic implications and consequences.

In one case, a female survivor was overprotective of her 16-year-old daughter. She did not allow her to date and tried to discourage her from having any contact with boys. The daughter was beginning to rebel by becoming secretive and distant from the mother, which only served to make the mother more suspicious and engulfing. The therapist had already processed the mother's childhood issues in the earlier part of the treatment and found the survivor to be quite open to seeing that she was going to the opposite extreme from her own mother, who had ignored the survivor's promiscuity as a teenager. But this insight, in and of itself, was not enough to create change.

The therapist, in an emotional session with the daughter and the mother, helped the daughter to express her experience of being suffocated by her mother. This helped the survivor to fully experience the effect of her overprotectiveness. At one key point in the session, her daughter said, "All I want is to be like the other kids." With the therapist's supportive presence, the mother was able to be nondefensive, and she cried. In a subsequent session with the survivor and her husband, the therapist asked the father why he had not done anything to intervene beyond feebly asking the survivor, "Why don't you lay off of her?"—and then dropping the matter. He responded that he saw what was happening and empathized with the daughter's position, but felt helpless to do anything about it. The therapist, aware of this client's own history of withdrawn and distanced parenting, coached the father on how to help his wife parent. The therapist also explored with him how he felt impotent and backed off from confronting his wife out of his fear that "she'd get really angry with me." The guise for his fear was his perpetual attitude that "she knows what to do with the kids better than I do." The therapist affirmed the husband's knowledge and authority and coached him specifically on how to help his wife proactively.

The therapist gave the following assignment to the wife and husband. The next time their daughter wanted to go out with a boy, Mom was to give her permission as unambivalently as possible, and he was to listen privately to her ventilate her anxiety and feelings about it. In individual sessions, the therapist coached the husband on how to listen actively, reflect, and be supportive of his wife through a series of role plays. The therapist was facilitating corrective experiences on several levels here—directly for the husband and indirectly for the wife and daughter. The husband's inner child experienced the therapist as a parent figure during these role plays. In Chapter 10, you will see how the therapist's role—in this case, as the director and activator of the change process—is adopted into the couple system.

In time, the survivor, through a letting go of the reins on her daughter, saw that her fears were unfounded. She was also able to feel listened to by her husband, which truly felt like a new experience. This increased her feelings of appreciation and love for him, which also served to move some energy out of the mother–daughter relationship and into the marriage. The husband felt more powerful and, therefore, was less apt to be passive-aggressive and withdrawn. After six months or so, the daughter was reported as having more fun and maintaining appropriate contact with boys, and the entire family reported less tension generally. In a later session with the mother and daughter, the therapist promoted a more honest communication about men, sex, and the survivor's own experiences growing up.

INDEPENDENT TRANSACTIONS

Difficulties, dissatisfaction, and failures in work and career often represent a major blockage in the healing process for survivors. Work provides a sense of identity and self-esteem, as well as an opportunity to express creativity and selfhood. Because of familial enmeshments and loyalties, childhood damage to self-esteem, and a lack of appreciation of their talents and abilities, survivors typically find themselves in unsatisfying and unproductive work situations.

By the midphase of treatment, survivors have begun to experience an entitlement to their feelings and they recognize their unhappiness about the lack of fulfillment, power, or generativity in their lives. The challenge for the therapist is to assist the survivor to explore and process these feelings and to fully envision exactly what it is that she would like to be or do in the world. Next, an action plan is developed in concert with the survivor to address the twin career issues of satisfaction and success.

The survivor's career problems fall into three major, often interconnected, areas: difficulties in interpersonal work situations, the choice of an inappropriate career or career path, and the tendency not to follow through on her chosen career path. First, the survivor may have major difficulties in interpersonal relationships, particularly hierarchical ones. The survivor may have repeated a familial drama with a supervisor, in which, for example, she felt out of control, exploited, and abused. The therapist must assist the survivor in understanding how to manage these situations effectively.

In one such case, a survivor was continually getting into conflicts and arguments with another woman, who was a supervisor, but in another department. The supervisor was behaving in a demeaning manner and was treating her disrespectfully. Although the survivor's employers and manager agreed that she was being mistreated, they were unwilling to do anything about the situation because the supervisor was a successful salesperson. The survivor had attempted many strategies, including approaching the supervisor directly and expressing her feelings, but to no avail. After several sessions of processing her feelings about the supervisor and manager, the client realized that she was reliving a repetitive triangle in which a perpetrator (the supervisor) was abusing her and a "parent" (the manager) was not protecting her.

The therapist then coached the client on how to deal with the supervisor. The therapist told the survivor how threatened the supervisor must be to act in such a way. He gave the survivor a strategic posture to utilize when interacting with the supervisor. The strategy was to be as emotionally nonreactive as possible, while also splicing in some knowing smiles and glances at the supervisor, as if to say, "I know what you're up to." To provide an anchor to the intervention, the therapist instructed the survivor to think about the therapist and what he might tell her to do, if she began to react emotionally to the supervisor. He also offered to be available by phone if she felt the need to call.

By playing the neutral role, the survivor felt more powerful and in control. As she no longer behaved like a victim, the survivor did not reinforce the supervisor's sadism and the tormenting behavior waned. A month later, the survivor reported that she no longer considered her work relationships a problem. In this case, the therapist took a repetitive familial drama and provided a corrective emotional experience by actively coaching the survivor on dealing with the abusive situation and the "abuser."

Shortly after resolving the dilemma, the client initiated serious discussions about her wanting to change careers for other, more appropriate reasons. The therapist's involvement and the client's success in handling the situation seemed to motivate her to gain even more control over her work life.

This brings us to the second major career difficulty of survivors. Many survivors have selected careers that have nothing to do with their own dreams and wishes. One female survivor became a teacher because her controlling father, who had sexually molested her as a child, wanted her to do so. Her dream, discovered one year into treatment, was to become a physician. Two years later, after taking the necessary courses, she was accepted into medical school. Another survivor had chosen to be an office worker mainly because her father had refused to pay her college costs, claiming that there was no money, despite the fact that he had paid for her five sisters to go to college.

Encouraging the client to explore her career dreams is a potent technique with a survivor. Going back into childhood and asking such questions as, "What did you want to be when you were 10, 15, or 20?" opens up a vista of possibilities. Another related technique is to help envision a career destination for the survivor. In this intervention, the therapist imagines and describes a scenario or picture of what her dream fully realized could look like. Often the survivor will scoff at such "silliness," but, if the practitioner maintains a serious stance, she will let herself go and explore various fantasies about what she can be or do. Old career dreams can be reharnessed particularly well at this juncture in therapy.

Survivors often choose compromise careers or no career at all. They may feel unworthy and tell the therapist that they could never make it in law, art, journalism, or whatever career calls them. They claim that they are not smart enough, can't take tests, are undisciplined, or just are too fearful. The therapist must challenge the reality of these assumptions and take on a believing posture in order to correct their distortions and remove negative introjects. The therapist should not underestimate the abilities and talents of the survivor. The emotional, behavioral, and cognitive impairments of the sexual abuse and family dysfunction have had far-ranging effects. The survivor can actually prove to be quite talented and capable once these impairments are removed. If the therapist is not focused on the survivor's potential, he or she may set an overt or covert barrier to the survivor's growth.

The third career block for survivors is their tendency to give up or to give in to their fears and anxieties. The survivors may talk about career dreams, but offer many reasons as to why they cannot pursue them. They maintain that they are too old, don't have the money to be retrained, or are too busy with the children. All of these complaints may be masks for the survivor's fears of progressing.

Career success and fulfillment arise out of a sense of deservedness, an okayness with personal power, and a belief in the self that transcends the adversity inevitably encountered. These factors are not the strengths of the survivor. In fact, the third factor may be the most problematic. Quite often, the therapist is effective at assisting a survivor in the initial creation and envisionment of a more fulfilling career path and has coached the survivor through various interpersonal difficulties, such as the one described above. Belief in the self, however, comes only through the tenacious and tedious contribution of the corrective transactional experience of the therapist as a patient booster of the survivor and the incremental successes the survivor experiences in confronting problematic circumstances. The therapist functions as a faithful and believing figure, someone who remains securely in the survivor's corner when she feels like giving up.

One survivor failed a professional licensure examination several times, and each time was ready to abandon her lifelong dream to be an accountant. The therapist remained steadfastly supportive, and at several points strongly encouraged her to take the examination again when she claimed, "It's no use . . . I'm just not smart enough." When she did pass the examination, she admitted that she would have given up had the therapist not taken such a stand.

Another survivor had a dream of opening a small children's clothing store. The therapist coached her through the process of developing a concept, finding investors, securing a lease, and so on. At each stage, when faced with a difficulty or problem, the survivor would complain to the therapist about how "nothing ever works out for me." Typically, she would become depressed and stop working on the project for a period of days. Each time, the therapist would confront her self-pitying attitude and tendency to give up. The survivor would eventually return to the project. Over a period of a year, there was a noticeable difference in that, after each of these interactions, she would come around sooner each time, and with increasing zest. As she got closer to realizing her goal, she would return to the task within a couple of hours without any contact from the therapist. After she had opened the store, she told the therapist that in reality the adversities were really helpful opportunities to look at the project differently. The therapist responded by telling her that "it's normal to get depressed when things don't go as you'd like," and that she could look forward to many more disappointments. The client smiled immediately and said, "But the key is not to give into it." Over a period of one hard year of focusing on her career, which was preceded by eight months of dreaming and envisioning, the survivor had internalized the belief in herself.

PREPARING TO CONFRONT THE FAMILY OF ORIGIN

An important part of the midphase work is the confrontation of the survivor's family of origin. The need to discuss the incest secret is crucial to the client's growth. To continue to maintain secrecy and protect her parents keeps her in the disempowered victim role. To continue a relationship with the family as if the abuse never occurred reinforces the unreality of the incest, which is one of the factors contributing to the survivor's psychological and physical symptoms. If she cuts off from the family without attempting to reconnect and heal the relationships, she still maintains the silence and retains her disempowered role.

Some survivors will claim to have "worked it out in their own minds," others will claim to have forgiven their parents, and some will talk about how their parents' own upbringing "was no bed of roses." Most survivors wonder what good talking to the family now will do. They may say, "What's done is done," "The past is best left in the past," or "My relationship with them now is totally different than it was then . . . my dad is really mellow now . . . my mom's much cooler, you know." A tone of resignation usually accompanies these claims and fear almost always underlies such comments.

While in some cases the survivor's parents may have grown as people and can actually relate to her in a healthier way, in many others, they have not. Often the relationship between the survivor and her family of origin may be "great now" because the survivor has compromised her integrity almost completely. Family relationships may be fine as long as the survivor maintains the silence, doesn't confront the issue of the incest, stays away from sensitive topics, and remains her false self. The forgiveness she claims to have achieved is a house of cards that may topple at any moment. Therefore, she defends her relationship with the family in the vague unrealistic hope of getting the good-enough parenting she still needs.

Confronting the family of origin about the incest is, perhaps, the most difficult part of the healing journey for the survivor. Her inner child still feels the family's power to abandon or annihilate her. While in reality the family's power has diminished, she still feels as if she might die if she were to tell the secret. On the other hand, if the secret already had surfaced in the past and nothing was done to stop the perpetrator or to protect her, she fears the horror of facing the same reactions again. The survivor's resistance may be great.

At the same time, the survivor holds the knowledge that she cannot be fully herself without facing the perpetrator and the nonprotecting members of the family. She senses that it is difficult to be empowered until she has a sense of mastery in the family. Therefore, the therapist's raising of the family confrontation issue creates an instantaneous internal conflict for the survivor. She becomes ambivalent, torn between wanting to assert herself and being fearful of the consequences.

In the midphase, the therapist and survivor grapple with the confrontation issue. The first goal is for the survivor to gain cognitive insight into why this is an important step for her. She then needs to come to a point of emotional readiness, accepting that the confrontation is a difficult but necessary step in her full recovery. The therapist must assure the survivor that she or he will remain a steadfast support throughout the process. The next chapter delineates the family-of-origin work and how to bring about a constructive resolution for the survivor.

SUMMARY

The therapeutic work in the midphase requires attention to the survivor's career and independent transactions, as well as to family-of-creation and family-of-origin issues and dynamics. Since there is a tendency for the survivor to become resistant in the midphase, primarily because of foundational fears of abandonment, annihilation, and engulfment, more active and directive techniques are required. If the therapist can assist the survivor in overcoming some of these fears, then the survivor will become sufficiently empowered to confront her family of origin regarding the incest. This important work is described in Chapter 9.

THE FAMILY-OF-ORIGIN WORK

"She's crazy and you're making her worse. If she keeps up these lies, she's going to make her mother get even sicker."
 —Perpetrator to therapist during family session

"She's not crazy. The incest happened and we're all going to face it and deal with it."

 —Therapist

This chapter deals with the family-of-origin work that is conducted during the midphase of therapy with the survivor and her family. The first half of the chapter details the goals of the family-of-origin work, which include the survivor's disclosure of the secret and its destructive effects, along with her rage and shame; the perpetrator's and nonprotective family members' acknowledgment of guilt and heartfelt apologies; the development of a reparation process that feels right to the survivor; and the survivor's development of a new relationship with the family that is healthy and safe psychologically.

The second half of the chapter describes the evolution of the survivor's identity as she moves away from the family, and how this creates the opportunity to move closer to her partner or to date more successfully. The chapter closes with a discussion of the impact of the individuation process on the survivor's intimate relationships.

149

PREPARATION OF THE SURVIVOR

Preparing the survivor for family sessions is critical. Preparation begins with education about the benefits of the family sessions. The clinician stresses that, although the process will be quite painful and difficult in the short term, growth will come in time, as the survivor masters the fears associated with the confrontation. Typically there are cognitive, emotional, and interpersonal gains that evolve over time which are attributable to the family therapy. These include increased courage and assertiveness; healing for the survivor's inner child, as she experiences the adult part of herself fighting and protecting her; becoming less shame-bound; reduction of anxiety and depression; changes in self-perception, as the survivor moves out of the victim/child role and acts like an adult in the family; the potential for restructuring family relationships in a healthier way; and, for the survivor and her partner, the potential for enhanced marital teamwork and satisfaction. There are some survivors who hope that the family sessions will magically "undo" all the damage. They need to be cautioned that although growth will occur, this is not the case.

The survivor needs to air and work through all the specific fears that she has regarding the confrontation. Often these terrors revolve around abandonment or annihilation, that is, she worries someone will die or there will be an irrevocable split and she will never see her family again. As the survivor processes each fear, the therapist must be empathic. He or she needs to reassure the survivor that although there are no guarantees, it is unlikely, based on the family's history, that death will take place soon or that a permanent rift will occur. However, the practitioner should point out that if things do not go well in the sessions, the survivor may choose temporarily to suspend contact with the family.

Bass and Davis, in *The Courage to Heal* (1988), describe a journaling process that we have adapted for use in family sessions. The survivor prepares accounts detailing the incestuous events, what she lost, and the effects the incest has had on her life, along with a list of meaningful reparations that she would find to be healing. In addition to working with the accounts in individual sessions, she can then read all or parts of each piece during the family sessions.

In the last few individual sessions before the family meetings, the therapist can use role-playing and behavioral rehearsal to prepare the

the survivor. In particular, the survivor should practice what she needs to say to various family members, and the therapist should rehearse their possible attacks on her and their denials of the abuse. In this way, the survivor is ready to handle whatever collusive, scape-goating, or double-binding maneuvers are thrown at her during the sessions.

PREPARATION OF THE SURVIVOR'S PARTNER

When the survivor is ready to face the family, her partner needs to be positioned as a strong ally and support system. He, too, must be educated about the benefits of the family sessions. He needs to understand that his role is critical to the survivor's growth. In individual or joint sessions, the therapist can role-play with him some of the survivor's likely reactions and behavior before, during, and after confronting the family. These responses include minimizing the damage she has suffered, expressing fears of being unable to confront the family, evaluating her in-session performance negatively, becoming depressed and melancholy, and verbalizing that she wants to disown or kill her parents or siblings. The clinician can then teach the partner appropriately supportive responses to each of these reactions. After the sessions are held, the partner can validate the survivor. They can plan a special dinner or weekend alone to process the experience and celebrate the survivor's successful completion of the process.

CONTRAINDICATIONS

The family therapy sessions are not held if there is ongoing substance abuse or the potential for dangerous acting out in the family of origin. The first responsibility of the therapist is to protect the safety of all the participants in the family drama. Before inviting the family of origin to participate, the therapist should explore the history of the various family members, with a focus on any dangerous acting out. Past history is the best predictor of future behavior. Thus a family member who has made suicide attempts in the past or has been very violent and abusive may tend to act out these tendencies during or after the confrontation process. The therapist can contact that member by telephone, assess the potential for danger, and bond with him or her by stressing the importance of the meetings.

In some situations, for example, the therapist may be told by other family members that the perpetrator or his spouse is acting strangely or talking about suicide or homicide. The therapist must work to defuse the situation before any sessions can be held. This may involve contacting the person directly and reassessing the danger, and, if appropriate, referring the problem family member for therapy or medication.

Often the survivor may magnify the possibility of danger by projecting her own angry wishes, anxieties, and childhood fears. The therapist, with the assistance of the partner, can point out the projections and encourage the ventilation of the rage, fear, and guilt. The therapist needs to reassure the client that he or she is in charge and that no one will be hurt in the process. We tell our clients that in over 15 years of conducting these family sessions, we have never had a suicide attempt nor has anyone been physically abused.

Another form of resistance is the claim that the parents are too old or too sick to be confronted in the sessions. This is actually almost never the case. Usually, if the therapist proceeds to meet the "sickly, decrepit" parents, they look fine and strong enough to handle the material. Even if a parent is near death, it may be helpful to get the trauma out in the open so that the relationship can have a peaceful conclusion.

Nevertheless, the potential for dangerous acting out is not to be taken lightly. If, after sifting through the family history and talking directly to the perpetrator, there remains a serious concern about safety, then family sessions should not be conducted. In these cases, the survivor ultimately will break off contact with the family since the system is dangerous to her well-being and that of her children. At the end of this chapter, we discuss this eventuality in greater detail.

ATTENDANCE

All family members who lived in the household at the time of the incest should be asked to attend various sessions with the survivor and her therapist. In addition, any extended family member who was a perpetrator should also attend. The therapist may meet with the survivor and the perpetrator first, or with the survivor and other family members. Decisions about who should attend each session should be made on a case-by-case basis. Usually the survivor will voice her preference about attendance, and it is best to follow her lead. The survivor's partner or spouse generally does *not* attend the family-of-origin sessions, lest he interfere with or take over the battle.

If the perpetrator is deceased, family sessions are still held. Those who did not protect the victim or those who maintained silence still need to be confronted with their behavior.

How Family Members Are Invited

Typically, either the survivor or the therapist calls the more sympathetic parent and asks for help in the therapeutic process. This is done, no matter how far away the family lives, or how long it has been since there has been any contact. The request to participate in the sessions is not framed in terms of dealing with the incest, but rather, more generally, around assisting or helping the survivor.

If the therapist is to call directly, he or she first secures the survivor's permission during the preparation process. In the ensuing call, the practitioner introduces himself or herself as the survivor's therapist, briefly indicates how important the family is to the survivor, and asks the parent to help organize everyone to meet in family sessions. If the family members are from out of town, they are encouraged to stay at a local hotel and not at the survivor's home. We normally conduct sessions with out-of-town families on weekends. The survivor and her family are also instructed to have contact *only* during the formal sessions. Usually, two to three family sessions lasting about two hours each are enough to complete the process.

ROLE OF THE THERAPIST

Throughout the confrontation and resolution process with the family, the therapist serves primarily as an ally, coach, role model, and champion to the survivor. The clinician must remain firmly on her side in the face of denial or of verbal attacks on the survivor, and even in the face of threats made against the therapist. The first and primary loyalty is to the survivor, barring any needs with regard to safety issues.

From this position of loyalty, the therapist acts as a firm director of the family's interaction process, encouraging the survivor to speak honestly and the family to listen and react appropriately, and stopping the family's accusations and "crazy-making" behavior. As the director, the clinician cannot allow other problems in the family, such as the parents' marital problems, to take the focus off the main agenda. Control of the session is also necessary so that the survivor can be empowered and the reality of the abuse can emerge rather than being swallowed up in the black hole of the family's patterns of denial and blame.

For example, in one session the therapist asked the perpetrator father to stop talking 15 times, because each time that he spoke, he sarcastically invalidated his daughter. By the end of the session, his timid daughter was actively telling him, "Be quiet and listen," as she followed the empowering lead of her ally. "I've wanted to say that for 35 years," she reported after the session.

In another session, the therapist told the client's mother, "Listen to your daughter for once in your life"—after the mother began diverting attention from her daughter's disclosures by focusing on herself. In that session, the survivor felt supported by her therapist and was then able to be much more assertive with her mother.

PHASES AND CONTENT OF THE SESSIONS

The sessions should follow a predictable series of phases. In the opening phase, the practitioner bonds with the family members and introduces the goals of the session, that is, the healing and letting go of the wounds of the past for every member of the family. He or she then outlines the structure of the process by saying, for example, that the survivor "needs to voice her pain, anger, and upset, while you listen, understand, and own your part of it. Then there may be a reparation process, a letting go of the pain of the past for all of you." The therapist then describes some of the survivor's difficulties and struggles in the context of the family history.

In the second phase, the survivor directly and openly confronts the various family members about the reality of the incest, the lack of protection, and the betrayal she experienced. She expresses her anger, shame, disgust, and pain. She reads her written descriptions of the incest, what she lost, and the effects the incest has had on her life.

In the third phase, the family is pressed to acknowledge the reality of the abuse and to examine how they could have allowed one of their own to have been sacrificed. Each family member is asked to apologize or to express empathy for the survivor.

In the fourth phase, the survivor presents her list of reparations and the family discusses how reparation can be made. After reparation is agreed upon or made, the survivor may choose to begin discussions of forgiveness. In a few cases, all of these phases can occur to some extent in one session. In most cases, several sessions and follow-up letters from the survivor to the family are required.

In the first phase, it is important for the therapist to maintain a demeanor that conveys a sense of safety, control, and structure. In this manner, the family members will feel that they can speak freely when the clinician introduces the discussion about the family dynamics.

Often the therapist has to push for a confrontation to begin phase 2. When the survivor is faced with the actual session, she may be quite anxious in spite of all the preparation. It is very important for the incest activities to be discussed in a detailed and nonambiguous way. The survivor should say, "Daddy touched my breasts," rather than just, "Something upsetting happened"; or "I came to you, Mom, and you were too drunk to help me," rather than, "You didn't help, Mom."

The survivor has to have worked through some of her annihilation and abandonment fears about confronting the family so that she can express hurt and anger toward them in a real way. Her emotional expression is a very important part of the confrontation process. It makes the abusive activities real.

If the perpetrator is deceased, the therapist may use an "empty chair" technique and "put" him in the chair. The survivor is then encouraged to speak to him in front of the family. This is a powerful technique that often results in other family members' joining in. The survivor may also be given a padded encounter or Bataka bat with which to beat the chair. The expression of anger to the deceased in front of the family can be very healing for the survivor.

In phase 3, the family has to acknowledge that indeed the incest and the denial did happen. The therapist must strongly support the client's recollections, and will often have to confront the family members directly by repeating or amplifying the survivor's statements. He or she may say, "This actually did happen—it's written all over her. Her symptoms are unmistakable. Just acknowledge it. Then you'll work to make it up to her!" Or to the mother, the therapist might say, "You were busy nursing your own depression and hurt. You *did* fail your daughter. You should have heard your 11-year-old when she came to you and told you what was going on."

Once acknowledgment has been made, the therapist should have the family examine how the abuse could have occurred. What were the precipitating factors? What stopped the survivor from telling the other parent? What made people afraid to speak the truth? The therapist must press for answers and explanations, which will also encourage the survivor to confront the perpetrator and others about their behavior.

After the abuse and the family dynamics are exposed, the therapist encourages the members to express remorse and apologize to the survivor. The clinician may say, "You hurt her badly," or "You need to apologize *now*. You may never get another chance." Siblings should also be asked to apologize for whatever part they played in the drama.

It has been our experience that the family members, and especially the perpetrator, usually carry a great deal of guilt about the way in which the survivor was treated, in spite of their denials. It is in their best interest, therefore, to be able to confess, feel remorse, and make reparation to the survivor. We often explain to our families that this four-step process will help them to be free from the debilitating effects of guilt and self-hate they feel concerning their involvement in the abuse. We also point out that acknowledging complicity and seeking forgiveness will bring them closer to a successful resolution of a deep-seated and long-lasting problem in the family.

In the fourth phase, the therapist asks the survivor what she needs from the various family members in order to help heal the wounds of the past. He or she prompts a discussion about possible reparation activities. When the survivor settles on meaningful plans for repara-tion, the therapist creates a contract between the client and particular family members to ensure completion of the tasks.

For example, in one case, the survivor had confronted her mother about the incest she had experienced with her stepfather, who was now deceased. Her mother had entered her own therapy to process the guilt she felt about her daughter's abuse, but their relationship remained strained. In the session, the mother begged her daughter for forgiveness. Weeping, she recalled how she had abandoned her to the stepfather's care so that she could take on additional responsibil-ities at work. The therapist pointed out that the mother not only had abandoned her daughter, but also had denied her accusations about the stepfather. The survivor's mother wept profusely with genuine remorse during the sessions. After the mother had apologized, the therapist asked the survivor what she really wanted from her mother to make it up. The survivor replied that she wanted her mother to take care of her daughter once a week so that she could attend a class. The request was important to the survivor because her mother had never encouraged her educational pursuits. The therapist then asked both the mother and the survivor to ensure that this actually hap-pened. In this case, when the mother fulfilled her part of the contract, the survivor was able to forgive her and let go of the pain.

RESISTANCE

The family's resistance can play out in different ways. In some cases, the family members will attend sessions, but maintain the denial. Usually, they do so by labeling the survivor as crazy or bad, making such statements as, "She's out to destroy us with these false accusa-tions! She's just trying to break us up," or, "She's always been crazy." In other cases, various key family members or the family as a whole simply refuses to come to the sessions. Or they make the appointment and then cancel or are no-shows.

To deal with these families, especially if the perpetrator is alive, the therapist may empower the survivor to confront the family mem-bers by phone or letter about their behavior. To do this she must steady herself, face and master her own abandonment terrors, and take a stand with the family. The strong stance represents her belief in her own innocence and the need to protect herself and her family from the ongoing emotional abuse and possible future sexual abuse of her children.

In order to help her take such a stance, the therapist must point out the tremendous emotional damage that the family is continuing to do to the survivor. For example, in one case, the therapist had recorded, with the client's permission, a portion of a session in which the client had finally confronted the awful truth that her parents and sister were colluding against her: "So now both of them (my parents) are abusing me, and my sister is a traitor who won't even tell the truth about what she listened to each night in my bedroom." The therapist played this back to the survivor at several strategic points in treatment so that she could maintain her stance vis-à-vis the family.

The therapist must also voice his or her concern for the safety of the survivor's children. Often a confrontational stance is needed and the therapist may have to keep bringing out the reality of the danger. In one case, in which the client's father had had sex with her throughout her early adolescence, the following exchange took place:

Therapist: Oh, you're taking the children (two daughters, ages 10 and 12) to *their* house for Thanksgiving dinner? Is he going to be vulgar and inappropriate at the dinner table again?

Client: I guess so.

Therapist: Is this really what is good for your children to hear? What is their experience when he talks this way?

Client: I don't think it bothers them that much. You know I never let them alone with him.

Therapist: He still acts vulgar. It is *humiliating* for them, just like it was for you. They are identified with you. And you relive the wound every time he acts like that.

Client: God, you may be right . . .

Therapist: Do you really want to perpetuate this situation, the way your mother did?

Client: No! (silence)

The client decided to take her own family of creation to Plymouth Rock in Massachusetts for a special, celebratory Thanksgiving dinner. She subsequently confronted her father about stopping his inappropriate behaviors and he agreed to come for family sessions.

It is useful for the survivor to take a strong stance with the perpetrator regarding her children, even if there is relatively little potential danger to them. This is so because the survivor is symbolically replaying the original trauma, with herself in the role of the protective mother. The process helps transform her self-concept from that of a helpless victim to one of an assertive adult. The survivor, through her actions, also models assertive and protective behavior for her own children.

FEAR-OF-LOSS STRATEGY

If the family continues to be uncooperative in attending sessions and maintains its denial, the therapist can suggest using the fear-of-loss strategy. The strategy consists of different behaviors that delimit contact with the family, all of which are designed to prevent further damage to the survivor and her family and to stir up separation anxiety in family members. The goal is to help the family to act more maturely, respectfully, and remorsefully vis-à-vis the survivor. For example, the survivor can refuse to attend an important family celebration, such as a shower, a wedding, or an anniversary dinner. She can refuse to participate in holiday festivities during Passover or Easter or Christmas. She can refuse to bring her children to the perpetrator's house or to any gathering at which he will be present. Or, in the extreme case, the survivor can refuse for herself, her spouse, and her children to have any contact at all with other family members, including not accepting any invitations or telephone calls and not answering correspondence. The actual stance must be chosen by the survivor, who needs to find a stance she feels is just and right for her.

When a survivor is married or is in a committed relationship, it is important for the therapist to enlist the partner's support during the fear-of-loss strategy. He should have been informed about how the family of origin is failing his partner, his children, and, ultimately, him, in not facing and coming to terms with the damage that has been done. It is important for the therapist to explain that, at this crisis point, the spouse can be either a champion or someone who fails her, and that each stance has strong consequences for the relationship. The partner then has to be coached to be the support, helpmate, and emotional ground for the survivor, as she takes her difficult stand. He needs to be instructed to help her in any way he can.

When the family refuses to attend the family-of-origin sessions, the survivor is encouraged to express her feelings in a letter. The letter is photocopied and distributed to the members of the nuclear family. For example, one survivor whose parents and perpetrator brother, Bill, had refused to attend sessions wrote as follows:

> Mom and Dad—I want you to realize that both me and Janet were touched sexually and fondled by Bill for many years while you both were drunk. This upbringing has ruined our lives. Neither you nor Bill seems to be interested in talking about any of this or fixing it. Therefore, I want nothing to do with you or my former brother. I will not put my children at risk to be sexually molested by your son.

After this letter was sent, the parents agreed to come to a session and began to talk about the past. Subsequently, Bill began to attend AA meetings.

This case example illustrates one of the goals of the fear-of-loss maneuver, that is, for family members to own the damage they have caused the survivor and to feel guilt and pain for her. Ideally, they will come in for family-of-origin sessions and act appropriately. They need actively to say that they are sorry and, at times, go into their own treatment or an AA program to work on behaviors that led to the abuse. They also need to offer to make reparation to the survivor. If the survivor is invested in the resolution process, she must creatively think of ways in which reparation can be made and allow them to do so. After three to six months of such a process, forgiveness may emerge. We have found that the act of forgiveness is a gift to all family members, including the survivor. However, the therapist *must* follow the survivor's lead vis à vis forgiveness.

LETTER WRITING

After the last family-of-origin session, the survivor often has a clearer, stronger position and voice in the family of origin. This can be solidified by a letter or series of letters addressed to the perpetrator/ nonprotective parents and siblings. The same letter is often photo-copied and sent simultaneously to all family members. It is an honest and clear statement of the survivor's thoughts and feelings about the trauma(s) and the dynamics and issues surrounding the trauma(s). Usually, the therapist works with the survivor on the letter, helping her to express fully what she means to say.

The letter typically covers the following content areas: the survi-vor's reactions to the family-of-origin sessions; the expression of thoughts and feelings that were unsaid at the sessions; a description of the new psychological role the survivor will play in the family of origin; a set of demands for any further reparation needed; and a structure for future family gatherings that include the survivor and her family.

Much of the letter's content will have already been discussed in the family-of-origin sessions. But the power of the written word is such that it positions the survivor as a more effective spokesperson for the truth in the family and mitigates against the repression and denial that tend to set in.

During the letter-writing phase, the survivor is often remorseful that she expressed anger to the perpetrator and nonprotective family members. Out of her own annihilation fears, she may believe that she has severely damaged or hurt various members. Thus the guilt, worry, and remorse may be great. The therapist needs to reassure the client that these reactions are normal. He or she also needs to develop an agreement with the survivor at this point that she will not act on any of these feelings by apologizing or making it up to family members in any way. Instead, the therapist and client agree to exam-ine all reactions fully in session and, if appropriate, with the partner. This type of contract usually prevents the client from abandoning the strong stand she has taken.

The therapist can also use psychodynamic and gestalt techniques to help the client unearth and process her fantasies and emotional reactions to the family sessions and letters. One very powerful tech-nique involves having the client role-play the part of herself who damaged a family member and engage in a dialogue with that part. The client can also talk with other parts of herself that are afraid of being killed off or abandoned. As the survivor explores her fearful and remorseful thoughts and feelings, she typically will begin to detach from them. She can then resume examining her own wounds and anger, and thus continue with the individuation process.

Sending letters can also be very constructive in dealing with family members who canceled their therapy appointments, didn't show up, or refused to attend the sessions. By sending copies of the letter to all family members, the survivor can have her chance to express herself and to break the taboo of silence in the family.

A letter can even be read by the survivor during a gravesite visit to a deceased perpetrator or family member. It is advisable for the therapist to accompany the survivor. The letter can be read aloud to the deceased, along with any additions, comments, and embellishments that occur to the survivor in the moment.

The only caveat with regard to letter writing is safety. The therapist needs to take a full inventory of previous suicidal thoughts, threats, or attempts, as well as previous threats or acts of violence made by family members. If the history indicates that a family member is potentially suicidal, physically abusive, or homicidal, the therapist and client may not want to disturb the system further by sending letters. However, such a situation is rare.

The following case example illustrates the power of letter writing with a family that resisted attending sessions, even though the perpetrator was deceased.

The Case of Peggy

Peggy, a 35-year-old homemaker, entered treatment for agoraphobia and depression. She was married with two children, and had a history of drug and alcohol use. The therapist invited Peggy's spouse into treatment and he complained of poor communication and a lack of sex in the marriage. While discussing these problems, he revealed that Peggy had been molested by her father.

Peggy came from a well-to-do Greek family. Her father drank heavily and would frequently beat both Peggy and her mother. Peggy was the oldest of four children and was often called upon to prepare dinner and get the others ready for bed. Her mother was quite depressed and withdrawn. When Peggy was 11, her mother attempted suicide and was hospitalized.

According to Peggy, her father began to abuse her just before this time and continued until she left for college. At first, he would come into her room to give her back rubs. Later, he started to fondle her, and eventually started having intercourse with her. When Peggy was a teenager, he began leaving money for her on her dresser. He died when Peggy was 21.

The therapy followed a standard course. Individual and conjoint sessions with Peggy focused on exposure to rid her of the agoraphobia. The therapist recommended a six-month course of Prozac to alleviate her chronic depression. As Peggy's fears diminished and her spirits lifted, she took a part-time job. The memory-retrieval work progressed well. Peggy remembered going to her mother and telling her that she was being molested. According to Peggy, her mother began to scream at her and called her a "whore." Peggy shared her memories in sessions with her husband, who was very understanding and comforting.

In this case, since Peggy's husband was so clearly supportive, the therapist opted to have him take her to her father's grave. There she read a letter aloud that detailed her feelings of rage and hurt over her father's actions. Peggy then spit on his grave and left. When she reported her experience to the therapist, he told her that she was ready to confront her mother and siblings.

Peggy called her mother, who lived out of town, and invited her to participate in family sessions. She told her mother that she was also calling her two sisters and brother to invite them as well. When Peggy's mother asked what would be discussed, Peggy simply responded: "My childhood." Peggy's mother and siblings refused to participate. In a series of phone calls to her mother, Peggy cried, screamed, and begged her to attend, but to no avail. She then sent the following letter to her mother and siblings.

To: Mom, Jean, Megan, and Nick,
I am writing this letter to you because I want you to know I quit. I quit trying to make you understand my pain, guilt, fear, and confusion. I will not endure any more sleepless haunted nights. I will not defend my actions or feelings to you ever again. I will not get into another screaming, crying phone call again.

I feel more desperate and consumed by this than I ever did. I guess I wanted my mother and siblings to understand me and the horrible things I went through. I'm not sure why that was so important to me. Maybe I was looking for your approval or your comfort. I know now that my childhood memories are mine and I can't jam them down anyone's throat. I didn't mean to. I didn't want to destroy your good memories of your marriage, Mom.

I do not want anyone to hate our father. I do not hate my father. I never did. He was a sick, troubled man who never forgave himself. I am sure that is why he started drinking. He had to kill the shame and pain. I tried that for a long time too. I felt so bad all the time.

I thought the truth would ease the pain. Right now the truth only hurts. I feel more alone now than when I was 15. Twenty years later and I am still haunted by my childhood. I know I cannot deal with this anymore. I will not lose any more sleep. I will not ignore my husband and children anymore because of this. I will not write down some things and then have a talk with you, Mom. I will not compare facts of when, where, how long, did he or didn't he. I will not defend that my mother treats me different from my siblings. None of this matters anymore. I quit.

Mom, neither of us knew how this would change my life. How I would feel different and confused because of this. That this was a terrible, unspeakable crime. He abused my body and my mind. He stole my childhood and my dreams. He made me feel crazy, bad, and unloved. He made me the whore when he left money on my bureau. He destroyed our chances of a normal mother/daughter relationship. He did that the first time he touched me. In a sick way, he made me the other woman, the mistress. How could we have a healthy relationship?

From then on I was doomed. I always felt guilty and bad, frightened and ashamed. From then on, I always tried to be good. I tried to erase and make up for what I did. I thought it was my fault. I wanted you both to love me even though I was bad. I wanted you to say I was good, a good little girl. This is what makes me so different from Jean and Megan. This is why I take everything to heart. My heart says I am still that bad little girl. This is why I am an alcoholic, and not Jean or Megan.

I had to tell you all the secret. It was the right decision for me.

After Peggy's family received this letter, her brother, Nick, called his sisters and mother and told them that it was a disgrace for them to keep protecting the father. He called Peggy and asked for permission to speak to the therapist. The therapist told him, "You are being a man now in supporting your sister. Please help by organizing a family meeting with me." Nick was successful in convincing the others to attend.

The family sessions proceeded smoothly and Peggy felt relieved and empowered. No longer did she feel like the crazy and bad outcast.

CREATING NEW FAMILY-OF-ORIGIN RELATIONSHIPS

The survivor has to be encouraged to envision and create the kinds of relationships she wants to have with family members. Guided imagery can be useful. She can be encouraged to envision scenes at their homes or her own, on specific holidays, and so on, in which she imagines the desired interaction and dialogues between (1) herself, (2) her partner, and (3) her children with each family member. The therapist must help the survivor sort out the more realistic scenes from the fantasies that are less likely to happen. In this way, the survivor is encouraged to become assertive and mature in the family of origin.

For example, one survivor envisioned her cold, unresponsive mother throwing her arms around her and her children and being very affectionate. The therapist talked with her about her unrealistic wishes and longings and pointed out that she could more realistically satisfy her needs for love with her husband. She then helped the woman to imagine her mother politely kissing her and the children hello and goodbye. The therapist role-played with the survivor, having her ask her mother for these warmer greetings, so that she could learn how to, at the very least, ask for and receive a warmer response from her parent.

As with any of the family-of-origin work we have described, it is impossible to predict how family members may respond to a survivor's needs and requests. It is important for the therapist to stress that the client is trying to develop a more separate self, to become the kind of person whom she likes and respects. All of these techniques are aimed at accomplishing that end. In truth, however, they may meet with failure, that is, the scenes the survivor envisions may never take place. And even if they do take place, the family members may enact their parts poorly or only sporadically. For example, in the case just described, the survivor's mother resumed her cold affect after greeting the client and her children more appropriately on only three occasions. But the therapist had prepared the survivor for this reversal, and she handled her mother assertively. Despite her mother's apology, the client expressed hurt and disappointment.

Such difficulties do not mean that envisioning and asking for reparative or healthy interactions with the family are not helpful to the survivor's growth process. The survivor will be able to look back and view her actions with self-respect. She will also be able to use the same creative and assertive skills in other interpersonal situations, where she probably will meet with greater success.

UNSUCCESSFUL FAMILY-OF-ORIGIN RESOLUTIONS

At times, because of serious family dysfunction or drug/alcohol abuse, a successful resolution of the incest trauma is impossible to achieve. Therefore, the survivor may have to accept a loss of contact with the family and may choose to sever the ties that are emotionally damaging to her.

The therapist then has to work with the survivor to process the grief entailed in losing her family. The clinician should facilitate the mourning process—which is similar to that which occurs when family members die. A mourning ritual, such as lighting candles for the dead, is often helpful to a survivor who needs to sever ties. The rift may only be temporary, and the client will know when she is ready to resume contact and under what conditions.

Even with an unsuccessful family-of-origin resolution, there is growth and individuation for the survivor. She still experiences herself as courageous and assertive. Her shame, anxiety, and depression tend to decrease. There are also changes in her self-perception, as she has moved out of the victim/child role and has become more of an adult in the family. In addition, the survivor usually creates a new healthier "family" by developing her relationships with her partner, loving friends, and those members of the extended family, such as cousins or more distant relatives, who treat her with respect and caring.

INDIVIDUATION AND LOVE RELATIONSHIPS

Individuation from the family of origin leads to a greater openness to other attachments and love relationships. Survivors who are single may want to begin dating and getting out more with friends. These women often do not enjoy dating because they do not trust men or are loath to engage in sex. When clients successfully confront their families, they feel empowered and less frightened. As a result, they are more likely to want to go out.

At times, the therapist may need to encourage clients to date. This is especially important with survivors who have received a lot of nurturance and support in therapy. These clients often become dependent on the clinician and expect most of their needs to be gratified in the treatment. This must be discouraged. Therefore, we urge our single clients to date and, ideally, to go out with three different men.

Dating: The Program of Three

Typically, the survivor has feelings of anger, mistrust, and anxiety with regard to men as a result of the sexual abuse. Because of this, she is likely to suffer from a range of difficulties in meeting and dating men, including an inability to tolerate any interaction with them. Some survivors, seeking to overcompensate for these feelings, become sexually promiscuous and addicted to sex.

In order to desensitize the client, the therapist encourages her to date three men *casually*, with no sexual intercourse and with no more than a weekly contact with each one. Within these guidelines, the survivor can learn to be friends with men—to view them as people. With more limited contact, she can slowly "warm up" to men and avoid precipitous idealization and fusion that lead inevitably to rejection and abandonment.

With three men to compare and contrast, the survivor can learn about what she wants and does not want from a man. She can feel desirable as a person and as a woman and begin to select men who treat her more positively. Often, of course, the survivor will scoff at these guidelines, claiming, for example, that she can't even find one man to date. The therapist needs to become proactive and directive in the face of this resistance. He or she has to secure a contract that the survivor will at least attempt to explore the world of men in a more mature manner. The therapist then can suggest activities, classes, groups, and workshops at which the survivor can learn and enjoy herself and meet more interesting men to date. The text *Comprehensive Family Therapy* (Kirschner & Kirschner, 1986) describes the dating program of three for single adults in greater detail.

At times, the survivor may be confused about her sexual preference. If she is confused, the therapist can suggest that she explore all her thoughts and feelings on the matter so that she can become clearer. Gestalt work with the various parts of herself that have different sexual preferences can be helpful. Some clients need to make exploratory forays into the local lesbian network by participating in discussion groups or workshops. We have had clients who were dating both men and women and eventually decided that they preferred women. The same program of dating three people is usually helpful, regardless of the client's sexual preference.

CASE EXAMPLE

Beth Torrence, whose case was described in Chapters 1 and 7, had a successful family-of-origin resolution. She then began to date for the first time in her life. Beth, an only child, had been sexually abused by her stepfather from age 6 to age 16. He would drink, then become verbally abusive, and then, if Beth did not submit to his sexual advances, would hit her. The therapist had three family-of-origin sessions with Beth, her mother, and her stepfather.

Beth's stepfather had gone to AA and had been sober for the past seven years. Even though he did not recall all of his abusive behavior, he was remorseful. Beth's mother had been physically abused by her husband and was seriously depressed during the period of the incest. She had subsequently attended Al-Anon programs and was significantly improved. She was able to own her part of the abuse— she would take sedatives and sleeping pills to escape the family horror and had abandoned Beth to her stepfather. In the first two sessions, all three of them wept as Beth recounted the details of being "tortured." She ventilated her anger and rage at her parents.

Both the mother and stepfather apologized to Beth and offered to make it up to her. In the third session, Beth explained that she was still too angry and was not ready to forgive them. She then sent them two follow-up letters, venting more of her rage about new memories that had surfaced. They phoned the therapist, who advised them to write back, saying that they understood and would wait patiently for Beth to work this through, no matter how long it took.

Meanwhile, at the therapist's urging, Beth had joined a local singing group and had met a man in the group who was quite smitten with her. Initially, she rejected him because he liked her "too much." The therapist paradoxically confronted Beth, saying, "Yes, be alone all your life. It's not really that bad!" Beth then began dating this man. The therapist encouraged her to date three men, and Beth laughed at the idea, claiming it was impossible. Beth had never dated in high school. In her early 20s, she had two horrible one-night stands during which she had been drunk and had had sex.

As Beth continued to date, she reported that she felt "normal" and "prettier." Her appearance and her self-esteem improved. Beth's stand with her parents and the attention she was getting by dating helped to empower her. Deciding that she wanted to change to a more satisfying and challenging career, she started taking evening courses and became interested in computers. After doing well in two courses, Beth reported that she had decided on a reparation plan. She wanted her parents to pay for her degree in computer science. They agreed to do so.

Beth decided that she wanted to forgive her parents. Following her lead, the therapist had the three of them come in for a follow-up session focused on the theme of forgiveness. Beth wanted a ritual to dispel the black cloud that had hung over the family. The therapist suggested that they release black helium-filled balloons as a symbol of letting the past go. At a subsequent session, the family released the balloons outside the therapist's office and Beth thanked her parents for their support.

At school, Beth met two other men in whom she became interested. She wanted to end her first relationship, but the therapist suggested that she just speak with her boyfriend about dating other people and continue to see him. Beth resisted this idea, but finally told him. The boyfriend was upset, but agreed to the arrangement. Beth reported that she felt very special, and laughed about having "all these men."

The Coupled Survivor

When a survivor is married or is seriously involved with a lover, the resolution phase often marks either a new benchmark in positive understanding and a turning point in the relationship, or a crisis of possible fragmentation and dissolution.

If the partner has been involved in the treatment process and has been willing to function as an ally for the survivor, he will have been included in the letter-writing process and the structuring or curtailment of family visits. In terms of the changes in family interactions, his role has ideally been, under the therapist's coaching, absolutely and unequivocally to support and team with the survivor. For example, in one case, a survivor's partner photocopied her confrontational letters and mailed them from his office. He then planned a skiing trip during the Christmas holiday so that the survivor, who had refused to attend her family's festivities, would not feel depressed and left out.

As a result of support like this, the stage is set for deepened bonding, positive reciprocity, and gratitude in the relationship. This process sets in motion a kind of healing for most couples. The partner feels competent, empowered, good, and giving—and thus more positively deserving. The survivor feels support, protection, and love in a way she had always hoped for. As a result, she, too, feels more deserving.

The survivor also is more ready to reciprocate by helping her partner. Couples sessions can be conducted more frequently and more successfully at this point in treatment. The therapist can help the couple develop a collaborative contract in which each partner asks for and receives what he or she needs emotionally from the other. This type of marital coalition is described in *Comprehensive Family Therapy* (Kirschner & Kirschner, 1986).

If the partner is a survivor himself, the whole process of therapy may shift to focusing on him. Even if he has not suffered sexual or physical abuse, he can more easily own his own wounds from the past, as the survivor begins to emerge from her pain. This is so because the survivor and the couple usually have less need at this point to keep her in the wounded "patient" role and the partner in the tough "sane" role. The therapist can then ask what the partner needs in order to feel better about himself or the relationship. The table has been set for further work on refining their teamwork as parents and/or lovers.

On the other hand, if the survivor has a partner who has been unsupportive, unwilling to attend sessions, and/or sabotaging of her family-of-origin work, her successful individuation from the family can often create a true crisis point. After the survivor has developed the courage to face "dumping" her family, she is ready potentially to leave her partner. The sword of the fear of loss then hangs over the couple's head. It is often in the phase of treatment after this that the fear-of-loss strategy for couples descibed in Chapter 8 can be successfully utilized by the survivor.

This crisis, however, poses a tremendous opportunity. The partner is frightened by the possibility of losing the survivor and often feels that he needs help in relating to her new strength. In addition, she is usually stronger in insisting that he participate in treatment. Thus he is ripe to enter treatment. At this point, with a slight encouragement by the therapist, even the most recalcitrant partner will usually come in to meet with him or her. In the ensuing couples sessions, the therapist strategically highlights the possible fragmentation of the relationship by using the fear-of-loss strategy (Kirschner & Kirschner, 1986, 1990a, 1990b, 1992). In our experience, this maneuver is most effective in generating a strong contract for marital therapy.

SUMMARY

Family-of-origin work involves a structured process of confrontational sessions with the family of origin, with the goals of the disclosure of the secret, the acknowledgment by the perpetrator and nonprotective family members of guilt and remorse, and the development of a reparation process. In some cases, the survivor may use a fear-of-loss strategy with the family in order to create interactional change. The process results in individuation and growth for the survivor. Typically, she becomes more authentic, assertive, and empowered. She moves her relationship with the family of origin to a healthier or safer level, and optimally, may be able to repair and let go of the wounds of the past. In addition, her dating or couple life tends to move forward significantly. Clients in committed relationships often enter more intensive couples therapy after completing the family-of-origin work. Chapter 10 details the strategies and techniques of couples therapy with survivors and their partners.

CHAPTER 10

THE ENDPHASE OF THERAPY

"I carried the blanket to a nice, secluded place . . . We ate and talked and pretty soon we made love there on the blanket. She said: 'Hey, this is great.' "

—A survivor's spouse

In the endphase, the therapist conducts couples and sex therapy with the survivor and her partner. Whereas the midphase focused on helping the survivor individuate from her family of origin, the endphase ideally focuses on the development of a healthier sexual and intimate relationship. As this occurs, the survivor moves out of her intense relationship with the therapist and the stage is set for termination. In this chapter, we describe couples and sex therapy techniques, present a transcript that illustrates the process of creating forgiveness, and discuss the concept of the intramarital coalition for mutual growth.

INTENSIVE MARITAL THERAPY

A natural outgrowth of the survivor's completion of the family-of-origin work described in Chapter 9 is an individuation of the self from the family system. A sense of her own personhood and emotional separateness emerges. Typically, by the endphase, unhealthy enmeshments and inappropriate cutoffs involving family members have been addressed and repaired to whatever extent possible. The survivor also feels less anxious and depressed, more settled and more confident in her career and as a parent.

The survivor's relationship with the therapist may still be quite intense, but she begins to sense that as good as that relationship is, it, too, will come to an end. As a result of the working through of the transference and the building of the couple's relationship, the specter of termination is not as frightening. Yet the survivor may be saddened by the prospect of the impending end of treatment.

The sense of losing the therapeutic relationship creates a void in the survivor, and she looks more to her partner to fill her needs for understanding and empathy. As a result, the survivor may approach the therapist with a more mature and assertive attitude of wanting a better and more need-satisfying relationship with her partner.

The prerequisite for intensive couples work is a strong commitment and the desire to create a positive win–win marital relationship. Although precursors to this work may have been attempted earlier in treatment, the partners must be now ready to implement their work more overtly in conjoint sessions. The readiness factor cannot be overemphasized. Often, there is an ill-timed recommendation of a course of marital therapy by the therapist or another practitioner. The appearance of relationship difficulties is not a signal to introduce intensive couples therapy. The dialectic among the needs of the survivor, those of her partner, and the growth of the couple cannot be approached via a knee-jerk eclecticism. Although the procedure may be technically correct, it may be out of tune with the needs of the survivor, who is still building her individual selfhood. Thus the marital work is doomed to fail. Most typically, intensive marital therapy is best conducted during the endphase of treatment.

The marital therapy of the endphase centers on three major foci. First, with respect to the construct of projective identification, the goal is for the partner to claim suppressed, split-off, and projected aspects of his personality for himself. The survivor, of course, must do the same. Second, there is an emphasis on the normalizing and enjoyment of sexual relating. Finally, the therapist assists the couple in creating a benevolent win–win relationship.

REVERSING THE PROJECTIVE
IDENTIFICATION PROCESS

As discussed in Chapter 5, one of the myths of coupled survivors is that the survivor is the only one of the pair to really have problems, emotional pain, and conflicted family-of-origin relationships.

As the veil of symptomatology, secrets, and shame lifts, the problems and issues of the partner quite naturally will rise to the surface as the survivor becomes less inclined to own her partner's projected pain. The projective identification process depends on the unconscious willingness of the survivor to behave as if she is the only one in the couple who feels wounded. As a result of treatment, the survivor is less inclined to project the more stable aspects of her self onto her mate as she is beginning to experience herself as truly more solid and together.

Still, having been consistently reinforced over time, the projective identification process remains resilient, particularly in distressed marriages. The role of the therapist, then, is to reverse the process by encouraging each mate to play out the disowned parts of the self that consistently project onto the other mate. This can be achieved best by direct therapeutic suggestion.

In one case, a survivor, Sandy, was in charge of the family finances. Sandy would become upset whenever her husband, Bill, made any purchase or even carried a credit card. In individual sessions, Sandy claimed that Bill "just could not be trusted with money . . . he's very impulsive, you know." Bill sheepishly agreed with Sandy when the issue was brought up in a conjoint session. In the therapist's view, Sandy was projecting her impulsiveness onto Bill, who, at one time in the marriage, fully owned and enacted it. Bill projected his cautiousness and compulsivity onto Sandy, who fully owned and enacted those traits.

The therapist seized an opportunity to break the homeostatic lock when Bill made an offhand remark in an individual session about how tired he was of Sandy's always needing to be in charge of the money. The therapist, after exploring his comment further, suggested that it would be great for Bill to take over that responsibility. After a few sessions, Bill agreed to confront Sandy. Sandy was quite resistant, but in an individual session with her, the therapist fully supported Bill, while reframing the switch as a much-needed break "for her."

By the following week, Bill had taken over the finances, and the therapist encouraged Sandy to "let Bill take over." Despite her continued claims that Bill would "screw it up," he actually did a better job than Sandy, as her compulsivity led her to make overly conservative financial decisions. Bill got to experience himself as capable. After six months, Sandy reported feeling much relieved. At that point, the therapist suggested that Sandy might want to "take another shot at the finances in a few years." This intervention aimed at completing the reversal of the projective identification cycle. It is critical to note that if this issue had arisen earlier in the treatment, the therapist would have supported Sandy's control of the finances.

Another therapeutic strategy to reverse the projective identification process is to highlight the problems of the survivor's partner. It may be useful to put the survivor in the consultant role at this point. Again, this may occur naturally in the treatment as the survivor's functioning improves. However, if it does not, the therapist may need to focus on the partner's issues, even though they appear not to be interfacing or presented as "problems." At times, the projective identification process is so strong that the partner's difficulties, which appear minor, are the proverbial tip of the iceberg. Unless the therapist is cognizant of the process, which preserves such suppression and denial, the couple's attempts to keep the partner as healthier or as having fewer problems than the survivor will prevail.

In one case, a survivor, Evelyn, constantly addressed issues regarding her upbringing and parenting. She had worked through most of her anger and resentment and was beginning to feel a sense of resolution. Her husband, Fred, on the other hand, continued to claim that his childhood was "just fine . . . oh, sure, I guess if you really wanted to look for something, you could tell me that my parents should have bought me that bike I wanted when I was 8." What lies behind such sarcastic comments is a demeaning of Evelyn's experience of herself and her healing; indeed, she felt as much, although she had a difficult time verbalizing it.

The therapist began to taper off individual sessions with Evelyn, even though she continued to present *as if* she needed continuous help. At the same time, he asked to meet with Fred more frequently. The therapist also began seeding for termination with Evelyn by talking about the many changes she had made in her individual work. Although this scared Evelyn, she started to own the "okay" piece in herself for the first time. Previously, she had only experienced herself as troubled or conflicted. This also represented the aspect of Fred that he denied in himself and projected onto her. As long as she enacted this piece, he could retain his feeling of "okayness" about his childhood experiences.

Even though Evelyn had made great strides, the projective identification process remained in place as Fred's needs to be okay about his childhood experience and her need to protect him from expressing his pain were overwhelming. However, the therapist's retaining a focus on Fred therapeutically and his "declaration" of Evelyn's "wellness" created a shift in the projective identification process. She became stronger and eventually began to detach from Fred, no longer needing to project her "okayness" onto him. Since she no longer denied that aspect of the self, Fred had to experience his "not okayness." Within 10 months, Fred had begun freely to discuss his own pain regarding childhood issues.

SEX THERAPY

Improving the sexual life of the couple is a second major focus of the intensive marital therapy in the endphase. The goals of this work are to remediate the sexual dysfunction of one or both partners, to normalize and heighten the couple's sexual pleasure, and, finally, to increase intimacy via the expression of sexual needs and fantasies.

Survivors and their partners often present with one or more sexual dysfunctions, among the two most common of which are disorders of desire and premature ejaculation. In most couples, disorders of desire are manifested by the survivor. Disorders of desire are best treated by Kaplan's (1974, 1979), array of sex therapy techniques. Because survivors experience physical touch and stimulation as instantaneously sexual and necessarily leading to a sexual act, they may avoid all contact and report a general lack of interest in sex. Kaplan's sensate focus technique is helpful in desensitizing survivors to touch stimuli. Moreover, the exercise will inform them and their partners and the practitioner as to what they enjoy and find physically pleasurable.

The exercise works as follows: The therapist may tell a partner to massage the survivor for one-half hour. An absolute injunction is given against having sex afterwards. This has the effect of relaxing the survivor, as she will not have to worry about the touch's leading to sex. The husband is instructed to do exactly what the survivor enjoys. If she likes being touched in a particular way, he is to continue. If she indicates that she doesn't like a particular kind of touch, then he is to stop. This instruction is particularly important because the survivor and spouse have often unconsciously recreated the sexual abuse trauma by the husband doing something in bed that the survivor does not find pleasurable or experiences as painful.

The technique in time may be adjusted to a particular level of erotic contact from the low end of a total injunction against sex to a moderate position of some erotic touch to a high end of mostly erotic touch. The technique has a paradoxical effect of building arousal by removing the pressure of impending sex. At some point, the partners will initiate sex on their own.

Quite often, the symptoms of the survivor mask the psychopathology of the partner. It is common for the survivor to project her sexuality onto her partner while maintaining that she has little interest in sex. When the survivor, working through the incest trauma, becomes more interested in sex, she begins to reclaim her projections. Suddenly, the previously high sexual interest of her partner decreases dramatically, or he may become impotent.

There are systemic explanations for such a switch, but, at this point in the treatment, it would serve the couple best to address the desire disorder of the partner. This kind of intervention will help break the couple's taboo against sexual intimacy and the homeostatic rule that only one partner can be sexual at any time by focusing on the previously disowned *new* role of each spouse. If there has been sufficient intrapsychic change in the survivor, she will not be likely to give up her newly claimed role, and this puts the onus of change on her partner.

If the partner suffers from premature ejaculation, the therapist may introduce the couple to one of two highly successful sex therapy procedures. Both techniques systematically raise the male's level of penile sensory awareness so that he can gain control over ejaculation (Kaplan, 1989).

In the Masters and Johnson's squeeze technique (Kaplan, 1974), the partner is asked to squeeze the head of the man's penis as he approaches orgasm. This can be done two to three times, each time with the man alerting his partner that he is ready to come. The squeezing prevents the ejaculation and gives the man a sense of control over his orgasm. In the span of six weeks, the symptom can be greatly improved.

The stop-start technique may be preferable for the spouses of survivors since the squeeze technique is sometimes viewed by couples as too harsh. In the stop-start method, the man is instructed to focus on his penile sensation while being manually and later intravaginally stimulated by the partner. When the man nears orgasm but prior to ejaculation, he is to tell the partner to stop. When he feels more in control of his level of arousal, he is to tell the partner to start again. The couple are instructed to do this three times and the man may ejaculate on the fourth time. The couple can repeat this exercise several times during the week in between sessions. Significantly, the therapist is to frame the technique as an "exercise" and not as a "performance." Finally, although the therapist must encourage the man to focus on his sensations during the procedure in order to be successful, he or she must also instruct the man to attend to his partner's sexual needs following the exercise. The reader is encouraged to read Kaplan's (1989) work detailing both techniques.

NORMALIZING SEXUALITY

The next goal is to normalize the sexual relationship by decreasing the heightened shame the survivor or her partner experiences with regard to sexual stimuli. The practitioner takes on the role of advisor and sex educator. Since the therapist has already served in a mentor role to the client, we cannot overestimate the healing power of simple permission, encouragement, programming, and reframing interventions. The therapist communicates a posture that sex is nothing to be ashamed of, sexual fantasies are normal and healthy, masturbation and pleasuring of the self are normal and good, and whatever sexually interests the couple is okay. The survivor and partner will internalize this role modeling.

In particular, the therapist may suggest romantic weekends at a couples-only resort or encourage them to dress provocatively for each other. The clinician should initiate frank discussions with both of them about their sexual histories, interests, and fantasies. Then she or he encourages the partners to have such talks with each other.

SEXUAL FANTASIES

The discussion of sexual fantasies is particularly fruitful for survivors, as they experience virtually any out-of-the-ordinary sexual acts or interests as weird, kinky, or perverse. These so-called perverse acts or fantasies may be as tepid as nonmissionary-position sex. Fantasies involving dominance and submission are very common in survivors, perhaps because they represent a recapitulation of the power dynamic in the childhood sexual abuse. Homosexual fantasies are also common.

Again, the survivor or partner feels ashamed of even reporting these fantasies. Therefore, the therapist must maintain a matter-of-fact attitude of openness. If the therapist unwittingly reinforces the taboos of the culture or religious subculture, the client will internalize this attitude as well. The therapist's homophobia and sexual timidity, no matter how disguised, will inhibit the client's expression and experience of sexual pleasure.

If the survivor and partner report that they "have no fantasies" or are having trouble talking about them, the therapist may suggest a romantic/sexual film or soft pornography, or popular books such as *The Joy of Sex* (Comfort, 1972) or any of the compilations of women's and men's fantasies, such as *My Secret Garden* (Friday, 1973). Of course, the therapist must respect the values of the client and proceed slowly and cautiously with clients who would be uncomfortable with such material. We should note, however, that many survivors and their partners have reported being "turned off" by certain books, films, or common fantasies, only to find later that they are excited and find the same fantasies pleasurable. The therapist must also be clear that fantasizing about something is not the same as doing it, and that a fantasy is a thought—one cannot be held responsible for what spontaneously comes into the mind.

Another very useful intervention is to encourage the partners to enact their sexual fantasies with each other. For example, a common sexual fantasy is the reversal of sexual roles. The survivor who is always in the passive/submissive role sexually may be encouraged to play the active/dominant role with her partner. This can be particularly healing for the survivor who was forced to engage in sexual acts as a child. It is not surprising, then, that the passive role is at once comfortable and highly conflicted. The encouragement by the therapist and her partner for her to take the active role is usually enough for her to become less passive. We have treated survivors who never enjoyed sex until they were "put in control" via their partner. In this sense, the survivor gets an opportunity to play the role of the perpetrator or to identify with the aggressor, but in a way that she can control and shape. She learns that she can express power in a safe and consensual manner.

Often the survivor has avoided the active/dominant position because she fears becoming exactly like the abusive perpetrator. When she experiences the dominant role without really harming her partner, the survivor realizes that her fears are unfounded, and that if she is given power, she will not become an abuser.

We have also found that the enactment of these power fantasies in the bedroom serves to decrease their enactment in other relationships. For example, the husband of one survivor was able to play out his submissive fantasy in the bedroom as opposed to at the workplace, where he had let co-workers and even subordinates treat him disrespectfully. Another common situation involves the sadomasochistic couple, in which the partners humiliate and verbally abuse each other. We have found success in getting these couples to see the sexual aspect of their relating and encouraging them to move this kind of relating into the safe confines of the bedroom. Partners who are not resistant to doing this often become less abusive toward each other outside the bedroom.

Homosexual fantasies may be enacted in which one partner plays an opposite-sex role. For example, the male partner may want to experience what it is like to have woman-to-woman sex. Since many men are aroused by this fantasy, many movies are available that portray lesbian sex. The survivor may feel less threatened by this type of sex, especially if the perpetrator was a man. The filling of sexual roles and fantasies allows the survivor to experience her sexuality as healthy and positive.

The overall result of the remediation of sexual dysfunction, sharing sexual fantasies, increasing the sexual arousal of the mate, normalizing sexual pleasuring, encouraging sexual role reversals, and fulfilling fantasies is increased intimacy on the part of the couple. Intimacy, in our view, is defined as the sharing of the deepest parts of the self with another. Exposure of fantasy life, the enactment of roles that are at the deeper parts of the personality, and the uncovering of shameful secrets bring the partners closer. Their bedroom becomes a kind of "magic theater" and the very heart of their marital life. Anxiety and conflicts about money, the children, and careers will usually take a back seat when the couple experiences this kind of intimate contact. The tendency toward workaholism, extramarital affairs, and other problems is reduced accordingly.

REPARATION AND FORGIVENESS

Increased intimacy will not take place if there are old wounds and hurts from prior points in the relationship. In the endphase, the therapist must encourage the couple to talk about these old hurts in a constructive manner so that the anger can be expressed and discharged, reparation made, and, ultimately, forgiveness offered by the angered party.

The reparative process is the key to a successful resolution (Kirschner & Kirschner, 1990b). Too often, therapists try to help a couple evolve without dealing with prior ghosts and hurts and without completing a process of forgiveness. The reparative act signifies the good intentions and willingness of the hurtful or abusive partner to right the wrong. It allows the hurt partner to feel empowered—she or he is getting something in exchange, which propels the letting-go process. Forgiveness can then be offered in an authentic and meaningful way.

The therapist must be active in assisting the couple during this process by encouraging the frank expression of feelings. This is accomplished by helping one see the pain of the other, as well as by ensuring that the hurt partner expresses his or her appropriate anger while offering the other an opportunity to make it right. She or he must also ensure that the hurt partner does not use the hurt as a destructive weapon, that is, be abusive in response. The practitioner may also offer suggestions about appropriate reparative acts.

In one case, the husband of a survivor had manipulated sex in such a way that his needs were always met and hers were not. The wife had been angry about this for a number of years, but because of the incest-influenced response of silence, did not complain actively. After validating this wife's anger and expression of feelings and helping the husband to listen to her feelings, the therapist suggested that the husband have sex with his wife in the way she wanted "for 100 times to make it up to her." The survivor was pleased with this, but said, "He would never do that." The therapist challenged the husband and the husband responded, "It will be tough, but I will do it on the condition that my wife forgive me when it is all over." She assured him that she would, since that would show her how much he wanted things to be different. After six months, the partners were relating to each other very differently. The husband was less defensive and less guilty and the survivor was more at ease and less angry. The couple then returned to a more reciprocal sexual pattern.

A CASE EXAMPLE

The following transcript is a clinical portrait of a prototypical work in the endphase. In this case, the daughter, Laura (see Chapter 1), was molested by her two brothers. After the ongoing incest was stopped, work began on the marriage. Nancy, age 40, the mother, and John, age 43, her husband, had sex infrequently. She herself was an incest survivor. This session describes a breakthrough in the marital work and the survivor's reclaiming of her own projected sexuality, and illustrates the importance of forgiveness in marital therapy. The transcript includes a six-month follow-up.

Therapist: John, get it out; let's get it over with.

John: I don't know. I want to be truthful with her. I want to tell her, I want her to tell me . . . find out what differences there are . . . and see if we can make this thing work. You know, I want to be happy and I want her to be happy. But every time we try to do something, it don't work out. I told her she could quit working if it's too much. I told her that last week. But I feel even though, if I went out on a limb, no matter what I did to try, she would not be happy with me. She said she would, but I don't think so. I think there is a hurt somewhere in her that, she just don't trust me and I don't think, as long as it's there, she won't let herself go and be what I want her to be.

Therapist: What about the other way, John? How about the hurt in you

John: Oh, I got a lot of hurt in me, yeah.

Therapist: So, when did she break your heart? You said you couldn't trust her anymore.

John: I don't know, I guess the worst time was when my brother died. I think that's when it happened. Just when I needed her the most, she wasn't there.

Therapist: What happened?

Nancy: You can tell her. You told me. You can tell her.

John: No, I can't.

Therapist: That's what you do. Do you see that smile that comes over your face, John? That's that bullshit. Instead of sharing the truth, you cover it up and then it goes on and on for years. It just eats away at you like a cancer, it just eats away and then nothing she says matters. It's all tuned out. You just tune her out. You don't believe a word she says to you, good, bad, or indifferent. Have you ever worked this out, this particular hurt? Have you ever talked about it in such a way that you could get some sense of satisfaction? You never did, right?

Nancy: We did talk about it.

Therapist: But it never got worked out.

Nancy: I couldn't reach him at that time because he was in a very deep shock.

Therapist: How did she disappoint you?

Nancy: I don't know how . . .

Therapist: Yeah, that's what we are trying to find out.

John: Well, you remember what happened.

Nancy: What are you talking about? How Tom was killed?

John: No, no, what happened afterward.

Therapist: This was a kid brother of yours?

John: Yeah.

Therapist: What happened?

John: He was killed by a truck tire.

Therapist: Did you see it happen?

John: Yeah. I was there. That part hurt me for a while. I learned to live with it. What really got to me was his wife. We look alike.

Nancy: Tommy and John.

John: Yeah. His wife tried to somehow hang on to me, thinking that he was still around. And when Nancy saw Tommy's wife coming to me, she thought that somehow we were seeing each other and she accused me of sleeping with her. Nancy even told other people.

Nancy: But John, how did she really turn out?

John: That's not important to me. It's a fact that I didn't sleep with her. I just tried to make her feel better. We both missed Tommy a lot. What you did to me then was awful.

Therapist: Go ahead.

John: Why! Why couldn't you understand?

Therapist: Listen, I want you to do something for your brother. I want you to forgive her. I mean, I think that you would have wanted someone to forgive you for not telling him how much you cared about him, how good he was doing, before he died. I think you would have wanted someone to forgive you then and there. Someone to take you aside and say, "John, you did your best, but we all make mistakes." Hey, we all make mistakes.

Nancy: Tell him what you did with all Tom's money. He bought a trailer with his money.

Therapist: It's not important. You two haven't been right since that time.

Nancy: We haven't been right since before that time. We haven't been right since Joey was born. Since I caught him with my girlfriend. I forgave him, because I went back to him. I had three more kids from him. But I changed an awful lot then. I did, because I was more cautious, more careful, and I was not going to let it happen again. I'm not going to be the fool and sit back and let you have your pleasure with other girls and then expect to come back to me when you want me again. I mean, who am I? I'm supposed to be your wife.

John: Yes, but if you had been that type of wife, I wouldn't even had looked at some of these girls at that time. I wouldn't have to be interested in them.

Nancy: You always would.

John: Yeah, I always would, but I would never chase them or go after them.

Therapist: What do you mean "that kind of wife"? What kind of wife?

John: What kind of wife?

Nancy: He means a "sex" wife, go to bed and have sex every night of the week kind, and I am not that type of a woman.

Therapist: Every night of the week?

Nancy: Yeah, he'd like that. That's right.

Therapist: So, what's wrong with that, he's a healthy guy?

Nancy: Plenty, because that's not me and he knows it. I can't. If he can come home at night and I have a nice meal for him when he comes home, and he curses me out, and calls my food slop.

Therapist: You wouldn't go to bed with him then?

Nancy: How can I go to bed and really enjoy myself with him?

Therapist: That would be hard.

John: Right now, I feel like I was 21. I got the energy and the drive.

Therapist: It's not just sex.

Nancy: It is.

Therapist: It is not.

Nancy: It is.

Therapist: When I asked him how he wanted you to change, he didn't even mention sex. He said more feminine, more gentle, more sensitive.

Nancy: It's still sex.

Therapist: How about starting this week with some dinners with just the two of you. Can we start with that?

Nancy: If he comes home at a civil hour.

Therapist: What's a civil hour?

Nancy: Seven o'clock.

Therapist: John, can you be home at an hour when you can get a little special TLC here? I know it's hard for you to take, John.

John: I can come home and I can go back and work again, you know.

Nancy: That's going to be real fun.

Therapist: What fun is that? That's no fun, John.

John: Well, I can't say when I can get home, you know.

Therapist: Sure you can. How about like eight o'clock? You can make eight o'clock.

Nancy: There's a difference between sex and loving. And when you come home, go to bed, and bang bang, and then you're gone again. That's my life.

Therapist: I hope it's not that bad.

Nancy: It is, it is, it is.

Therapist: We'll get to that next. Can you come home and stay home at eight o'clock, so this lovely woman can have a special meal ready for you?

Nancy: What would you like, honey, T-bone steak or porterhouse? I'll even go out to the store and buy you wine, which I don't really approve of buying any kind of booze. How's that? How about some champagne? If that's your cup of tea, I'll give it to you. But you'd better know what to do with it afterward, buddy, or your goose is cooked.

Note: The survivor owns her own sexuality in a demanding way here, in contrast to her earlier statements that John wants a "sex" wife and that's "not me." She goes on to indicate that John is the one with a sexual problem:

Therapist: He knows what to do with it.

Nancy: I don't think so.

Therapist: John, John.

Nancy: I'll be anything you want me to be, but you have to stop condemning me or you're not going to get it. I need a couple of kind words. If you do that, you'll get a heck of a lot more out of me. But I can't, I cannot be anything more, when the hurt is in there. I get hurt very badly too.

Therapist: So John, do you forgive Nancy for that hurt?

John: For that hurt. Does it make that much difference if I say yes or no?

Nancy: I know I'll be honest with you. I never knew I hurt you that bad. I feel terrible now. I'm really really sorry, honey. Not ever, did I know. May the Lord strike me dead if I'm lying.

Therapist: No, that's the truth, that's the truth. That's why I'm making such a big deal about talking about it, and getting past the pain. You two have suffered enough. I see the pain. It's like I've been living in that house.

John: No, you could say that, but when I say it, I'm going to mean it.

Therapist: Yeah, that's right.

Nancy: So, you're saying it's that hard to forgive.

John: No, it would be a turning point. If I say I forgive you and I'm truthful about it, I expect you to be truthful about everything from now on.

Nancy: Is that so bad?

John: No, that's not so bad, if that's what you want me to say and you're willing to work from this point.

Therapist: Yes, she said she would be willing to work.

John: All right, then, I'll forgive you for hurting me when Tommy died.

Therapist: All right!

John: I told you I'm tired of being an island, I'm tired of being a one-man fighter. I don't want to fight the world by myself any more.

Therapist: You're doing the right thing.

John: I hope so.

Six months later

John: Just a couple of weeks ago, Nancy had a bad day at work. She was taking care of an old lady and the patient died. When she came home, this was on a Sunday, she was real upset. I said, "The heck with supper, the heck with the kids. Get in the car, bring a couple bottles of beer for me and bring a blanket." She said, "What do you want with a blanket?" I said, "Just bring it along, we'll get something to eat, we'll eat on the blanket." But I had other ideas.

Therapist: Right.

John: So, we got something to eat at a little stand, you know, and we took it with us. I carried the blanket to a nice, secluded place, and she said, "What are we doing here?" I said, "Well, you wanted to be away, you know." It was a nice place near the water, everything. We ate and talked and pretty soon we made love there on the blanket. She said, "Hey, this is great."

Therapist: Good, see that!

John: She said, "I like this. We have to do this again." I said, "I thought you didn't like this." She said, "I'd like to do this every Sunday, even Saturday, if I can."

As in the case of Nancy and John, the healing of old wounds helps to solidify the gains in caretaking, intimacy, and sexuality for the couple. As this occurs, the survivor owns her own sexuality and can begin to organize the couple's sex life for personal fulfillment.

THE INTRAMARITAL COALITION

The stage is now set for the therapist to begin actively to introduce the concept of the intramarital coalition. Like Napier and Whitaker (1978) and Framo (1976), we believe that marriages have the tendency not only to replicate, but also to transcend the transactional qualities of the past. Wynne (1984), in his research on healthy marriages, corroborated this hypothesis. The intramarital coalition is a vehicle by which the spouses can transcend the wounds of the past and help heal each other. In this type of relationship, each partner serves as a kind of remedial growth agent for the other (Kirschner & Kirschner, 1986).

The needs of the survivor and her spouse, depending on the extent of the abuse and deprivation in childhood, require that the marriage serve as much as possible as a therapeutic respite for each. To the extent possible with each couple, the therapist teaches each partner to provide the healing inputs, such as nurturance, discipline, programming, and support, for the other. The therapist determines the healing input of the survivor, based on his or her knowledge of her culled from hours of extensive individual therapy. With regard to the survivor's partner, the therapist attempts to have more individual sessions with him at this phase, to determine what he needs in order for the marriage to be more satisfying.

Ideally, the final step of the marital work in the endphase focuses on the establishment of the coalition for growth. The therapist conducts couples sessions to discuss what inputs each partner needs from the other to facilitate continuing growth in the absence of a relationship with the therapist. This step represents the detriangulation of the therapist out of the couple system.

The spouses learn to assist each other progressively and regressively. In the progressive aspects of family life, each spouse can be taught to promote the other's individuation and self-actualization in career or child-rearing roles. He or she learns to help the other to become more and more competent and successful in the world. In the regressive trend, each learns to provide for the other a safe haven for self-disclosure and the satisfaction of rapprochement needs. The partners practice active listening and mastery of the nurturant responses each needs. Thus the partners learn to fulfill needs for autonomy and needs for intimacy.

The survivor's partner may ask for more progressive input, perhaps asking that the survivor continue to be tough with him and not let him get away with anything. The survivor may ask for more regressive input, perhaps asking her partner for continued support as she deals with her family of origin, or more progressive help, with encouragement in career endeavors. These inputs are generally not new requests, but rather represent an extension of what the therapist has done or has directed the partner to do previously. The therapist helps the partners fine-tune the inputs needed, teaching when and how the input is to be delivered. The therapist also highlights the psychological basis for the inputs so that each partner gains more knowledge of the needs and motivations of the other.

Ideally, as the partners evolve, they become more adept and sophisticated as growth agents for each other and adjust/refine the therapist's suggestions. As they "outdo" the therapist in understanding and relating to each other, the stage is set for termination. *Comprehensive Family Therapy* (Kirschner & Kirschner, 1986) presents a more detailed discussion of the flowering of the intramarital coalition and the termination process.

SUMMARY

The endphase of treatment is focused on couples and sex therapy with the survivor and her partner. The spouses are helped to reverse their projective identificatory processes, to transcend sexual problems, to develop a creative and fulfilling sex life, and to forgive and let go of old wounds. Ideally, as the therapy winds down, the practitioner facilitates the development of a collaborative set for growth, the intramarital coalition, and the partners assume their roles as healing agents for each other.

CHAPTER 11

THE MALE SURVIVOR

"When I look back on my sexual experiences with my brother, I can't honestly say that I didn't enjoy them. In fact, I looked forward to fooling around with him."

—A 35-year-old male survivor

This chapter focuses exclusively on the male survivor, including the typical dynamics in father/stepfather–son incest, older brother–younger brother incest, and mother/stepmother–son incest. It covers issues that differentiate male survivors from female survivors and the implications these differences have for treatment. The chapter also includes a case study of a homosexual survivor who experienced extra-familial abuse.

PREVALENCE

The prevalence of the sexual abuse of males has not been well established. Different studies have yielded different ranges of victimization. Finkelhor (1984) reported a range of 2.5% to 8.7% of boys being sexually abused, whereas Sebold (1987) suggested an incidence figure closer to 8%. Risin and Koss (1987) found a similar figure among college-aged men who gave self-reports of having been sexually abused as children. Swift (1977), on the other hand, surveyed 20 clinicians in an urban mental health center and found that 33% of the male children in treatment reported sexual abuse, while 19% of the male adults reported childhood abuse. Other studies, including that of Porter (1986), put the figure at closer to one out of six boys. There are, as yet, no adequate baseline data showing the general prevalence of incest with boys.

According to both *The Spada Report* (Spada, 1979) and *The Hite Report on Male Sexuality* (Hite, 1981), over 80% of gay men were sexually abused as children. Johnson and Shrier (1987) found that eight of 11 male adolescents at an adolescent medical clinic who identified themselves as being homosexual also reported having been molested as children.

FATHER/STEPFATHER–SON INCEST

One of the most confusing and least studied areas of sexual abuse is same-sex incest. Most of the literature on the sexual abuse of males focuses on victims' statements or on generalized descriptions of issues that arise in treatment (Lew, 1988; Grubman-Black, 1990). Courtois (1988), echoing Dixon, Arnold, and Calestro (1978), has argued that father–son incest is an underreported problem because of the mislabeling of the incest as homosexual behavior or the practitioner's failure to consider this form of molestation as even possible. Since studies like those of Finkelhor (1984) and Porter (1986) have estimated the sexual molestation of boys at one in six, it is quite likely that the prevalence of homosexual incest has been underestimated. In an interesting study conducted among homosexual men (Simari & Baskin, 1982), incest with their fathers was reported as highly negative with traumatic aftereffects. First-person accounts reported by Lew (1988) and Grubman-Black (1990) also have emphasized the aggressiveness of the violation and the betrayal of trust.

Our experience with father–son incest has been with survivors who came from male-dominant families. In these systems, the mothers generally did not know what was going on between the father and son. The sons did not tell them because they feared their fathers who ruled the families with iron fists. In one particular case, however, the mother participated in the activity by encouraging both children, the son and daughter, to have sex with their father.

OLDER BROTHER–YOUNGER BROTHER INCEST

Sexual play between siblings is the only type of familial sex that has been acknowledged as a more normal part of a child's psychosexual development. This attitude of normality, especially toward siblings who are close in age, has tended to minimize both the reporting of these experiences and the establishing of some reasonable rate of prevalence in society.

Of Finkelhor's (1979) sample, 13% reported sibling sexual experiences, 74% of which were heterosexual and 26% homosexual. We have found that two types of sibling incest inevitably have traumatic aftereffects for the survivor—older brother–younger sister incest and older brother–younger brother incest. In both kinds, the age of the perpetrator, his relative power over the victim, and certain family dynamics tend to play significant roles in the trauma of the molestation. In Chapter 3 we discussed older brother–younger sister incest, whereas here we describe same-sex sibling incest.

While it has been less studied than heterosexual sibling incest, same-sex sibling incest does occur and, in our view, with greater frequency than has been reported in the literature. This may be due to a tendency among clinicians to consider same-sex sexual play, especially among boys, as part of normal maturation. For example, Harry Stack Sullivan (1953), in his classic volume *The Interpersonal Theory of Psychiatry*, argued that it was normal for chums or preadolescent boys to have homosexual contact with each other. He went on to describe how a group of juveniles attending the same school in Kansas had routinely engaged in "mutual masturbation and other presumably homosexual activity." Another boy, who was at the school at the same time, and whom Sullivan knew, admitted that he did not participate in those activities. Sullivan reported that this boy became a homosexual as an adult whereas the others married and had children. In Sullivan's view (not the authors'), the group members, by sharing a mutual intimacy, were able to overcome their feelings of being different and isolated. The nonparticipant, on the other hand, was arrested developmentally in the chum era because he was still seeking an intimate same-sex companion.

Our belief, however, is that mutual masturbation with peers, or with a brother who is close in age, is very different from most older

brother–younger brother incest. The former activity is usually initiated mutually and is under the control of all participants, whereas the
latter is almost always initiated by the older and physically stronger
brother. In this case, the participation of the younger boy is not
necessarily voluntary. In many instances, it is secured by threats of
violence or by actual violence, or is disguised as "horseplay." At
other times, the older boy may coerce his brother to have sex with a
neighbor or to masturbate in front of others. Because some victims
are naïve or immature, they may initially see these acts as play or fun.
Only later does the younger boy realize what is happening. Survivors
have reported feeling shame, anger, and betrayal about being exploited in these ways.

HOMOSEXUALITY OR ABUSE?

We have frequently been asked two important questions with regard
to same-sex incest: Is the activity a homosexual act? Is the perpetrator
a homosexual? Contrary to what Courtois (1988) and Mrazek (1981)
have written, our view of same-sex incest is that it is not a homosexual
act—it is *child sexual abuse*. When we talk about a father's molesting
his daughter, we do not refer to the act as heterosexual behavior but
as sexual abuse. The same is true for same-sex incest. As Lew
(1988) points out: "The question, then, is not one of homosexuality or
heterosexuality, but of child sexual abuse and its results" (p. 61).

In a similar vein, some writers, including Mrazek (1981) and more
recently Courtois (1988), have described the father or stepfather who
molests his son as a homosexual or "latent homosexual." Mrazek,
for example, writes: "Latent or conscious struggles with homosexual
impulses usually have been a major determinant for some of the
father's long-term behavior and character style." In the same para-
graph, however, he continues his description of these fathers in this
way: "The father may also foster other incestuous relationships, such
as between siblings, ... or engage in additional sexual activities
himself with his other children, *both male and female*" (italics added)
(p. 102).

Mrazek's description of these perpetrators is more consistent with
a diagnosis of sex-addicted pedophiles who are also voyeurs than
one of latent homosexuals. Furthermore, these pedophiles prey on

daughters as well as sons because they are child abusers, not homosexuals. In our clinical experience, most perpetrators of same-sex incest, including fathers, stepfathers, uncles, and grandfathers, are *not* homosexuals. Rather, as Lew (1988) has noted, they are pedophiles who would identify themselves as heterosexual in orientation.

MOTHER/STEPMOTHER–SON INCEST

Russell (1986) found that 5% of all sexual abuse of girls and 20% of all abuse of boys involve women, but no data were reported, specifically, for the incidence of mother–child incest. Maternal incest with sons, the more prevalent form of mother–child abuse, has received some attention in the literature. Courtois (1988), following Meiselman (1978) and Ward (1985), has categorized mother–son incest as either son-initiated or mother-initiated incest. According to these authors, son-initiated incest occurs when older adolescents or young adults "rape" their mothers. Rather than holding the mothers responsible for all forms of incest, Courtois argues that, as with other forms of rape, it is time to hold the older male child responsible for the sexual act. Ward (1985) has also claimed that this type of incest is underreported because mothers have difficulty acknowledging that their sons have raped them.

In our combined clinical experience, we have never seen a single case that could be construed as son-initiated incest. Yet, some survivors have confessed in therapy that, as they matured, they came to enjoy sex with their mothers, and that, under the influence of drugs or alcohol, they were able to initiate the sex. These cases, however, illustrate that while sons may have initiated the incestuous activities at some point, they had already been victimized by their mothers and, in some instances, this had gone on for many years. Nevertheless, it is possible that under certain extreme conditions mother rape may occur.

Whereas most of the various types of incest discussed in Chapter 3 are found in intact or two-parent families, incest between mothers and sons seems to take place more frequently in single-parent families. In these families, the mothers have turned to their sons to satisfy their needs for affection and sexual gratification. Single-parent families, like stepfamilies, are highly vulnerable to stress and dysfunction because they often lack both emotional and economic support systems. Under these conditions, mothers and sons come to rely on each other to meet their mutual needs for support. Over time, they may become increasingly isolated from outsiders and more dependent on each other. In this vulnerable state, for example, the son's need to be special to someone may be exploited by the mother through her initiating sexual contact.

CLINICAL DESCRIPTIONS OF INCESTUOUS MOTHERS

In the absence of empirical data on women perpetrators, we have only clinical descriptions and a few first-hand accounts from survivors of maternal incest. These descriptions, like those of male perpetrators, have tended to defuse the myth that these mothers are more psychotic or evil than most outpatients. Instead, they have portrayed the incestuous mother as having been victimized herself, as lacking resources, and as suffering from alcoholism and other problems.

Survivors have reported to us that their mothers were alcoholic or chemically dependent. Alcoholism and substance abuse in female perpetrators have also been found by McCarty (1986), Chasnoff et al. (1986), and Groth (1982). Some of these accounts have described the incest as occurring during bouts of drinking, much as other survivors have reported with male perpetrators. Indeed, there seem to be other parallels between male and female perpetrators. Alcoholism, sex addiction, a history of physical or sexual abuse as children, and a greater tendency to abuse the opposite-sex child have all been found to be associated with both male and female abusers.

SURVIVORS OF MATERNAL INCEST

A recent study by Carnes (1991) of 290 sex addicts illustrates the potential impact of maternal abuse. The findings showed that 15% of the males and 9% of the female addicts had been "sexually fondled" by their mothers. Carnes also reported that 11% of the males and 3% of the females were forced to have sex with their mothers. Unfortunately, no data were presented on how many of these sex addicts had themselves become abusers.

One of the surprising outcomes of Carnes' work with sex addicts was that when he asked men to rank order their five worst abusers, they listed their mothers at the top. Women addicts did not list their mothers among the top five. It is likely, then, that women are molesting their sons at a greater rate than they are their daughters, just as fathers are molesting daughters at a greater rate than they are their sons.

The following case example illustrates how some families cope when the fathers have to leave their homes because of the demands of their careers or of military service. The latter situation has also been documented by Crigler (1984) in his case study of a military family in which mother–son incest occurred.

THE CASE OF TONY

Tony was conceived on one of his father's leaves from military service and was 2 years old before meeting his father for the first time. Tony and his mother then moved from base to base following his father's postings.

When Tony was 7, the Navy gave his father an important promotion that involved a mandatory move to Alaska. Tony's mother refused to leave the South, where they had lived for a time, because she had made a few friends there. Tony's father left without them, and Tony remembered seeing him only three times over the next three years. It was during this period that Tony's mother began to molest him.

In therapy, Tony related how the incest had started. Much to his shame, his mother had continued to bathe him even though he felt "too old." One day, when she was cleaning his penis, he objected, whereupon his mother told him that she could make him feel good there. His mother began to fondle and caress him and Tony remembered getting his first erection. According to Tony, he experienced both shame and pleasure.

This pattern of "special time" during bathing, as Tony's mother referred to it, continued until, one day after school, Tony's mother called out to him from her bedroom. Tony remembered that she smelled funny, probably from alcohol. His mother lay on the bed dressed in a housecoat with nothing on underneath. She told Tony that she was very sad and needed a back rub to make her feel better. The back rub ended with her taking Tony's hands and showing him how to make her "feel good." Within a year of their special times in the bathtub, Tony and his mother were engaging in mutual masturbation and oral sex.

When Tony was 10 years old, his father returned and his mother consented to move the family to California. The incest stopped completely, and with it, the overly enmeshed relationship.

Tony's adolescence was marked by school failure, truancy, and some petty thievery. He explored both homosexual and heterosexual activities, but was unable to maintain a steady relationship. As a young adult, Tony still could not create a relationship and went from job to job. He finally entered treatment at age 30 because of depression, low self-esteem, some drug use, and intense feelings of loneliness.

DIFFERENCES BETWEEN MALE AND FEMALE SURVIVORS

Male survivors differ from female victims in several key ways, including defensive denial around the initiation of the abuse, identity confusion with regard to sexual preference, and, in some cases, identifying with and becoming perpetrators.

Male survivors often minimize and qualify the sexual abuse they have suffered. For example, victims of older brother–younger brother incest have reported that the sexual interactions were just playing around or "horseplay." For them, the early sexual experiences have been reframed into more normal sibling transactions. The denial or minimization of the abuse can be interpreted in light of gender-based differences. Victimization is often seen by men as a feminine or weak position. Admitting or acknowledging "weakness" is not a quality that comes as easily to men as it does to women.

A second difference between male and female survivors revolves around the impact of the abuse on sexual identity. For heterosexual male victims, there seems to be an additional layer of shame that they feel which most females do not feel. In treatment, these clients often report that the abuse caused them anxiety over their identity as males. They worried about becoming gay or losing their manhood. These reactions are difficult to admit, even to members of the family. Our goal in treatment is to help these survivors overcome their shame and disclose the abuse to their families, whether it was extra- or intrafamilial abuse.

The identity confusion reported by some males may also be a by-product of certain gender-related expectations. Blatt and Shickman (1984) have theorized that psychopathology may follow a gender-based path. In their view, dysfunction in males is often expressed in symptoms that center on self-concept, living up to performance expectations, and fulfilling obligations. This is in contrast to women whose predominant concerns revolve around issues of intimacy and interpersonal relationships. For some men (LoPiccolo & Blatt, 1972), these struggles with self-concept take the form of confusion in sexual identity.

As noted in Chapter 3, male perpetrators were often abused themselves. Two different reports have shown that between 30% and 50% of male offenders were either sexually molested or had witnessed incest between their fathers and sisters (Pelto, 1981: Kaufman & Zigler, 1987). No such finding about female victims has yet been documented.

Some writers have suggested (e.g., Courtois, 1988) that the findings of gender differences with regard to becoming perpetrators can be explained on the basis of cognitive and perceptual differences between the sexes. Carmen, Rieker, and Mills (1984) found that male victims tended to deal with the trauma by externalization, whereas females usually coped through internalization. In this schema, males would externalize by becoming perpetrators, while females would become depressed.

Implications for Treatment

The differences between male and female survivors have consequences for treatment. In our experience, male clients require somewhat more confrontation to overcome their denial, especially if they are also perpetrators. Thus the therapeutic stance required in treatment is somewhat stronger and has more of a paternal element.

In general, male survivors lack positive male role models. As the poet Robert Bly (1990) has observed, many men suffer from a wound, a void where their fathers' input should have been. This is particularly true for male victims. For them, being a man is connected with being either abandoned or victimized. They may suffer from a weak sense of male identity or even have confusion over their sexual preference. Therapy, therefore, must aim at transforming these internalized models of manhood into more positive and constructive ones.

In our work, we provide "fathering" input to our clients in several ways: role playing, direct guidance, and sending them into the world of men. Role-playing situations from a male standpoint can be very helpful to some clients. For example, some clients don't have a clue as to how to discipline their sons because they themselves were either abused or neglected. Role playing a father disciplining his child, with the therapist as "parent" and the client as "son," can serve two functions. First, it models appropriate limit-setting behavior. Second, the "as if" exercise gives the survivor a corrective transactional experience of limit setting from a transference figure and usually results in the strengthening of the therapeutic alliance.

Direct guidance is something many survivors did not get from their fathers. Male survivors often lack basic information and so are unable to make appropriate decisions. Sending them to take courses where they can learn about managing money or investments or suggesting books and newsletters to read is just one example of the kind of guidance many survivors need. Another example is in the area of education. Some survivors need to be encouraged to go back to school to improve their careers. An active therapeutic stance coupled with a realistic belief in the client can help transform the identity of the person from that of being a victim to one marked by self-pride and empowerment.

Confrontation is often necessary with male survivors when direct guidance is ignored. But, because confrontation threatens certain clients, it must be undertaken only if the therapeutic alliance is strong. In the case of Andy, discussed later, the client's hostility toward the clinician does not deter the clinician from pressing the survivor about meeting with his parents. The therapist's determination to stay on track ultimately leads to a breakthrough in the therapy.

The third strategy in helping male clients is perhaps the most important. We ask our clients to seek out the world of men. We may suggest going to a health club or "Y" to play in a basketball or tennis league. With some clients, we may recommend a men's group so that they can learn that other men have feelings of weakness or confusion. Some men prefer a male survivor group or a group for homosexual alcoholics. Whatever the preference, however, the emphasis should be on a strictly male activity because the experience with other men will help build a masculine identity.

Special Issues of Homosexual Survivors

We have often been asked if homosexual incest or extrafamilial homosexual abuse leads to the choice of a homosexual life-style. It is true that some homosexual victims will question their preference given the incest or the abuse. In these cases, there is usually substantial confusion about their identities in general, and their preference in particular. But in our view, sexual preference is not a result of the victimization. For most survivors, the incest certainly affects how they are sexually and how they conduct relationships, but their preference is based on other factors, most notably, biological ones.

Homosexual men have reported that when same-sex incest or abuse involved coercion, their sexual enjoyment was greatly diminished. Even those men who reported knowing at 6 or 7 years of age that they had a homosexual preference claimed to have ambivalent feelings about the incest. On the one hand, they were greatly attracted to the perpetrator's much larger genitals; on the other, they were afraid of being hurt. At the same time, they also confessed to using these sexual experiences as fantasy material during masturbation, even though they ended up feeling somewhat guilty and ashamed.

In some instances, the victim who is homosexual is molested by a neighbor or older brother who is not. In these cases, we have found that the abuse becomes even more traumatic if the perpetrator teases or taunts the victim about being a girl or in some other way refers to him as feminine. In one case, the abuser was the older brother, who would call the victim "Lila," which happened to be his girlfriend's name. When the younger boy ran to his father and cried, the father only laughed heartily.

Another major issue for both male and female homosexual survivors is "coming out" to their parents. While disclosing their sexual preference is difficult for nonvictims as well, we have found that survivors who have not revealed the abuse or confronted their families about it are less likely to admit their homosexuality. They lead secretive lives in which the pain of the past and the fear of being found out in the present are inextricably bound up. In our treatment of gay survivors, we try to help them find the courage to deal with their families, not only about the abuse, but also about their choice of life-style. The case example in the next section illustrates how these two issues can be dealt with simultaneously.

EXTRAFAMILIAL ABUSE

As Finkelhor (1984) and others have shown, most boys, unlike girls, are sexually abused outside the family. However, survivors of extra-familial abuse often have difficulty acknowledging being molested by camp counselors, neighbors, older boys, clergy, or teachers. Many of our clients, especially those who are gay, have characterized these experiences as "affectionate," "caring," and not harmful. Indeed, for some boys who are starved for affection from their own fathers or who have no male figures in their lives, the perpetrator's interest in them is special and welcomed. They are extremely vulnerable to perpetrators who operate through subtleness and seduction. Survivors, who are clients, have described how at the preadolescent ages of 11 to 13, they would lie to their parents about where they were going and then go to an older male's house or a known cruising place for homosexuals in order to have sex. The allure of affectionate males was for some survivors "too strong to resist." These survivors experience less guilt about the activities.

The following discussion of the treatment of a male survivor includes a transcript of a session in which he is helped to talk to his parents about two issues: being sexually abused and being a homosexual.

THE CASE OF ANDY

Andy, a 27-year-old white, gay male, initially presented in psychotherapy for depression, feelings of isolation, and a sense that his life was going nowhere. About six months into treatment, Andy casually reported that he believed that he had been sexually abused as a young child by a man, but had no firm memory of either the abuse or the abuser. The therapist contracted with Andy to help him recover the memories.

Eventually, Andy retrieved the dissociated memories. He remembered that he was molested by a man who was a relatively close friend of the family, and who was like an "uncle" to Andy. But the most

troubling and haunting memory was one in which he told his mother
of the abuse shortly after the second time he had been abused. She
had cleaned him up, he reported, and sent him to bed, telling him
not to talk about it to anyone. While the abuse did not continue, Andy
remembered that neither his mother nor his father ever asked him
about it or ever comforted him.

While in therapy, Andy made steady progress toward his career
and social goals. However, there remained a distinctively false quality in his interactions with significant others. As part of his false
façade, Andy had not told his parents about his being gay. In the
therapist's view, not "coming out" to them was also connected to
the issue of confronting his parents around their reaction to the
abuse. Often, when a male survivor confronts his parents about
extrafamilial sexual abuse, other unspoken issues surface and can be
addressed. In fact, some survivors have told us that they cannot talk
about the sexual abuse because their parents may find out about
other secrets.

In the following session transcript, the therapist, David MacFarlane, M.A., confronts Andy on his fears of being more honest with
his family. The session begins with the therapist's focusing on the
goals of empowering Andy to be more real with his parents and to
confront them on the sexual abuse. He also ties Andy's lack of openness with his parents to other relationship difficulties.

Therapist: You are not real with them. How can you expect to have
    a real relationship with anyone?

Andy: What is this bullshit? Like everything in the world revolves
    around my mother and father. Give me a break (laughs).

Therapist: How can you expect a genuine relationship with anyone if
    you can't be real with your parents?

Andy: How can I expect it? Because I expect it, that's why.

Therapist: That's fantasy land.

Andy: Is it?

Therapist: Yeah.

Andy: What if they die tomorrow?

Therapist: God hope they don't.

Andy: Oh, because if they do, I'm doomed?

Therapist: Look, Andy, do you want an honest relationship with
    someone or don't you?

Andy: Oh, please, we've been through this before, haven't we? I've thought about this all right. So, fuck you.

Therapist: What's to think about?

Andy: What do you mean what's to think about? There's a lot to think about.

Therapist: What's to think about? Andy, we have thought this through 10 times.

Andy: Have we? Well, maybe we'll think it through 10 more before I actually do it.

Later in the session

Therapist: Real people address the issues.

Andy: But my parents don't even live around here, why are they an issue?

Therapist: You have never left home because you're still frightened to be honest with them.

Andy: (Laughs) And once I do this, I will be all grown up, a free and independent person, and my life will just take off, right? I'll be fixed. I'll be cured.

Therapist: It's a necessary step.

Andy: I know that, all right? (Laughs)

Therapist: So what's the problem?

Andy: How should I know? You're the therapist here. You tell me. What's the problem?

Therapist: Oh no, you tell me.

Andy: Oh no, no, I insist, really. I am depending on your superior knowledge and expertise and training. It's cold in here.

Therapist: I told you it can get even colder.

Andy: (Laughs)

Note how the therapist disarms Andy by remaining doggedly persistent and essentially ignoring Andy's defensive hostility and resistance.

Therapist: So, what's the problem here?

Andy: You already know. You ought to know.

Therapist: What? Come on, say it.

Andy: (Laughs)
>Long pause.

Therapist: All right. I'll help you out here. Are you ready? Repeat after me.

Andy: (Laughs)

Therapist: "I'm afraid."

Andy: (Laughs)

The therapist is using a psychodramatic technique in which he verbalizes the client's fears. This allows him to go underneath Andy's resistance and access the underlying anxiety-provoking thoughts.

Therapist: I'm afraid,

Andy: I'm afraid,

Therapist: that if I tell my parents,

Andy: that if I tell my parents,

Therapist: that I'm gay,

Andy: that I'm gay,

Therapist: and that they were no help to me at all when I was molested,

Andy: and that they were no help to me when I was molested,

Therapist: that I'm afraid,

Andy: that I'm afraid,

Therapist: that they will behave,

Andy: that they will behave,

Therapist: Now, fill in the rest.

At this key point, the therapist tries to get Andy to voice his fears as to why he is so reluctant to confront his parents.

Andy: the same way.

Therapist: Which is?

Andy: Worse.

Therapist: Which is?

Andy: A)—like they don't give a shit.

Therapist: Not likely, but go ahead.

Andy: B)—(pause). Well, I think my father would probably be pissed off. My mother may be sort of condescending.

Therapist: Tell me what she's likely to say.

Andy: "Oh, you poor thing, you should have told us a long time ago."

Therapist: And that will drive you wild.

Andy: (Laughs) You're right. That's right. It will piss me off. It will make me so damn mad that . . . just like when they said to me, "we're worried about you."

Therapist: (In a sickeningly sweet voice) "We're worried about you."

The therapist's knowledge of how Andy's parents relate to him is reassuring to him. By facilitating the expression of his fears, the therapist has helped the client move past a barrier to being more authentic. Now the previously hidden emotions can emerge and the client becomes more assertive rather than hostile.

Andy: I used to disappear for three and four days, over a whole weekend, and nobody ever asked where the hell I was.

Therapist: Yeah. Talk to them in those chairs (pointing to empty chairs).

Andy: (To imaginary parents) What do you mean you are worried about me?

Therapist: Go on.

Andy: What do you mean you care about me? Where the fuck were you when I was 8 years old?

Therapist: Role-play their answer.

Andy: (As his mother) You are imagining it, it never happened. You're crazy, you're crazy, you're imagining it. (Andy's mother used to tell him that he was crazy.)

Therapist: And you'll say?

Andy: I don't know what I'll say. Maybe part of me believes it. Part of me does believe that I'm crazy. That it never happened and I'm crazy.

Therapist: Right. And what would an honest person say to them now?

Andy: No, I'm not crazy.

Therapist: (As Andy, pointing to the chairs) I'm not crazy.

Andy: (Laughs) They're going to tell me I'm crazy. They always tell me that I'm crazy.

Therapist: And you're going to tell them that you're not. You damn well know you're not.

Andy: But what if they sit there and they tell me about how much they love me and all that bullshit?

Therapist: Do you believe that they handled the abuse situation with love?

Andy: No, I don't.

Therapist: Love isn't something you say to someone, it's something you do.

Andy: See, the issue here isn't really telling them that I'm gay. The issue here is confronting them over the guy who screwed me, isn't it?

Therapist: Yes, yes. It's telling them how you suffered with that, how ashamed you were, how helpless you felt, and how he betrayed your trust. And no one cared enough to listen to all that.

Andy: And why I haven't been able to tell them about being gay and my life-style. It's because I never really believed that they cared or that they were interested.

Therapist: They do care. But they're frightened of facing the truth.

Andy: It's why I don't tell people anything about myself unless they ask because I just learned a long time ago that if people wanted to know, they would ask. I just stopped telling people what was going on because I know they did not want to know.

Therapist: You mean your folks didn't.

Andy: Right. That's what I mean.

Therapist: Not everybody is your folks.

Andy: But at the time they were everybody.

Therapist: I know.

Significantly, the therapist corrects Andy's perception that people don't care, a belief that prevents the client from forming meaningful relationships. Also, compare this last interaction with Andy's opening statement, "What is this bullshit? Like everything in the world revolves around my mother and father."

Therapist: Not everybody is your parent.

Andy: I know. Well, maybe I don't know. I don't know.

Therapist: You don't know that. You still act that way with people.

Again, the therapist corrects Andy's distorted perception of people. The client becomes even more open about his concerns.

Andy: But I just don't know if I can do it. Sure, I can see myself picking up the phone and calling them and saying, "Mom and Dad, I'm gay."

Therapist: You don't say that.

Andy: I know, but I don't know if I can do all the other stuff.

Therapist: Tell me your fantasy about it.

Andy: I'm just gonna lose and they're gonna win. They are going to tell me I'm crazy.

Therapist: You need some help with this. Of course, they're going to tell you that.

Now the therapist begins to press Andy for a commitment to action.

Therapist: So, we need an agreement here.

Andy: When I do this?

Therapist: We need an agreement. First, we have to agree that you're going to do it.

Andy: I know I'm going to do it.

Therapist: Great.

Andy: I've been thinking that anyway, even without talking to you.

Therapist: Great.

Andy: You're just a tool here.

    (Laughter by both)

Andy's assertion that the therapist is a tool still carries a hostile tone, but it is also absolutely accurate. The therapy is a tool or vehicle for the client's growth. Andy has, in his own way, organized the therapist to confront and challenge him so that he can face his parents honestly and maturely.

Therapist: So, how much time do you need to decide to talk to them?

Andy: I don't know. October 11 is Coming Out Day, or is it October 12?

Therapist: What's that?

Andy: It's National Coming Out Day.

It becomes clear that Andy had been thinking long and hard about coming out and has organized the therapist to push him past the fears.

Therapist: All right. There's your deadline.

Andy: That only gives me two to three weeks.

Therapist: That's right. You're going to need some rehearsal here. Right?

Andy: You know I don't like that role-playing stuff. You know I don't.

Therapist: It will do you good.

Later in the session, Andy's resistance reappears as the reality of the deadline sinks in. In Chapter 6, we described how normal development follows a zigzag course of progress to regress to progress, a process called progressive abreactive regression (PAR) (Kirschner & Kirschner, 1986). In this case, progress for Andy was agreeing to tell his parents and break the silence. Having agreed to move forward, we would expect that he would regress in that he would become fearful and resistant. The therapist encourages Andy's expressions of fear while he remains firm in not allowing the regression to interfere with the commitment to go forward with the confrontation.

Andy: No, I don't want to. I'm not going to do it.

Therapist: You are.

Andy: I can't. I can't.

Therapist: Yes, you can. Yes, you can.

Andy: It will probably traumatize me and I'll experience a setback.

Therapist: So, when?

Andy: I can't do it.

Therapist: You can, too. I'll be here. I'll help you with it. You know I'll help you with it. I've helped you with lots of hard things, haven't I?

Andy: I don't know, have you?

Therapist: So what about it?

Andy: What if they come up here? They come for dinner or something.

Therapist: Yeah, so?

Andy: And we go through all of this?

Therapist: Yeah, and . . .

Andy: Then they have to leave and they go home . . .

Therapist: Okay, so they have to go home.

Andy: They are so upset they have an accident and they both die. Or worse yet, they don't die, they live.

Therapist: That's your wish coming out here.

Andy: No, they live and they end up like . . .

Therapist: You'd love to kill them off.

Andy: . . . stuck on a respirator or something.

Therapist: Ah, you'd love that, wouldn't you? Stop worrying about them. They'll be fine. They'll be who they are. You are not going to kill them off.

Andy: What if they kill me?

Therapist: They're not going to kill you either.

Andy: Don't be so sure.

Therapist: You know very well they are not going to kill you.

The therapist allows Andy to express his foundation fears of annihilation and abandonment. The therapist retains a posture of realistic reassurance so that Andy can feel safe.

The therapist, in subsequent sessions, explored with Andy how, if he did not confront his parents, his core fears would continue to influence his intimate relationships. Andy needed to have an experience of speaking, confronting, and challenging his parents in the face of his fears of losing everything, of killing them or being killed or rejected by them. On the other hand, if he were able to confront his parents and have a successful resolution, the experience would be very corrective. Andy would then be able to feel more okay about saying the truth and being real with the important people in his life. He would view himself as a stronger person, and as someone who was more willing to confront his own doubts and fears.

Epilogue

Shortly after this session, Andy invited his parents to his home. In an emotional disclosure, he revealed to them that he was gay. Just as Andy had predicted, the parents were vaguely supportive. In a subsequent session, Andy told the therapist that he was also going to tell his parents that he had been molested as a child.

SUMMARY

Male survivors differ from female survivors in three ways: defensive denial around who initiated the abuse, identity confusion about sexual preference, and, in some cases, identifying with and becoming perpetrators. In our view, homosexuality is not an outcome of childhood abuse, but rather a product of biology. It is true, however, that homosexual boys are more vulnerable to the advances of perpetrators because of their sexual preference. The therapeutic stance with male survivors emphasizes a "fathering" or paternal quality because these men often were raised without the benefit of positive male role models.

EPILOGUE

This comprehensive treatment program for adult incest survivors provides a step-by-step structure designed to deal with the emotional, cognitive, and psychosomatic problems, as well as the interpersonal difficulties survivors face both in their families of creation and families of origin. We view this program as an optimal model for treatment. Obviously, not every case proceeds through every step of the program. But having the comprehensive model for treatment in mind allows the clinician to have a map for growth that both maximizes the potential for gain and also guards against the creation of a ceiling barrier to the survivor's healing and personal development.

The current zeitgeist of openness to the realities of childhood abuse leaves the practitioner vulnerable to errors that he or she may create such ceiling barriers. The therapist may overly magnify the extent or effects of the abuse or inadvertently help to create painful cutoffs from the family of origin. If confrontations with the family of origin are discouraged as totally hopeless, or conducted without preparation or without the goal of resolution in mind, they may result in the client becoming further hurt and estranged. Neither of these actions are in the best interests of the survivor.

We feel that it is important for the practitioner working with incest survivors to guard against these errors. The survivor needs to become conscious of the incestuous experiences and the damage caused by them, but this is only part of the healing journey. The journey ideally ends with a letting go of the past and the active creation of a new present and future.

The approach described in this book has shown itself to be powerful and effective. It is more easily applied by clinicians who are comfortable with directive techniques and those who are familiar with couples and family therapy. Clinicians who do not have such experience should use the approach under appropriate supervision.

REFERENCES

American Psychiatric Association (1987). *Diagnostic and statistical manual of mental disorders* (3rd ed., rev.). Washington, DC: Author.

Angelou, M. (1980). *I know why the caged bird sings.* New York: Bantam.

Barlow, D.H., O'Brien, G.T., & Last, C. (1983). Couples treatment of agoraphobia: Initial outcome. In R. Spitzer & J.B. Williams (Eds.), *Psychotherapy research: Where are we and where should we go?* New York: Guilford.

Barlow, D.H., O'Brien, G.T., & Last, C. (1984). Couples treatment of agoraphobia. *Behavior Therapy, 15,* 41–58.

Bass, E., & Davis, L. (1988). *The courage to heal: A guide for women survivors of child sexual abuse.* New York: Harper & Row.

Bass, E., & Thornton, L. (1983). *I never told anyone: Writings by women survivors of child sexual abuse.* New York: Harper & Row.

Bateson, G., Jackson, D.D., Haley, J., & Weakland, J. (1956). Towards a theory of schizophrenia. *Behavior Science, 1,* 251–264.

Benward, J., & Densen-Gerber, J. (1975). Incest as a causative factor in anti-social behavior: An exploratory study. *Contemporary Drug Problems, 4,* 323–340.

Black, C. (1981). *It will never happen to me: Children of alcoholics.* Denver: MAC.

Bland, K., & Hallam, R.S. (1981). Relationship between response to graded exposure and marital satisfaction in agoraphobics. *Behavior Research and Therapy, 19,* 335–338.

Blatt, S.J., & Shickman, S. (1984). Two primary configurations of psychopathology. *Psychoanalysis and Contemporary Thought, 7,* 187–254.

Bly, R. (1990). *Iron John.* Reading, MA: Addison-Wesley.

Brady, K. (1979). *Father's days: A true story of incest.* New York: Dell.

Briere, J. (1984, April). *The effects of childhood sexual abuse on later psychological functioning: Defining a post-sexual abuse syndrome.* Presented at the third National Conference on the Sexual Victimization of Children, Washington, DC.

Briere, J., & Runtz, M. (1985, August). *Symptomatology associated with prior sexual abuse in a non-clinical sample.* Presented at the annual meeting of the American Psychological Association, Los Angeles.

Briere, J., & Runtz, M. (1986). Suicidal thoughts and behaviors in former sexual abuse victims. *Canadian Journal of Behavioral Science, 18,* 413–423.

215

Browne, A., & Finkelhor, D. (1986). Impact of child sexual abuse: A review of the literature. *Psychological Bulletin, 99*, 66–77.

Calof, D. (1987, March). *Treating adult survivors of incest and child abuse.* Workshop at the Family Therapy Networker Symposium, Washington, DC.

Carmen, E.H., Rieker, P.R., & Mills, T. (1984). Victims of violence and psychiatric illness. *American Journal of Psychiatry, 143*, 378–383.

Carnes, P. (1991). *Don't call it love: Recovery from sexual addiction.* New York: Bantam.

Chasnoff, I.J., Burns, W.J., Schnoll, S.H., Burns, K., Chisum, G., & Kyle-Spore, L. (1986). Maternal-neonatal incest. *American Journal of Orthopsychiatry, 56*, 577–580.

Comfort, A. (1972). *The joy of sex.* New York: Simon & Schuster.

Courtois, C.A. (1979). Characteristics of a volunteer sample of adult women who experienced incest in childhood and adolescence. *Dissertation Abstracts International, 40A*, 3194A.

Courtois, C.A. (1988). *Healing the incest wound.* New York: Norton.

Coyne, J.C. (1987). Depression, biology, marriage, and marital therapy. *Journal of Marital and Family Therapy, 13*, 393–407.

Crigler, P. (1984). Incest in the military family. In F. Kaslow & R. Ridenour (Eds.), *The military family.* New York: Guilford.

Dixon, K.N., Arnold, L.E., & Calestro, K. (1978). Father–son incest: Underreported psychiatric problem? *American Journal of Psychiatry, 135*, 835–838.

Ellenson, G.S. (1985). Detecting a history of incest: A predictive syndrome. *Social Casework, 66*, 525–532.

Ellenson, G.S. (1986). Disturbances in perception in adult female incest survivors. *Social Casework, 67*, 149–159.

Ellis, A., & Harper, R.A. (1975). *A new guide to rational living.* North Hollywood, CA: Wilshire Books.

Emslie, G.J., & Rosenfeld, A.A. (1983). Incest reported by children and adolescents hospitalized for severe psychiatric problems. *American Journal of Psychiatry, 140*, 708–711.

Erikson, E. (1950). *Childhood and society.* New York: Norton.

Evert, K. (1987). *When you're ready: A woman's healing from childhood physical and sexual abuse by her mother.* Walnut Creek, CA: Launch Press.

Finkelhor, D. (1978). Psychological, cultural and family factors in incest and family sexual abuse. *Journal of Marriage and Family Counseling, 4*, 41–49.

Finkelhor, D. (1979). *Sexually victimized children.* New York: Free Press.

Finkelhor, D. (1984). *Child sexual abuse: New theory and research.* New York: Free Press.

Fossum, M.A., & Mason, M.J. (1986). *Facing shame.* New York: Norton.

Framo, J.L. (1976). Family of origin as a therapeutic resource for adults in marital and family therapy: You can and should go home again. *Family Process, 25*, 193–210.

Friday, N. (1973). *My secret garden.* New York: Trident.

Garber, J., & Seligman, M.E.D. (1980). *Human helplessness: Theory and application.* New York: Academic.

Glueck, B.C. (1965). Pedophilia. In R. Slovenko (Ed.), *Sexual behavior and the law.* Springfield, IL: Charles C. Thomas.

Groth, A.N. (1982). The incest offender. In S.M. Sgroi (Ed.), *Handbook of clinical interventions in child sexual abuse.* Lexington, MA: Lexington Books.

Grubman-Black, S.D. (1990). *Broken boys/mending men.* Blue Ridge Summit, PA: Tab Books.

Hafner, R.J. (1977). The husbands of agoraphobic women and their influence on treatment outcome. *British Journal of Psychotherapy, 131,* 289–294.

Herman, J. (1981). *Father–daughter incest.* Cambridge, MA: Harvard University Press.

Herman, J., Russell, D., & Trocki, K. (1986). Long-term effects of incestuous abuse in childhood. *American Journal of Psychiatry, 138,* 967–970.

Hite, S. (1981). *The Hite report on male sexuality.* New York: Knopf.

Johnson, R.L., & Shrier, D. (1987). Past sexual victimization by females of male patients in an adolescent medicine clinic population. *American Journal of Psychiatry, 144,* 650–652.

Kaplan, H.S. (1974). *The new sex therapy.* New York: Brunner/Mazel.

Kaplan, H.S. (1979). *Disorders of sexual desire and other new concepts and techniques in sex therapy.* New York: Brunner/Mazel.

Kaplan, H.S. (1989). *How to overcome premature ejaculation.* New York: Brunner/Mazel.

Kaufman, J., & Zigler, E. (1987). Do abused children become abusive parents? *American Journal of Orthopsychiatry, 57,* 186–191.

Kempe, R.S., & Kempe. C.H. (1984). *The common secret: Sexual abuse of children and adolescents.* New York: Freeman.

Kinsey, A.C., Pomeroy, W.B., Martin, C.E., & Gebhard, P. (1953). *Sexual behavior in the human female.* Philadelphia: Saunders.

Kinston, W. (1983). A theoretical context for shame. *International Journal of Psychoanalysis, 64,* 213–226.

Kirschner, D.A., & Kirschner, S. (1986). *Comprehensive family therapy.* New York: Brunner/Mazel.

Kirschner, D.A., & Kirschner, S. (1990a). Comprehensive family therapy. In F. Kaslow (Ed.), *Voices in family psychology* (Vol. 2, pp. 231–243). Newbury Park, CA: Sage.

Kirschner, D.A., & Kirschner, S. (1990b). Reparation and forgiveness in marital life. *The Family Psychologist, 6,* 30–31.

Kirschner, D.A., & Kirschner, S. (1992). Comprehensive family therapy in the treatment of spouse abuse. In R. Weitz (Ed.), *Psychotherapy in independent practice: Current issues for clinicians.* (pp. 67–76). New York: Haworth Press.

Kohut, H. (1977). *The restoration of the self.* New York: International Universities Press.

Lazarus, A.A. (1976). *Multimodal behavior therapy.* New York: Springer.

Lees, S.W. (1981). *Guidelines for helping female victims and survivors of incest.* Cambridge, MA: Incest Resources.

Leupnitz, D.A. (1988). *The family interpreted.* New York: Basic Books.

Lew, M. (1988). *Victims no longer.* New York: Harper & Row.

LoPiccolo, J., & Blatt, S.J. (1972). Cognitive styles and sexual identity. *Journal of Clinical Psychology, 28*, 148–151.

Lundberg-Love, P.K. (1990). Adult survivors of incest. In R.T. Ammerman & M. Hersen (Eds.), *Treatment of family violence: A sourcebook.* New York: Wiley.

Lundberg-Love, P.K., Crawford, C.M., & Geffner, R.A. (1987, October). *Characteristics and treatment of adult incest survivors.* Presented at the annual meeting of the Southwestern Psychological Association, New Orleans.

Lundberg-Love, P.K., Mannion, S., Ford, K., Geffner, R., & Peacock, L. (1992). The long-term consequences of childhood incestuous victimization upon adult women's psychological symptomatology. *Journal of Child Sexual Abuse, 1*, 81–102.

Machotka, P., Pittman, F.S., & Flomenhaft, K. (1967). Incest as a family affair. *Family Process, 6*, 98–116.

Maltz, W., & Holman, B. (1987). *Incest and sexuality.* Lexington, MA: Lexington Books.

Maslow, A.H. (1971). *The farther reaches of human nature.* New York: Viking.

Masson, J.M. (1984). *The assault on truth: Freud's suppression of the seduction theory.* New York: Farrar, Straus, & Giroux.

McCarty, L.M. (1986). Mother–child incest: Characteristics of the offender. *Child Welfare, 65*, 447–458.

Meiselman, K. (1978). *Incest: A psychological study of causes and effects with treatment recommendations.* San Francisco: Jossey-Bass.

Miller, A. (1981). *Prisoners of childhood.* New York: Basic Books.

Miller, A. (1983). *For your own good: Hidden cruelty in child-rearing and the roots of violence.* New York: Farrar, Straus, & Giroux.

Miller, A. (1984). *Thou shalt not be aware: Society's betrayal of the child.* New York: New American Library.

Miller, A. (1990). *Banished knowledge.* New York: Doubleday.

Milton, F., & Hafner, R.J. (1979). The outcome of behavior therapy for agoraphobia in relation to marital adjustment. *Archives of General Psychiatry, 36*, 907–911.

Morris, M. (1982). *If I should die before I wake.* New York: Dell.

Mrazek, P.B. (1981). The nature of incest: A review of contributing factors. In P.B. Mrazek & C.H. Kempe (Eds.), *Sexually abused children and their families.* New York: Pergamon.

Napier, G., & Whitaker, C. (1978). *The family crucible.* New York: Harper & Row.

Pelto, V.L. (1981). Male incest offenders and non-offenders: A comparison of early sexual history. *Dissertation Abstracts International, 42*, (3-B), 1154.

Porter, E. (1986). *Treating the young male victim of sexual assault.* Syracuse, NY: Safer Society Press.

Putnam, F. (1989). *Diagnosis and treatment of multiple personality disorder.* New York: Guilford.

Rappaport, R.L. (1991). When eclecticism is the integration of therapeutic postures, not theories. *Journal of Integrative and Eclectic Psychotherapy, 10*, 164–172.

Rieker, P., & Carmen, E. (1986). The victim-to-patient process: The disconfirmation and transformation of abuse. *American Journal of Orthopsychiatry, 56*, 360–370.

Risin, L.I., & Koss, M.P. (1987). The sexual abuse of boys: Prevalence and descriptive characteristics of childhood victimizations. *Journal of Interpersonal Violence, 2,* 309–323.

Rosenfeld, A.A. (1977). Sexual misuse and the family. *Victimology, 2,* 226–235.

Rosenfeld, A.A. (1979). Endogamic incest and the victim–perpetrator model. *American Journal of Diseases of Children, 133,* 406–410.

Rush, F. (1980). *The best kept secret: Sexual abuse of children.* Englewood Cliffs, NJ: Prentice-Hall.

Russell, D. (1986). *The secret trauma: Incest in the lives of girls and women.* New York: Basic Books.

Schorer, L.R., Friedman, J.M., Weiler, S.J., Heiman, J.R., and LoPiccolo, J. (1980). *A multi-axial descriptive system for the sexual dysfunctions: Categories and manual.* Stony Brook, NY: Sex Therapy Center.

Sebold, J. (1987). Indicators of child sexual abuse in males. *Social Casework, 68,* 75–80.

Sedney, M.A., & Brooks, B. (1984). Factors associated with history of childhood sexual experience in a nonclinical female population. *American Journal of Child Psychiatry, 23,* 215–218.

Seligman, M.E.D. (1975). *Helplessness: On depression, development and death.* San Francisco: Freeman.

Sgroi, S.M., Blick, L.C., & Porter, F.S. (1982). A conceptual framework for child abuse. In S.M. Sgroi (Ed.), *Handbook of clinical intervention in child sexual abuse.* Lexington, MA: Heath.

Simari, C.G., & Baskin, D. (1982). Incestuous experiences within homosexual populations: A preliminary study. *Archives of Sexual Behavior, 11,* 329–344.

Spada, J. (1979). *The Spada report.* New York: New American Library.

Sprei, J., & Courtois, C.A. (1988). The treatment of women's sexual dysfunctions arising from sexual assault. In J.R. Field & R.A. Brown (Eds.), *Advances in the understanding and treatment of sexual problems: Compendium for the individual and marital therapist.* New York: Spectrum.

Steele, B.F. (1986). Notes on the lasting effects of early child abuse throughout the life cycle. *Child Abuse and Neglect, 10,* 283–291.

Stein, A. (1980). Comprehensive family therapy. In R. Herink (Ed.), *The psychotherapy handbook* (pp. 204–207). New York: New American Library.

Sullivan, H.S. (1953). *The interpersonal theory of psychiatry.* New York: Norton.

Swift, C. (1977). Sexual victimization of children: An urban mental health survey. *Victimology, 2,* 322–327.

Trepper, T.S., & Barrett, M.J. (1989). *Systemic family treatment of incest.* New York: Brunner/Mazel.

Virkkunen, M. (1974). Incest offenses and alcoholism. *Medical and Scientific Law, 14,* 124.

Ward, E. (1985). *Father–daughter rape.* New York: Grove.

Waterman, J. (1986). Family dynamics of incest with young children. In K. MacFarlane & J. Waterman (Eds.), *Sexual abuse of young children.* New York: Guilford.

Westermeyer, J. (1978). Incest in psychiatric practice: A description of patients and incestuous relationships. *Journal of Clinical Psychiatry, 39,* 643–648.

Wooley, M.J., & Vigilanti, M.A. (1984). Psychological separation and the sexual abuse victim. *Psychotherapy: Theory, Research and Practice, 21,* 347–352.

Wynne, L.C. (1984). The epigenesis of relational systems: A model for understanding family development. *Family Process, 23,* 297–318.

Zubin, J., & Spring, B. (1977). Vulnerability: A new theory of schizophrenia. *Journal of Abnormal Psychology, 86,* 103–126.

NAME INDEX

221

SUBJECT INDEX

223